BEYOND SCHOOLS

BEYOND SCHOOLS

Education for Economic, Social and Personal Development

Edited by
Horace B. Reed
and
Elizabeth Lee Loughran

Citizen Involvement Training Program
Community Education Resource Center
School of Education
University of Massachusetts
Amherst, MA

Production Coordinator: Ruth Benn
Graphics and Cover Design: Patricia Zembruski
Design, Layout and Paste-up: Ruth Benn, Beth King
Typesetting: North Valley Typesetting & Graphics, Greenfield, MA.
Printing: Common Wealth Company, Inc., Hadley, MA.

Library of Congress Catalog Card Number 84-70668

ISBN 0-934210-10-1

Table of Contents

Contributing Authors

Donald K. Carew Professor in the Division of Human Services and Applied Behavioral Sciences, School of Education, University of Massachusetts, Amherst, MA.

Stanley Gajanayake Doctoral candidate at the School of Education, University of Massachusetts, Amherst; his research focuses on the training needs of village-level leaders for participatory development.

Elizabeth Lee Loughran Assistant Executive Director at the Center for Human Development, Springfield, MA.

Jeanne Martin Training specialist for the Mt. Auburn Hospital Alcohol Education and Training Center; instructor at Simmons College Graduate School of Social Work and Massasoit Community College, Boston, MA.

James E. Masker Coordinator of Education Services, National Center for Appropriate Technology, Butte, MT.

Ismael Ramirez-Soto Attorney at Law and Managing Attorney of the Community Services Unit, Greater Boston Legal Services, Inc., Boston, MA.

Horace B. Reed Professor of Education and Director of Community Education Resource Center, School of Education, University of Massachusetts, Amherst, MA.

Robert G. Ross Director of Counseling Services, Bunker Hill Community College, Boston, MA.

Judithe D. Speidel Associate Professor of Education and Director of a graduate program in museum education, University of Massachusetts, Amherst, MA.

Sue E. Sturtevant Doctoral candidate specializing in museum education at the University of Massachusetts; a museum consultant for the Massachusetts Heritage Park program in Paxton, MA.

PREFACE

The editors of *Beyond Schools: Education for Economic, Social and Personal Development* have brought together a set of perspectives that will contribute greatly to our further understanding of education learning and development. The editors' long-term interest in the community as the fundamental unit of education is deep-rooted in their own philosophy and practice. Their intent is to provide the reader with a broadened framework. It has been known for some time that learning extends beyond the schools, but this knowledge has not always led to a vision of education which is broader than schooling. In fact, the evidence points to the other direction. Even in recent years, a series of prominent national studies on achieving excellence in education have, for the most part, focused squarely on the schools as if to say that improving the schools would equal improved education. The editors effectively remind us that the system of human learning encompasses a variety of educative environments, only one of which is the school. A great part of our human learning takes place in nonformal, nonintentional formats and contexts. The editors have continued to develop the conceptions of education advanced in the earlier part of the century by John Dewey whose concern for school and society dictated a broader possible view of education. This not only expanded our vision of education, but enabled many to see education as a tool and as a process by which people are empowered to fulfill their noblest aspirations as free and just individuals. Consequently, the reader will be pleased and fascinated by the unique contemporary perspectives that are brought to bear in this compendium volume. The presentations are offered as tools for action that if implemented can have a profound bearing not only on one's philosophy of education, but on the very practical tasks of improving learning settings both in school and in nonschool situations. *Beyond Schools* brings together such contemporary themes as nonformal education, appropriate technology, worklife, self-help groups, and community education. *Beyond Schools* creates a new map of education that will help clarify where we have been, where we are, and where we need to go, if we are to develop further an educational system based both on quality and equality.

Reed and Loughran bring to the volume both the theory and the practice of looking at education as it extends beyond schools. They also bring an international perspective, having worked in settings other than the United States. They have carefully woven into this collection special sensitivities which can only have been the product of actual work in a variety of cultures. In many so-called developing countries, nonformal education is given as much, if not more, weight in public policy than formal education. Thus, clarifying conceptions of nonformal education, as it fits into an expanded definition of education, is extremely valuable to national and global audiences. There is increasing and broad interest in many varied community-based organizations that have a significant educational function. While other writers have focused on out-of-school education, there is, I believe, still a serious lack of descriptive and prospective analysis for gaining a handle on the diversity of organizations, agencies, and groups that are all involved in educative functions. This book provides a cogent, imaginative group of concepts and variables which serve as a framework for analyzing educational theory and practices in and out of school education.

The data base for this study consists of ten essays dealing with twenty educational nonschool settings and subsettings. The editors have developed a coherent conceptual base to inform the collation of the vast amount of educational data into a useful and informative set of findings. It is clear from the results of this study that education takes place in out-of-school settings in a way that is practical and has theoretical relevance from one setting to another, as does formal schooling. Each of the ten essays is interesting and informative in its own right. Several chapters explore approaches to out-of-school education that have seldom, if ever, been previously explored, such as appropriate technology, community legal education, the quality of worklife movement, self-help groups as education, and human services as education. Both the editors and the contributors to this volume, *Beyond Schools: Education for Economic, Social and Personal Development*, provide any who are interested in improved education with insights that are helpful to policy and practice. In a period in which American education is in the process of review, and when reform and excellence are being advanced, it is exceptionally timely. A careful examination of the contents of this book will enhance the debate now going on in terms of improving the quality and equality of education in the United States.

Mario D. Fantini
Dean, School of Education
University of Massachusetts
Amherst

BEYOND SCHOOLS

Education for Economic, Social and Personal Development

PART I

1
INTRODUCTION

In a rundown storefront in a New England mill town, a young woman is talking to a group of a dozen people of various ages. She is giving a workshop in Spanish about how to file a claim in the small claims court. Questions are frequent on all kinds of issues: What kinds of rights do tenants have? What kinds of repairs do landlords have to make? What can be done if new merchandise is faulty? What is the maximum interest a merchant can charge?

Across town in the modern facilities of a computer factory, a group of workers are quizzing a panel of technicians. These workers are part of a "quality control circle" which meets monthly to improve the quality of its product. The workers are acquiring the scientific background they need in order to be able to suggest technical improvements in their part of the manufacturing process.

In a nearby church basement, a group of people are spending their lunch hour attending a meeting of Alcoholics Anonymous. One after another, members share their experiences. One woman recounts her sense of hopelessness. Another man talks about his daughter's reaction to his drinking. Another describes the difficulty of avoiding going to the bar on Friday nights.

Across the world in a Thai village, a group of villagers gathers in the village square to talk about the water supply. A staff member from the regional community development office has come at their request to talk about repairs and improvements to the village's three major wells.

Education beyond schools takes many forms and serves many purposes. It is a major way that adults learn new skills in order to qualify for better jobs, to solve personal problems, or to enrich their lives in other ways. Simultaneously, education is a major vehicle for collective growth and development. Business, industry, as well as a wide variety of social and community groups see education as one way to foster desirable change in their organizations.

Out-of-school education is also much more varied and flexible than school education. Schools have a remarkable degree of similarity that transcends the majority of cultures; classrooms, blackboards, chalk, 25-35 children all the same age, a teacher, all are familiar components of schools in most parts of the world. The examples given above, however, demonstrate that nonschool, educational approaches are different not just from schools but from each other. They represent a fascinating array of methods, settings, and organizational approaches to the basic teaching-learning interaction.

Additionally, far more education takes place outside of schools than inside. In the United States alone, one nonschool educational approach, the training of workers by business and industry, is a 30-40 billion dollar operation. When one adds the multitude of other out-of-school settings such as libraries, museums, community study groups, agricultural extension workshops, radio and television courses, and so on, the enormous scope and extent of the effort becomes clear.

Research on this vast effort, however, is in its infancy. A quick trip through any library or research guide demonstrates how small the literature is in comparison to the importance of the topic both in terms of its size and effect on the individuals and organizations involved. Even less frequent are studies that attempt to look at education beyond schools as a whole phenomenon which encompasses an enormous number of component parts.

This study is a substantive addition to the research on the characteristics and underlying assumptions of education beyond schools. It presents a detailed analysis of ten approaches as separate and varied as the brief examples described above. Additionally, it presents a method for analyzing and comparing these very distinct approaches and demonstrates the important kinds of generalizations this method can generate.

A Learning System

Out-of-school education for the most part takes place in nonformal settings and, as such, is one part of a larger educational system. This educational system results in only a small part of all the learning that occurs throughout life. Learning is the larger concept which involves any modification in an individual or group that results in behavioral change. Some learning results from education—any intentional, overt and organized effort to influence a person or group with the aim of improving quality of life.

All of the learning occuring in any society can be conceptualized as a system of which schools are only one part. The largest part of this system consists of informal settings, including the home, neighborhood, or peer group, where major skills such as languages, interpersonal behavior, and survival strategies are acquired through a complex of unorganized, but highly effective, teaching-learning interactions.

The educational portion of this system consists of nonformal and formal settings. The nonformal part of the system is larger and includes settings like churches, scout groups, self-help groups, businesses, government agencies, libraries, unions and similar groups. Nonformal educational groups are organized, are designed to make an intentional effort to influence people, and are responsible for much of the learning that fills specific needs. People learn job skills at work, health maintenance from doctors and clinics, legal skills from lawyers, sports skills from being on teams, and psychological skills from counseling clinics and support groups.

The smaller part of the educational system is the formal school system, the component responsible for teaching basic symbol systems, for fostering abstract thinking, and for conserving the culture. Through the formal system, we learn to read, write, and compute; to read music and program computers; to think logically and critically; and to articulate the basic beliefs of our culture. The construction of new knowledge has much of its basis in this part of the educational system.

A Study of Education Beyond Schools

This study concentrates on the many nonschool approaches found in the nonformal part of the educational system. All of them are organized, and they represent open, intentional efforts to influence participants and increase the quality of life. Some of these approaches have a long and rich history: museums, human services and adult evening programs come to mind. Others are more recent: community development, appropriate technology projects, and self-help groups are examples. Some look more like educational settings because, like schools, they are aimed at individual development. Others, however, like legal education and community development approaches, represent collective or organizational efforts aimed more usually at economic or social development.

All together, ten approaches were chosen for detailed study here. The selection is neither inclusive nor representative, but presents some very distinct and interesting examples from the field. A study of these examples results in a heightened awareness of the tremendous variety of settings and methodologies in the field.

The data for this study have been collected over a three-year period by researchers with considerable background in their respective approaches. Each researcher reviewed the literature and other resources in his/her field, selecting a number of the most significant for annotation. A summary of each of these sources was then prepared as well as a precise description of the contents using approximately thirty variables, related both to educational and other factors. In addition, each source was cross-referenced with 19 other nonschool approaches. The data were then computerized, thus providing access across many significant educational approaches not previously widely available.

The data base is available to the public in several ways. This volume summarizes the approaches and the most important interconnections; an annotated, cross-referenced bibliography of the entire study is available through the Community Education Resource Center at the University of Massachusetts.

The book is divided into two major sections. Part I has three chapters: first, an introduction; second, a description of the methodology developed to analyze the broad range of data; and third, the results of the analysis across the ten approaches. Similarities and differences are highlighted, and some basic characteristics of nonschool education are suggested. Part II consists of ten chapters describing each approach. Each chapter contains a useful resource section.

The Increasing Importance of Out-of-School Education

Out-of-school education has always been significant even if it has only recently been a subject of much interest and examination. One can point to the tremendous power of voluntary associations in this country, as noted by deTocqueville and more recently by Commanger (1979). Much of the learning in this society, both of individuals and of collectives, has occurred in the process of working with these nonprofit and for-profit enterprises.

There are two major reasons why study of these educational settings is more necessary today than in the past, as well as some interesting indications that the formal educational establishment is beginning to notice and react to the phenomenon.

The first reason has been vividly presented by Cross (1978). She documents convincingly the changing demographics in this country. Both modern medicine and the post World War II baby boom have contributed to a population bulge in the middle adult years and an increasingly large elderly population. Nonformal learning is the predominant learning mode of this age group, in contrast to the importance of formal learning for children and youth.

For similar reasons, it is no longer necessary for this country to devote such a large portion of its educational energy to youth. The schools are built; enrollments are declining; the surplus of teachers is growing. There is both the reason and the opportunity to devote more resources to adult learning styles, in other words, to learning in nonformal work and community groups.

A second reason why research into out-of-school learning approaches is increasing in importance derives from the failure of the formal system to reach significant groups of disenfranchised people. The formal system has not completely met the needs of Blacks, Hispanics or other minority groups, except as individuals from those groups wish to "melt" into the dominant society. Nor for that matter has the system ever adequately met the needs of nonacademically oriented students of whatever background. What is different today is that these groups are developing power bases from which to demand more effective education for their members. Largely using the judicial system, they have demanded, and to some extent received, more equal treatment from the formal system. What has happened to a lesser extent is an investigation of whether many groups of youth, as well as adults, would learn more effectively in nonformal out-of-school settings. Results of the research in vocational education, experiential learning, internships and apprenticeships, is an important indication of the vitality of these approaches for youth from many different backgrounds.

Perhaps more important is the collective learning of entire groups of people as they become involved in the power structures of society. Significantly, much of this learning has occurred in nonformal settings. Churches became important educational settings for Blacks in the 1960's as they explored nonviolent resistance; community organizing on the Alinsky model (1971) occurs primarily in community groups. This collective learning, along with individual learning, has improved the quality of life for minority persons. In like fashion, many of the education projects for workers have had a similar effect in modifying major business and industrial power structures.

Out-of-School Research to Date

During the last decade, some exciting reformulations of educational theory have taken place, most commonly using the terms *lifelong learning* or *the learning society*. Related ideas may be found in the fields of nonformal education, continuing education and community education. The most important concepts developed by these schools of thought are the following: (a) that learning occurs throughout the lifespan; (b) that learning occurs in nonformal and informal settings; and (c) that learning is aimed at improving the quality of life (Dave, 1976). These three concepts are essential to the ideas under investigation in this book.

Lifelong Learning

Basically, the theory of lifelong learning is being developed in two parallel settings. The first is the UNESCO Institute for Education. Edgar Faure in his book *Learning To Be* (1972) signaled the beginnings of UNESCO's effort to put its considerable resources to use in developing a theory of lifelong education, including its nonformal, as well as formal, aspects. Faure's document provided a worldwide signal that schooling in the developing nations could not by itself be expected to provide the needed educational resources. Stressing broad goals of scientific humanism, creativity, social commitment, and the whole person in a global setting, Faure called for a system of education that gives focused attention to nonformal education, where learning is lifelong and involves both individuals and groups.

Since the publication of Faure's volume, the Institute has published a series of research reports on lifelong education (Cropley, 1977, 1979; Dave, 1973, 1975, 1976). Together, they represent an important beginning, particularly for developing a theoretical foundation for lifelong learning. Of these reports, one of the most significant is R.H. Dave's *Foundations Of Lifelong Education* (1976). Using the three elements of the definition presented above (lifespan, nonformal, and quality of life), Dave and associates synthesize foundational essays in philosophy, history, psychology, anthropology, ecology, sociology and economics. Both the breadth of their approach and the findings of the strengths and weaknesses of formal and nonformal education are important to an understanding of the topic. However, Dave's work is limited by the fact that it is largely theoretical, and its emphasis is on individual development. Dave makes clear that in lifelong learning theory, the individual is at the center of the educational process with community development left unattended.

Nonformal Education

Another school of thought, which also cites Faure's work as an important initiating force, is nonformal education, largely occurring in the context of adult education and rural development projects in the Third World. In contrast to the Institute's work, descriptions of nonformal education projects are more practical and specific rather than theoretical. There is a collective emphasis as well as the individual emphasis of the Institute. Philip Coomb's (1968) analysis of education and the world crisis is another germinal study that lays the groundwork for conceptualizing education as a system. Presenting the ways that education and national societies interact, the author points out the complex problems confronting schooling in the world given its failures to meet social needs. One solution rests in an inclusive view of education where a wide range of organized agencies are seen as having significant educational functions. Similar moves in the direction of seeing education as encompassing both formal and nonformal education agencies are strongly supported by the World Bank, UNESCO and other units of the United Nations, and the foreign missions of many of the industrialized nations. What is lacking, however, is an integrated approach that makes significant comparisions across various settings.

Adult and Community Education

In the United States, the research on lifelong learning has been a further development of the adult and community education theorists. K. Patricia Cross (1974, 1978, 1980) has developed a useful rationale for the increased interest in the field, citing the aging of the population. She along with Vermilye (1975), Jessup (1969), Tough (1971), Gross (1977), Hiemstra (1976), Knowles (1970), and others has developed an extensive series of innovative approaches to adult learning. Peterson and Associates' (1979) summary is the most complete account of the field, with a series of essays that explore an expanded concept of education. This is a fine resource with useful overall concepts, an excellent bibliography and resource lists of relevant agencies, organizations and federal level activities.

Emphasis on Individual Learning

The limitations of the above literature are similar to that of UNESCO's Institute. The focus is on the phenomenon of individual learning. The movement ignores the phenomenon of collective learning and thereby misses a significant portion of the learning aimed at change that occurs in any society. Only a few isolated works in this country have developed this theme and then usually only in a fairly specific field. Hunter and Harmon's (1979) discussion of adult literacy in the United States, for instance, advocates a more collective approach, but their work is restricted to the topic of literacy training.

The current status, particularly of educational practice in the United States, reflects a long history of emphasis on individual learning. The formal school is dedicated to individual learning; very few of the reforms aimed at increasing the degree of influence by and interchange with the community have had widespread effect. The relatively mild impact of such noted theorists as John Dewey and Theodore Brameld on formal education as it is currently practiced is a case in point. Dewey (1918) saw education as social and environmental interactions. He tried to construct both a theory and broad implementing guidelines that would transform formal schooling into practicing such a view of education. Brameld (1971) carried this position further, seeing schooling as future-oriented, providing a leadership role in moving social, economic and political structures of communities towards more just and humane values. There is little evidence to suggest that these visions of nonformal learning have become central to past or present formal schooling.

Significance of this Study

This present work, therefore, presents a significant addition to the existing literature for three reasons. First, it describes the educational functioning of ten differing settings, agencies, and approaches. The cross-referenced data base of this study affords practitioners in any one setting opportunities to learn new or more effective ways of serving individuals and the community. Additionally, the potential for fruitful collaboration across settings is enhanced by increasing the awareness of practitioners in one field of the innovations in another field.

Secondly, it investigates the phenomenon of collective education co-equally with individual education. It seeks to investigate the education that occurs as businesses, work groups, volunteer agencies, community development projects and the like seek to make an impact on basic structures of their societies.

Thirdly, this work provides a set of concepts and variables that serve as an organizing framework, creating a fruitful balance of theory and program description. The UNESCO effort and much of the United States' lifelong learning education literature is largely theoretical, whereas the nonformal education and community development literature suffers from the opposite emphasis. This work describes theoretical elements from a very detailed investigation of operating programs, thus bringing the two approaches more in balance.

To return to the four vignettes presented at the beginning of this chapter, they represent in microcosm the scope and potential of this book. The problems these out-of-school approaches are confronting could not be more crucial to the lives of the people concerned, nor for that matter, to the organizations to which they belong. Water supply, personal health, the quality of major industrial products, and the rights of minorities are major issues of individual and societal existence. Yet the educational methods employed by these groups are quite diverse as are many of the other educational variables involved. Through acquainting the reader with a wide selection of these approaches, together with a methodology for further study, and some potentially interesting generalizations to explore, readers will be introduced to the richness and variety of education beyond schools.

Suggested Resources
Introduction

Bibliography

Alinsky, S.D. *Rules for radicals.* New York: Vintage Books, 1971.

Brameld, T. *Patterns of educational philosophy.* New York: Holt, Rinehart and Winston, 1971.

Cremin, L.A. *Public Education.* New York: Basic Books, Inc., 1976.

Commager, H.S. Volunteerism: New structures of power? Address presented at Amherst College, Amherst, Massachusetts, January 19, 1979.

Coombs, P.H. *The world educational crisis: A systems analysis.* New York: Oxford University Press, 1968.

Cropley, A.J. *Lifelong education: A psychological analysis.* Oxford, England: Pergamon Press, 1977.

Cropley, A.J. (Ed.). *Lifelong education: A stocktaking.* Hamburg, West Germany: UNESCO Institute for Education, 1979.

Cross, K.P., Valley, J.R., and Associates. *Planning nontraditional programs: An analysis of the issues for postsecondary education.* San Francisco, CA: Jossey-Bass, 1974.

Cross, K.P. *The missing link: Converting adult learners to learning resources.* New York College Entrance Examination Board, 1978.

Cross, K.P. Our changing students and their impact on colleges: Prospects for a true learning society. *Phi Delta Kappan,* May 1980, 61, 627-30.

Curle, A. *Educational problems of developing societies with case studies of Ghana, Pakistan, and Nigeria.* New York: Praeger, 1973.

Dave, R.H. *Lifelong education and school curriculum.* Hamburg: UNESCO Institute for Education, 1973.

Dave, R.H. (Ed.). *Reflections on lifelong education and the school.* Hamburg: UNESCO Institute for Education, 1975.

Dave, R.H. (Ed.). *Foundations of lifelong education.* Oxford, England: Pergamon Press, 1976.

Dewey, J. *Experience and education.* New York: Macmillan Publishing Company, Inc., 1938.

Faure, E. *Learning to be: The world of education today and tomorrow*. Paris, France: UNESCO, 1972.

Freire, P. *Education for critical consciousness*. New York: The Seaburg Press, 1973.

Gross, R. *New paths to learning: College education for adults*. New York: Public Affairs Committee, 1977.

Hart, J.K. *The discovery of intelligence*. New York: The Century Company, 1924.

Heermann, B., Enders, C.C., and Wine, E. (Eds.). *Serving lifelong learners*. San Francisco, CA: Jossey-Bass Publishers, 1980.

Hiemstra, R. *Lifelong learning*. Lincoln, Nebraska: Professional Educators Publications, 1976.

Hunter, C.S.J., and Harmon, D. *Adult illiteracy in the United States*. New York: McGraw-Hill Book Company, 1979.

Jessup, F.W. (Ed.). *Lifelong learning: A symposium on continuing education*. Oxford, England: Pergamon Press, 1969.

Knowles, M.S. *The modern practice of adult education*. New York: Association Press, 1970.

Oliver, D.W. *Education and community: A radical critique of innovative schooling*. Berkeley, CA: McCutchen Publishing Corporation, 1976.

Olsen, M.E. (Ed.). *Power in societies*. New York: Macmillan Publishing Company, Inc., 1970.

Peterson, R.E., and Associates. *Lifelong learning in America*. San Francisco, CA: Jossey-Bass Publishers, 1979.

Toffler, A. (Ed.). *Learning for tomorrow: The role of the future in education*. New York: Vintage Books, 1974.

Tough, A. *The adult's learning projects: A fresh approach to theory and practice in adult learning*. Toronto: The Ontario Institute for Studies in Education, 1971.

Vermilye, D. (Ed.). *Lifelong learners: A new clientele for higher education*. San Francisco, CA: Jossey-Bass Publishers, 1975.

Vliet, W.V. (Ed.). *Lifelong education and community learning: Three case studies in India*. Hamburg: UNESCO Institute for Education, 1978.

Wagschal, P.H. (Ed.). *Learning tomorrows: Commentaries on the future of education*. New York: Praeger, 1979.

Journals

Convergence

Lifelong Learning: The Adult Years

Prospects

Resource Centers

Community Education Resource Center
School of Education
University of Massachusetts
Amherst, MA 01003
Tel. (413) 545-1587

National Association for Human Development
1750 Pennsylvania Avenue
Washington, D.C. 20006
Tel. (202) 393-1882

National Council on Community Services and Continuing Education
One Dupont Circle, N.W.
Suite 410
Washington, D.C. 20036
Tel. (202) 293-7050

2
METHODOLOGY
OF THE STUDY

A brief look at the origins of this study on out-of-school approaches to education throws light on the exploratory nature of the methodology used. The editors and contributors have had many years of professional involvement with formal schooling at all levels. This experience has resulted in increasing conviction that significant problems of society, here and abroad, are not effectively addressed through the schools. At the same time, the writers have also had extensive experience with a range of out-of-school educational agencies. This latter involvement has provided a more optimistic perspective on the power of education to serve as one force for social change.

The editors' intuitive belief that many agencies and institutions of society are deeply involved in education became articulated and subject to analysis through the gradual development of an instrument called the *Lifelong Learning Scale* (Table 2). Over a period of several years, the scale had been refined through its use as a diagnostic and training tool in connection with staff development workshops for people representing varied out-of-school agencies. The discussions that evolved out of these many contacts provided further clues concerning social change and learning theories that inform educational decisions. Additional questions arose about the similarities and differences in the ways that out-of-school approaches conceptualized and implemented education.

In brief, the inductive, experiential origins of this study lead to the present effort at logical analysis of these experiences. A group of scholars representing many different fields agreed to examine their fields using the same analytical framework. Their intention was to generate data, which for the first time could easily be compared, and to create an analytical tool that others might use in similar endeavors. This chapter describes the development of the research framework, and the next chapter centers on the comparisons that were generated when the scholars applied the methodology to their respective fields.

Selection of Out-of-School Approaches

The selection of out-of-school categories included in the study was made by the editors. Using their personal awareness of the large number of interesting and diverse agencies and approaches with significant educational functions, the decisions were influenced by the availability of experienced practitioners who had strong theoretical groundings, who were willing to contribute the considerable time for the literature search and writing of essay drafts, and who had an interest in the overall design of the study.

It is important to realize that the selection of approaches is neither inclusive nor balanced. Many extremely important approaches were omitted; libraries, religious groups, unions, government, the arts, the media, the military, and recreational approaches are some of the more important omissions. The inclusions, on the other hand, probably involve more collective rather than individual educational approaches than one might find in a comprehensive study of education. The intention of the study, therefore, is to provide some beginning insights as to the many varied settings where education occurs and to develop a framework for examining education across settings.

Contributors were provided with a set of instructions which included the expectation that each essay would reflect a thorough search of the relevant literature as well as the personal insights of the writer. In the review of the literature, the writers used a list of over thirty variables and concepts which they referred to as they reviewed each literature source. Information on these variables was recorded on cards and forms the data for this study and another publication entitled *Lifelong Learning In The Community: An Annotated Cross-Referenced Bibliography* (Reed, 1982). In writing their essays, each used a common framework so that collation of information across essays would be facilitated.

Framework For The Essays

A rationale for the framework was constructed around four objectives. There was the need to clarify distinctions, as well as similarities, among the approaches concerning their varied descriptions of education. A related purpose was the identification of the issues and concerns (pervasive themes) that are persistent focal points for practitioners and theorists of each approach. A third guideline called for an exploration of the social change and learning theories underlying each setting. A fourth objective of the rationale was to describe how education was delivered or implemented.

Thus the writers, in constructing each essay, organized their information (from the literature sources and personal experiences) around four components or lenses: (a) Description of the approach; (b) Pervasive Themes; (c) Social change and learning theories; and (d) Delivery variables. (Table 1)

Table 1
List of Concepts and Variables

DESCRIPTIONS OF APPROACHES*

Twenty units (basic approaches and subsets): Economic, Social, and Personal emphasis.

PERVASIVE THEMES

THEORETICAL COMPONENTS

Social Change Theory

- Object of change (individual or group)
- Sources of change (top-down or bottom-up)
- Type of change (evolutionary or basic change)

Learning Theory

- Authority (external or internal)
- Level of Reduction (incremental or Gestalt)

DELIVERY VARIABLES

Objectives
Content and Sequences
Time Units
Learners
Staff
Teaching Learning Approaches
Rewards and Evaluation
Curriculum Materials and Resources
Financial Resources
Building Resources
Power, Control and Administration

*(See Table 1, Chpt. 3 p. 26)

Description Component

An initial task for each writer was to clarify, individually, what to include when gathering information. For example, within the general field of appropriate technology, subsets might need to be distinguished depending upon varied basic assumptions and values. The adult education movement, as another example, is vaguely described by some authors as being the same as all out-of-school education, while most adult education practitioners mean something much more specific. In the essays then, the writers describe the distinctions of what is and is not being included in the selection of sources and the writing of the essay. This section of the essay may also make comparisons with other overlapping categories. The writers often approach this description problem by providing a brief historical context to shed further light on the evolution of an approach with its variations and subsets.

Another important task in describing some of the approaches is to distinguish the educational aspects of the approach from the noneducational aspects. While some of the approaches such as adult education are clearly educational and accepted as such, many others such as appropriate technology or quality of worklife have many noneducational components as well. It is important, for instance, to distinguish education for social change from the larger concept of social change. The former concept includes the many organized and intentional efforts to influence change while the latter has many informal, intuitive processes as well. It is just as important to distinguish education from generalized activity or work. Education is much more clearly organized and includes a higher degree of reflection about what is occurring. Education never just happens. Further the purposes of education are overt, while other forces for change may not be subject to conscious examination.

Identification of Subcategories

In the process of analyzing each essay, using the four components or lenses, it became apparent that there were significant differences within some of the approaches as regards one or more of the components. Thus, within some of the approaches, subsets were identified and treated as separate units. For the ten approaches, a total of twenty separate units are included in the comparative study.

Pervasive Themes

Much of the vitality and essence of an approach can be gleaned by identifying its pervading issues, concerns, and problems. These pervasive themes continually crop up in the literature, at conferences and workshops, and during informal daily discussions at the work place. Such issues are frequently reflected in the guidelines provided to agencies by funding sources.

Each author was asked to describe themes that appeared to pervade the literature and/or practices of the approach. A theme is an issue, a concern, a piece of rhetoric, and/or a topic which is regularly mentioned and discussed. Of all the components the authors were asked to address, this one is perhaps the most open-ended. Each writer was asked to describe and discuss the implications of those topics or issues which repeatedly appeared in the literature and were most evident to someone investigating the approach.

In the early stages of this study, the editors had no specific hypotheses about these themes. We planned to inventory them, and then see if, when collated, there were themes which cut across a number of approaches. We could then group approaches according to a theme and see if similarities occur on other factors we have identified. Examples of themes that were found to be characteristic of more than one approach included concerns about participation, funding, cost-effectiveness, human potential, academic versus functional learning, etc. Some themes persist over many decades in an approach, while others are more topical.

Theoretical Component: Social Change and Learning Theories

All educational approaches—whether formal settings like schools or nonformal out-of-school settings such as the ones being described in this book—have behind them certain assumptions about how and why things occur. Of primary importance to education is the question: How and why do people learn? Of equal importance are the questions: What is the nature of the change that occurs through the educational setting? and, How does it occur? Learning and social change theory are the more fundamental fields of knowledge from which the more applied profession of education derives its roots (Burrell and Morgan, 1979).

In this study, we hypothesized that the ten approaches included with their subsets would contain a wide variety of answers to these basic theoretical questions. We assumed that we would be able to group the approaches and subapproaches according to the answers to these questions. We then planned to see if the groups contained within them marked similarities, differences, and relationships relevant to other variables in the study.

Social Change Theories. All educational approaches, both formal and nonformal, imply change. However, they differ markedly according to the *object of change* (individual or group), the *source of change* (top-down or bottom-up), the *nature of change* (evolutionary or basic change).

Many approaches—particularly in North America—see the object of change as the individual. Personal development or individual growth is the primary aim. However, a number of the approaches included in this volume see the object of change to be some sort of group: an organization, a community or society at large. Community or organizational development is the major goal.

Similarly, approaches differ according to the source of change. Change can emanate from the top and ripple down (or from the center to the periphery) or the reverse can be true. Generally, these approaches imply major value differences as well. Top-down change is conceived of and implemented by the more powerful, wealthy, enfranchised groups in the organization, community or society, while bottom-up strategies involve empowerment of the disenfranchised.

The last aspect involves the question of whether change is seen as a slow, evolutionary process or whether change only occurs when the approach challenges the basic structures and processes of the group or society. If an approach largely reinforces the major institutions of society (e.g., corporation, government, bureaucracy, institutions, agencies, etc.) and provides the support for further improvements of these institutions or individuals within them, then it is an evolutionary approach. If it criticizes and seeks to change these structures, for instance by challenging the economy's dependence on nonrenewable energy, or by advocating nonhierarchical structures, or by seeking empowerment of the disenfranchised, it is a more basic change approach.

Whether social change is seen mainly as an individual or more collective phenomenon, top-down or bottom-up, evolutionary or basic structural change, we hypothesized these to be major sources of information of similarities, differences and relationships among the variables of our study and across the approaches.

Learning Theories. One way distinctions can be made among learning theories is by estimating the *sources of authority,* the motivating forces, for learners' educational decision making. Roughly speaking, the sources of authority can be seen as largely internal or external to the learner. If internal, decisions are made by the learner based on self-awareness of one's wants and needs. If external, decisions are made on the basis of what other people or forces (professionals, government bodies, tradition, etc.) perceive are the needs of the learner.

Generally, the selection of a source of authority for educational decision making has a substantial effect on the teaching-learning approach employed. If the assumption is that it is internal sources of knowing that must be tapped, then techniques are more usually experiential and participatory. The intent is to involve learners in an exploration of their own experience in order to come to a new conceptualization of a particular phenomenon. On the other hand, if sources of knowledge are seen as largely external, then other kinds of techniques make more sense: lectures, demonstrations, media presentations, and the like.

Another way learning theories can be distinguished is by looking at the concept of *level of reduction:* estimating the emphasis on sequential learning increments versus a Gestalt approach. Incremental learning stresses separate bits of information or stimuli, while Gestalt learning stresses relationships of many areas of information or stimuli with concern for the whole person (head, heart, body). The concepts of *sources of authority* and *level of reduction* were perceived as additional fruitful ways to compare the approaches and look for relationships with the other variables.

Delivery Variables

Out-of-school educational approaches can be compared and contrasted by separating the concept of education into a set of delivery variables, each variable being seen on a formal-nonformal continuum. Examples of such variables include objectives, content, and methods.

Each essay was written to include information about this component by using the Lifelong Learning Scale (Table 2). This instrument presents eleven educational variables along the vertical column. Each variable has a scale made of a continuum, with one end being described as more formal, more structured, more abstract, and more objective. The other end of the continuum is labeled more nonformal, more flexible, more concrete, and more subjective. As refinements to these general descriptions of the continua, each variable has specific descriptors that help identify where on the continuum an educational approach falls. Connecting the eleven points on the continua establishes a profile for a given approach.

Data Analysis

The analysis of the data integrating the variables and concepts of the four components or lenses, for each approach and across all approaches, provides a coherent framework for understanding, studying, and implementing out-of-school education. This analysis is presented in Chapter 3.

The processing and integrating of the large amount of information in the essays were greatly facilitated by the fact that the writers developed the essays using the same general guidelines consisting of the four components. The first step in the analysis was to abstract from the essays a short description of each approach and any subapproaches. The next step was the identification of a set of constructs that help classify the pervasive themes: economic emphasis, social emphasis, and personal emphasis. The third step was the development of generalized, contrasting views of social change theories and of learning theories. Social change theories were distinguished on three elements: source of social change (top-down or bottom-up); object of change (individual or group); type of social change (evolutionary or basic change). For learning theories, distinctions were made on two elements: authority (external or internal) and level of reduction (incremental or gestalt).

The analysis of the data from the delivery variables involved coding the twenty approaches and subapproaches on each of the eleven Lifelong Learning Scale variables, using a "1" for the formal end of the continua, a "3" for the middle section, and a "5" for the nonformal end.

Similarities, differences, collations, and relationships among the twenty approaches and across pairs of variables were made using simple matrices. These matrices serve to organize and classify the data so that observations could be made concerning the several questions posed by the study.

Limitations

The inclusion and exclusion of out-of-school approaches in this study are not intended to convey value judgments as to their relative social importance. As noted above, some categories not included at this stage of the study are obviously of major significance, such as religious organizations, business and industry training, and military training. We are also aware that additional components or lenses (variables and concepts) can be used in the analysis of out-of-school education. We have attempted to cast a net that captures many of the basic questions that are of interest to theorists and practitioners.

Table 2
The Lifelong Learning Scale

EDUCATIONAL VARIABLES	DESCRIPTORS ON CONTINUUM	
	1 2 3	4 5
	More Formal More Structured More Abstract More Objective	Less Formal More Flexible More Concrete More Subjective

Objectives	Building and conservation
	  of knowledge
	More cognitive
	More delayed
		Applying knowledge for
		  personal and community
		  development
		More psychological and
		  physical
		More immediate

Content And Sequence	Abstract symbol systems Logically organized Scholarly disciplines Predictable sequence Requirements and prerequisites	Concrete; experiential Psychologically organized Interdisciplinary Sequence less ordered Few requirements
Time Units	Long-term Full-time Tightly scheduled Preset time periods	Short-term Part-time Flexible schedule Situational time periods

Learners	Age selective
	Selection criteria predictable
	  and more precise
		Age inclusive
		Selection criteria less
		  predictable and more
		  general

Staff	Professionals A major life aim Highly trained Distinct roles Credentials	Lay oriented Ancillary life aim Short-term training Less distinct roles Noncredentialed
Teaching-Learning Approaches	Teacher more directive Teacher more responsible Learner is receiver	Teacher more facilitating, advising, linking Learner more responsible Learner more active

Table 2 continued

Rewards And Evaluation	Extrinsic rewards	Intrinsic rewards
	More competitive	More cooperative
	Evaluation of knowing	Evaluation of performance
	Product oriented	Process oriented
	Quantitative evaluation	Qualitative evaluation
Curriculum Materials and Resources	Complex technology	Simpler technology
	Commercial production	Local production
	Written and spoken media	Multi-media
Financial Resources	Larger expenditures per learner	Smaller expenditures per learner
	Long-term investment	Short-term investment
	Mostly government sponsored	Varied sponsors
	More elaborate accounting procedures	Less elaborate accounting procedures
	Less flexible allocations	More flexible allocations
Building Resources	Major permanent constructions	Minor temporary constructions
	Specific, set spaces	Flexible spaces
	High maintenance cost	Less maintenance cost
	Less often user constructed	More often user constructed
Power, Control And Administration	Adherence to rules, forms, and routines	More personal
	More hierarchical	More horizontal
	Power partly function of status and resources	Power largely function of competency
	Decision making by role	Decision making shared
	Workers in established organizations	Workers less organized
	Leaders viewed as managers	Leaders viewed as coordinators

Conclusion

This net is potentially of as much interest to researchers and practitioners as are the results of its application here. One of the major difficulties in studying education as a field is its extreme fragmentation. Though an extraordinary amount of creative education occurs daily, it is rare for a practitioner in one field to have any knowledge of innovations elsewhere. Even the terminology varies tremendously so that it is difficult for potential teachers (facilitators, trainers, etc.) to talk to each other across fields, much less learn from each other.

The methodology developed here has the value of wide applicability across fields. The four components are basic to all educational approaches and are easily translated into distinctive terminology. Additionally, the four components represent a balance of inductive and deductive approaches combining the benefits of both the intuitive and the rational. Together they provide a coherent way to explore the fascinating and highly diverse field of out-of-school education.

Suggested Resources
Methodology of the Study

Bibliography

Brandon, J. and Associates (Eds.). *Networking: A trainer's manual.* Amherst, Massachusetts: Community Education Resource Center, School of Education, University of Massachusetts, 1982.

Burrell, G. and Morgan, G. *Sociological paradigms and organizational analysis.* London: Heinemann Educational Books Ltd., 1979.

Frith, M. and Reed, H.B. *Lifelong learning manual: Training for effective education in organizations.* Amherst, Massachusetts: Community Education Resource Center, School of Education, University of Massachusetts, 1982.

Reed, H. and Associates. *Lifelong learning in the community: An annotated, cross-referenced bibliography.* Amherst, Massachusetts: Community Education Resource Center, School of Education, University of Massachusetts, 1982.

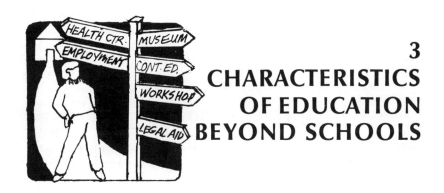

3
CHARACTERISTICS
OF EDUCATION
BEYOND SCHOOLS

School's out
School's out
The teacher let the monkeys out

Schools traditionally put a major emphasis on endings. Examinations, final papers, grades, plays, concerts, picnics, field trips, and at last graduation all lead rather strongly to the conclusion that education ends. The teachers let the monkeys out, and life begins.

Of course the most frequent sequel to graduation is that one gets a job (and begins on-the-job training) or enters the military (and goes to boot camp) or goes on a trip (and stops at a museum or historical village) or gets involved in a political cause (and develops slogans and organizes rallies). Education pervades life. While the notion that school ends is quite accurate, and a relief to many participants, education remains a crucial component of the work, recreation and community activities of most adults.

The purpose of this chapter is to begin to describe and draw some conclusions about education that has been let out of school. What does it look like? Where do you find it? What are its purposes? What underlying assumptions support it? What basic methods and organizational strategies are commonly used?

The data that have been used to construct this chapter have been derived from educational approaches described in the essays that follow. They are only a small section of the approaches that might have been chosen and no rigorous attempt was made to balance the selection. However, they represent concrete examples of what one might get into if one ventures into the field of out-of-school education.

The value of the data base is its concreteness and specificity. The broad characteristics and conclusions suggested here must, of necessity, be considered tentative; however, they emerge from the specific detail of many out-of-school educational ventures. They are both the results of the study and emergent proposals about the nature of education seen broadly, of education freed from classrooms and lessons and grades.

The underlying assumption, of course, is that this purpose is important, that education occurring out-of-schools is just as important as education in schools and deserves the same degree of study. The authors of this volume would push this assumption further and say that education after graduation is more interesting, varied, relevant, engrossing, difficult and fun. There are lessons in it for schoolmasters as well.

Location: Where is Out-of-School Education?

The definition of education upon which this book is based is "any overt, organized effort to influence individuals or groups that improves the quality of life." It follows that one begins a search for out-of-school educational approaches within the organizations that impact on people's daily lives. Work organizations, political, community and government organizations, recreational, volunteer and inspirational organizations come to mind. Each of these organizations has at times a message which it wants to convey to others. As it organizes to deliver its message, it becomes an educational approach.

Education for Economic, Social and Personal Development

The educational approaches chosen for study here fall into some of the basic organizational categories suggested above. Sometimes they fall into more than one category. For example, the essays on the educational aspects of the human services and quality of worklife movements clearly discuss education as a part of work. The human services essay sees education not only as necessary training for staff but also as an integral part of services delivered to clients or patients. The quality of worklife essay discusses the enormous extent of the training provided to workers in business and industry and also discusses how education can be integrated into a major social change movement within the work world.

Four of the approaches selected discuss education as it is delivered by local, regional or nationally focused groups. These groups have as purposes the improvement of social, economic and political conditions in the community or nation. Community development groups use a broad range of educational techniques to improve both material and nonmaterial conditions in the community. Nonformal education is a process these groups often use. Nonformal education projects have a wide range of purposes from fostering basic literacy, to improving agricultural techniques, to fostering social equity. Legal education uses a variety of educational approaches to teach legal literacy particularly to those racial and ethnic groups which do not have easy access to normal legal institutions. Appropriate technology education efforts operate at both local and national levels to change basic attitudes and practices towards use of energy, growing of food, and manufacture of necessary products.

Four other approaches selected are embedded in organizations which are devoted to interesting use of leisure time and/or personal growth. Visiting a museum is a part of a vacation or Sunday afternoon. Adult education classes, either at a local high school or as part of a community education program, fill many evenings, summers, and weekends. A self-help group such as Alcoholics Anonymous may be an important factor in an individual's ability to change and grow.

Clearly, too, many of these approaches cross the boundaries between work, community, and leisure-time organizations. A women's consciousness raising group may be devoted to the personal growth of its members and also aim its message at the community and nation. Appropriate technology groups have a major focus on the community and on the way work is performed in society. Community development and nonformal education projects have a similar dual focus. Most community education projects serve individuals in the community, but occasionally they organize educational efforts aimed at the whole community.

The major point is that education is an important factor in many of the organizations which impact on the daily life of individuals. These groups have as diverse interests and purposes as do the people they serve. It follows that there are many other organizations that could be studied as important members of the nonschool educational system. Examples of important omissions in this volume include religious organizations, political parties, labor unions, volunteer and fraternal organizations, government, the mass media, libraries, the military, and so on. Again, selection for inclusion in this volume is not based on any inherent importance in relationship to other approaches, but represents the specific interests of the authors who participated in the study.

Education as Auxiliary

What then are the major conclusions one can draw simply from looking at where education is found after school ends? The first is that by far the majority of the approaches are embedded in organizations which would not define their basic purpose as educational. Businesses exist to produce a product and make a profit; human services to cure the sick and/or enable people to live better lives; community development projects want to improve the water supply or farming practices. For the most part, if one were to ask practitioners in these fields whether they consider themselves teachers or whether they would like to study teacher training techniques, they would consider the question odd in the extreme.

There are exceptions, of course, adult education being the most obvious one. The thesis advanced here, however, is that approaches that define themselves only as educational are less numerous and for that reason less significant than their harder-to-see counterparts. Education in the adult world is a means to do something else and thus is most likely to be found highly enmeshed in other activities.

This basic characteristic of most out-of-school educational approaches has both negative and positive ramifications. A negative aspect for the authors of this volume was the amount of energy that had to go into devising ways of studying education when it was not called education, did not use common educational terminology, and was severely entangled with things that were not education. The second chapter in this book describes that effort in more detail. More positively, the reader will be able to study the following ten essays and only rarely encounter any mention of discipline or motivation. Education occuring as a by-product of accomplishing something else benefits from the internal drive and self-discipline behind that desired end. The power behind it is much more intrinsic and important than a letter grade.

In Summary

Several major conclusions occur from an initial examination of where education occurs beyond schools. The first is that it is, to a greater or lesser degree, part of every organization's function. All organizations must train their own members; a great number educate as part of their overall function and/or use educational techniques as part of major change efforts. The second conclusion is that a significant majority of the education occuring outside of schools is highly integrated into other purposes and activities of the organizations. This integration is a primary difference between these approaches and schools. While this difference makes out-of-school education quite difficult to study, nonetheless it is a major factor in eliminating some of the more persistent problems facing professional school people.

Out-of-School Education: Definition

The first topic each of the authors in this volume was asked to address was the question of definition: Describe the approach, make any distinctions necessary within the approach, and distinguish the approach from similar ones in the field. Before getting into any analysis of the content of that exercise, it is interesting to explore what was initially an unexpected result of the process.

Distinctions Within Approach

Suddenly there were not just ten approaches to be studied but some forty. Even after rigorous elimination, twenty remained to be analysed. Appropriate technology consists of at least two educational approaches.

The attempt to get individuals in small community groups to take charge of their lives by using renewable energy sources is very different from the effort to change the nation's energy policy. Adult basic education is very different from noncredit adult education, which in form is quite distinct from credit approaches, and so forth. Many of the approaches had within them numerous subsets. Others, such as the quality of worklife movement, had a lesser tendency to subdivide because they themselves were already subsets of a larger field (business training).

This tendency to multiply obviously creates some difficulties for this chapter in extending the scope and complexity of the descriptive effort. It is close to impossible to grasp twenty complex phenomena simultaneously. On the other hand, immense variety of approach emerges as a major characteristic of out-of-school education and a major way the field differs from school based approaches. Despite all the rhetoric of the professional education journals, one can walk into a high school in Maine, Texas, France, or Indonesia and be impressed more with similarities than differences. In contrast, a doctor's office, Alcoholics Anonymous, a cake decorating class, and village development project impress one with their differences, one from the other.

The variety available as soon as education is seen as a phenomenon distinct from the physical school building and the traditional characteristics of schooling is one of the more exciting aspects of out-of-school education. Numerous different models exist and their effectiveness with different populations and purposes can be studied. Similarly, for those involved in conducting new educational approaches, there are numerous possibilities to examine and try. There is no sense of being locked into a singular approach.

A Categorization

Variety as a basic characteristic, however, does present a problem when one's intent is to arrive at some overall grasp of a field. It brings about a need to simplify and to categorize, just in order to make sense out of what is basically a multifaceted phenomenon.

The categorization that follows is no doubt only one such scheme that might be applied in order to encourage some greater understandings out of the data available. It is based on the idea explored above that education occuring outside schools most usually happens in the process of accomplishing something else. Thus a basic way of categorizing numerous specific approaches is to categorize their goals.

Economic development, social development, and personal development represent three major goals which organizations commonly serve. Organizations dedicated to economic development are concerned with material progress, increased production, better and more cost-effective products, and products with fewer negative by-products. Organizations concerned with social development are interested in such things as the quality of interpersonal relationships within a community. Organizations fostering personal development focus on such varied things as helping individuals overcome physical, emotional or financial problems, enriching the use of their leisure time, learning something useful for either their personal or professional growth.

These three categories can be represented as a circular continuum with many approaches crossing the line between categories. Figure 1 presents this representation.

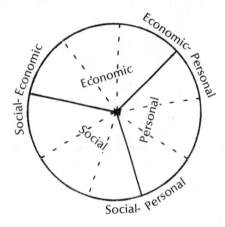

Figure 1

Again, the intent is less to limit a specific approach by forcing it into a specific category, but to begin to collate the data in order to gain greater understanding of it.

Brief Description of the Approaches

Table 1 lists the ten approaches included in this volume along with the subapproaches chosen for study here.

Table 1
Descriptions of Approaches and Subapproaches

ADULT EDUCATION: Programs designed to provide organized opportunities for adults, especially those who have not had adequate schooling experiences, but also others who are interested in lifelong learning.

Adult Basic Education—Mostly federal/state funded programs to provide basic literacy and numeracy education to the large numbers of people who are seriously handicapped by illiteracy.

Adult Noncredit— Programs offered through continuing education through schools, colleges and universities, libraries, etc., which meet a wide range of adult learning interests from gourmet cooking to foreign languages.

Adult Credit—Opportunities for adults to complete or continue their formal schooling, often through approaches that are more adaptable and flexible than traditional schooling.

Table 1 continued

APPROPRIATE TECHNOLOGY: The movement to improve the quality of life through the creation, adaptation, and implementation of technology which is selected to best fit the specific situation of a community or nation.

As Hardware—An emphasis on technology as material tools and equipment with concern to promote more effective, efficient economic and material development and higher standards of living.

As Software—That segment of the movement which is interested in the view that all human creations are examples of technology, including social structures; enhanced development includes many areas of life in addition to material needs.

COMMUNITY DEVELOPMENT: Based on the belief that the abilities and energies of the people in a community can be used to improve their own lives through the use of democratic processes and voluntary efforts. Development refers to the institutions and structures that act as vehicles for fulfilling the peoples' needs and desires.

National Focus—Building a sense of community at local levels is seen to require major input from national resources; implicit is the view that local communities need direction and motivation provided by leaders and trainers at the national level.

Local Focus—The emphasis is on local initiative to decide what the community needs and for local power and resources to carry out development projects.

COMMUNITY EDUCATION: A movement that encourages the cooperation between school systems and various groups and segments of local communities or neighborhoods; community participation in education is stressed.

COMMUNITY LEGAL EDUCATION: CLE works largely with the poor and disenfranchised groups in society to help them understand and improve their capacity to use the legal system; an additional purpose is to work to reform the legal system.

HUMAN SERVICES: The field that includes the entire range of programs offering physical and mental health services to communities.

Medical Model—The most common approach, with the medical expert providing help to cure the individual's illnesses.

Welfare Model—Services to individuals who are seen as the victims of forces beyond their control: unemployment, poverty, old age, youth, handicap, discrimination.

Social Change Model—The organization of groups of people concerned with significant community problems; programs are designed to create better living conditions within neighborhoods. There is an awareness that structures of the social order may need to be improved.

Table 1 continued

MUSEUM EDUCATION: Museums function educationally, both formally and non-formally, as a major part of their activities. They have direct relationships with schools, provide their own formal classes and programs, and also serve the public through a variety of approaches: browsing, slide shows, tape recordings, etc.

   Cultural Preservation—The assumption is that the museum is the repository of creative products, and that these are for public display only under carefully controlled conditions.

   Public Service—The museum staff are seen as responsible for active involvement of the public in what is offered; major efforts are made to increase the public's interest (including minorities, handicapped, etc.) in using the museum.

NONFORMAL EDUCATION: The pedagogy of many out-of-school agencies with characteristics that emphasize flexibility, inclusiveness, relevance, participation, low cost, functionalism, adaptability.

   Process—The delivery aspects of this alternative pedagogy and its distinctions from schooling delivery. Less attention is paid to what goals the pedagogy is designed to promote.

   Maintenance—Seen as a low cost way to reach the masses of people, especially in Third World countries, with the purpose of increasing allegiance to national objectives and of decreasing the unrest of the disenfranchised.

   Social Change —Seen as a way to help empower the lower social classes, minorities and other disenfranchised groups; an explicit effort to modify basic social structures.

QUALITY OF WORKLIFE: A movement in business and industry concerned with both productivity and with worker nonmaterial satisfaction, including self-actualization, participation in decisions, concern for both the organization and the individuals; a belief in workers' abilities to have control over processes which directly affect them.

SELF-HELP: Groups that are usually community-based, with agendas aimed at specific group interests, needs or problems; strong belief in self-help as a way for individuals to help themselves and others. Membership is voluntary.

   Inner Focus—Personal needs and interests are the main concerns of the members, such as in support groups and recreation groups.

   Outer Focus—A major focus is to unite members having common interests in a community or national issue; often called issue-oriented groups.

Categorizing the Approaches

The table of necessity condenses much of the data described in the essay and will be difficult to absorb in detail if one does not first read the essays. The problem intensifies if one categorizes each of the twenty subapproaches using a second circular scheme, represented in Figure 2.

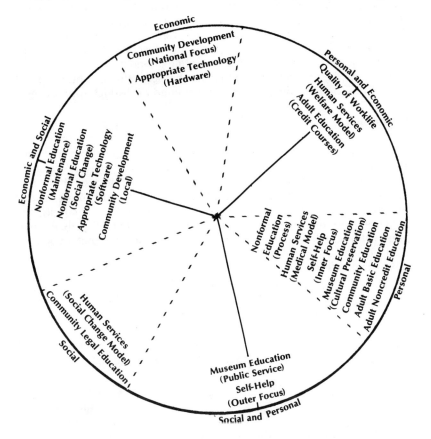

The Importance of Objectives. Clearly the more detailed specific learnings about these varied definitions will come from reading the individual essays. However, there are some general observations that can be made as well. The most significant one is that what often differentiates one subapproach from another within the same field is a shift in objectives. For example, when community development is discussed on a national level, it most usually is equated with economic development: generating electricity, diversifying the agricultural or industrial base, increasing the standard of living. Community development on the local level more often is concerned with improving local groups. At issue is the quality of life in the community. Similarly, some museums which aim primarily at preserving various objects lead to the personal enjoyment and development of the people who visit them. Other museums with a public service emphasis promote various social objectives such as heightening awareness of different cultural heritages or of the effect of various physical handicaps.

Again, this finding supports and in turn is supported by the finding that education outside of schools generally occurs in the process of doing something else. Education in schools has a uniform purpose: to educate. It is perhaps not surprising that schools are largely a homogenous phenomenon. Adult education has similar purposes and tends in practice to be more similar to schools than many other approaches described here. In contrast, education outside of school is a highly mobile phenomenon. As objectives change, so do the educational approaches that serve them, so much so that they must be defined differently and examined as distinct approaches.

In Summary

Two major observations emerge when one examines the effort of each educational approach to define itself. The first is that there is a distinct tendency towards differentiation. Many approaches quickly multiply into an array of distinct settings, and those that did not were already very small components of a larger field composed of many subsets. Secondly, the distinctions within a field often involve a difference in overall goals. As goals shifted within the field, the approach became so different that it could no longer be seen as similar enough to warrant a common definition.

The next section continues this self-definition exercise by examining the pervasive themes generated by each approach. In examining the major concerns suggested in each approach, we will be investigating whether or not this tendency towards variety of goals is supported through a second form of analysis.

Pervasive Themes

In another effort to generate basic characteristics about nonschool education, each author was asked to describe major concerns or issues which are frequently discussed by both practitioners and commentators in their field. The purpose of the request was to generate a list of important themes in order to see if there were any broad concerns which occur across the fields. Themes that were of wide interest in turn might provide further clues about the more general nature of nonschool education.

Table 2 summarizes the themes that received wide mention across approaches; the following sections discuss items of note in relation to each theme presented in Table 2.

Table 2

Pervasive Themes of the Approaches

ECONOMIC DEVELOPMENT

Community development—a central thrust until the last two decades; recent concern for development to include other areas of life.

Nonformal education—a most important goal for this approach's processes.

Appropriate technology—efforts are directed to encourage research that relates to specific economic situations.

Quality of worklife—one of the two main concerns.

Human services, welfare approach—focuses on a decent standard of living for people who, through little fault of their own, are unable to earn a reasonable living.

EMPOWERMENT

Community development—an underlying objective with dialogue as to whether efforts largely empower those who already have power.

Nonformal education—processes are believed to be especially useful and available for the disenfranchised.

Appropriate technology—one segment of the movement wants to relate to the poverty-stricken in both devleoped and developing nations.

Quality of worklife—interest in the power of workers of modern corporations.

Self-help—includes the concept of lifting by one's bootstraps relevant to those in need.

Human services, social change—this issue is taken seriously.

Adult education—implicit faith that literacy and other basic skills will empower the learner.

Community education—some attention to empowering community groups, largely through linkages with schools.

Community legal education—a main thrust is to provide access to the legal system for either advocacy or protection.

HUMAN POTENTIAL

Nonformal education—a way to provide aspects of schooling, using other means to reach out-of-school populations.

Quality of worklife—a way to enhance the life of the individual worker.

Self-help—a way to improve one's life situation.

Human services—a way to help individuals become active, contributing members of the community.

Museum education—a way for individuals to appreciate the creative achievements of culture.

Adult education—a way for the individual to improve him/herself.

Community education—a way for individuals to gain access and some control of schooling resources.

Legal education—a way for the disadvantaged to exercise their individual rights and address their grievances.

SENSE OF COMMUNITY

Community education—a strong value with schools as a major common bond.

Table 2 continued

Appropriate technology, software approach—sees a community working together to solve local problems as well as building common bonds.

Community development—an explicit objective is to bring people together to work on basic problems and concerns of life functions.

Self-help—many groups are strongly centered on community building.

Human services—some approaches see individual health closely related to the health of the community.

LINKAGES

Community development—an integrated effort is seen as requiring planned interagency cooperation.

Nonformal education—nonschool pedagogy implies that many community-based and national level agencies share and work together.

Quality of worklife—intra-agency linkages are sometimes seen as a concern.

Self-help—some interest in coalitions to achieve selected objectives.

Human services—much is said about the need for agency linkages, but there is difficulty in developing these.

Community education—a central theme linking schools and communities.

CULTURE CONSERVATION

Nonformal education—this is one major objective related to national unity and stability.

Self-help—many groups are formed to help preserve and encourage the values and traditions of the community and its culture.

Museum education—a powerful motivating force.

Adult education—inherent in the literacy and vocational emphasis there is the belief that the masses of people will learn to appreciate the ongoing economic, social and political structure of the culture.

Economic Development

It is first interesting to look at the nature of each theme and the source of its support. Economic development, which includes such concerns as increasing productivity, decreasing costs, increasing employment, developing more environmentally sound technologies and increasing standards of living, is supported by the three educational approaches which have the largest following in the Third World (community development, appropriate technology and nonformal education). At the same time the theme is equally important for the quality of worklife movement and for the larger field of business training to which it belongs. Statistics indicate that more money is spent on education in business in the United States than on all public education combined. When one adds the money spent on such related educational efforts as vocational education, the results are even more dramatic. Both the quantitative nature of the interest in this theme and its worldwide appeal speak to its importance as a crucial concern of out-of-school education.

Empowerment

While economic development may be the most pervasive theme in terms of money spent on educational approaches involved in its pursuit, the theme of empowerment had the broadest support across fields selected for study here. Empowerment and related concerns of increasing participation, self-reliance, autonomy, involvement, and civil rights was a central theme for every major approach selected here except for museum education. Again, it is not safe to extrapolate this overwhelming interest to out-of-school education as a whole because of the very probable bias in the sample presented in this volume. However, its importance seems well demonstrated.

One possible suggestion for the wide appeal of this theme, which seems supported both by this concern and a number of others with broad cross-category interest, is that out-of-school education is strongly connected to the hopes, dreams, and aspirations of its participants. It is a way to improve, correct, develop and change the status quo. In contrast to the basic attitude towards compulsory school, out-of-school education is more consciously idealistic. It is possible for people to take charge of their own lives, to act autonomously if one can remove the artificial boundaries that perpetuate discrimination.

Human Potential

It is clearly no accident that the theme of development of human potential has wide mention across categories as well. It is the belief in the possibility of further developing human potential that is the basic assumption behind the idea of empowerment. Again there is an optimism behind the themes that is an important characteristic of the field.

Sense of Community

The interest in forging a sense of community is an equally optimistic concern which again has strong roots in a belief in human potential. There is an interest in strengthening bonds among groups of people, improving the quality of those interactions, and creating a sense of common identity. While this theme is mentioned by fewer approaches, it nonetheless is central to those who suggest it.

It also is a theme which suggests a reason for the strong tendency of out-of-school educational approaches towards heterogeneity and variety. To be cohesive, a community must be small and particular. Variety of approach serves the specific needs of the community better than uniformity.

Linkages

The interest in interagency linkage is strongly related to the interest in forming a community. Communities always struggle with the tension between a desire for cohesiveness and the need to respect the autonomy and freedom of individual members. Organizations struggle with the same tension, but more frequently solve the issue using quite authoritarian lines of command. The interest in forming interagency linkage reflects the desire of many educational approaches to live with the tension or to attain resolutions that fulfill both needs simultaneously. It also provides a means to build a community without depowering numerous groups of people.

Culture Conservation

If one were to compare all the themes described above to those that would emerge from a similar analysis of schools, one would be struck with a quite noticeable difference in tone. Common themes in school literature include the importance of "basics", the need for discipline, accountability, and the importance of scholarship. However, this last theme that had wide support among out-of-school approaches studied here is very familiar to schools as well. It is the importance of conserving the culture. It has always been a function of schools to act as a stabilizing force through preserving the basic focus and heritage of the culture. Many nonschool approaches have similar values and concerns as well.

If one looks at these pervasive themes as a whole, the desire for a reasonable standard of living, a chance to develop one's potential, to live in a stable, cohesive and just community, what one discovers are some quite common aspirations. The pervasive themes that recur most frequently across approaches are the individual and collective hopes of participants. What is reinforced again is the basic characteristic of out-of-school education as being a means to other ends, as being a vehicle for people to work towards some very basic and understandable goals. Out-of-school education in this sense is very functional; equally important, it is idealistic, optimistic, and a way of accomplishing some very important life goals.

Pervasive Conflicts, Tensions, Compromises and Frustrations

Another unanticipated result stemming from the request that the author of each essay discuss important themes and concerns was that a substantial number of the concerns were actually descriptions of conflicts or tensions within the movement. While there are some common characteristics of the goals of out-of-school education, there is a great deal of conflict about how to attain these goals. This section summarizes some of the most widespread conflicts in the field.

Funding

The single issue that produces conflicts, tensions, compromises, and frustrations for all ten categories concerns funding. The particular variety of conflict and frustration differs among the categories. For example, adult education is concerned that with federal aid in jeopardy, there is the need to charge learner fees—yet the major groups of learners adult education wishes to serve are poor. Another example, community development in Third World countries requires considerable support from outside agencies (World Bank, missions representing industrialized nations, foundations), yet these funding sources often have "strings" attached which seriously tilt or impede the purposes and processes of local projects.

Other conflicts revolve around the unpredictability of funding, with results of overextension of project activities with little chance to follow-through; the enormous amount of time and energy and resources required periodically to obtain continued or new funding; the agony of competition among some categories for the same funding sources; the difficulty of locating funding by those approaches which are especially interested in counter-culture objectives, or purposes that are designed to make significant modifications in the underlying structures of a social order; the difficulty of locating funding for purposes which the mainstream of a culture does not consider very important. It should be no surprise that funding is so pervasive an issue, for what is at stake here in many instances is the issue of agency survival.

Participation

With the exception of legal education, all the categories find that the issue of learner (client) participation raises unresolved conflicts. Quality of life in the workplace is premised on the belief that worker empowerment will increase production and worker satisfaction, yet management is concerned about just what sorts of decisions workers should participate in and with what levels of power. Another example is that of nonformal education in Third World countries. It is dedicated to addressing the felt needs and involvements of the learner participants, but what does a nation do when what the participants want to accomplish through use of nonformal education is counter to basic national priorities?

The theme of participation raises tensions and frustrations around a number of questions: Who is to be included in the participation? What issues are fair game for decision making? Is participation advisory or more decisive than that? Are all (or even most) learners of a given approach capable of levels of participation which can basically affect the organization? How can participation be encouraged with groups who are alienated or out-of-touch? What does a group do when the time it takes to attend to and achieve participation is greater than the time available to achieve the purposes of a project? What happens when participants are not yet conscious of the underlying sources of the problems they face? What should happen when the local decisions of participants are counter to national interests or to values of a special, elite group? Participation is a rose with thorns.

Role of the Professional

Most of the categories have a continuing problem with matching values about learner participation and the role of the leader (teacher, counselor, facilitator). The leader's power, inherent in knowing more than the learner as well as power related to perceived status and leader access to human and material resources, establishes an interpersonal dynamic that can run counter to learner empowerment. For example, the advice given by the professional to a disenfranchised client in legal education is heavily loaded with the professional's own values about the social system. Often the purpose is to empower the learner. Another example, the technical expert in appropriate technology may see the impact of a better, more relevant way of people dealing with energy at the local level as being carried out through a grass roots approach. Often the expert has technical information and understanding of implications of implementing the technology that weighs heavily as local level decisions are made.

For self-help and nonformal education there is considerably less of this sort of conflict. Self-help relies largely on volunteer, lay leadership; nonformal education also recruits village experts. One of the problems these two categories do face is how to keep from gravitating towards the mean—moving towards increased professionalism by the lay leaders as a program becomes established over a period of years. A case in point is the adult education movement which, at one time, was uninterested in issues of leadership credentials; in recent years there has been a significant effort to get government acceptance of procedures which will lead to certification and a sense of professionalism.

Other Major Conflicts

A majority of the categories in varying combinations are faced with several other types of conflicts; five are briefly mentioned here. There is a strong leaning toward social change through an evolutionary approach, yet there is a persistent undercurrent of concern that the actual working-out of this position usually results in disguising the weaknesses of poorly functioning social structures.

Another related conflict is whether the root problems of a social system are largely economic or whether there must be major inclusive efforts made to address change and development through institutions that are connected to all life functions.

A third conflict has its origins in the difficulties of evaluating program cost efficiency, although there may be convincing evidence of its successful achievement of program services and other objectives.

An enduring conflict lies in trying to choose the criteria for selecting the target population of learners. Given limited resources, time and energy, this conflict involves decisions about age, sex, minority status, ethnic status, and location of learner groups.

A fifth source of tension is between the program objectives that promote local interests and those that promote regional and national interests. While these two sets of objectives may sometimes be complementary, they can also be somewhat independent of each other or even contradictory. A frequent expression of this conflict is demonstrated by a concern about local parochialism versus concern about national hegemony.

If one looks at the conflicts that have emerged from the initial study, a fairly common characteristic is that they are conflicts over means rather than ends. The conflicts center on how to get sufficient funds without subverting basic goals, how to allow participation and still accomplish something, how to staff a project and accomplish dual purposes of efficiency and empowerment. These conflicts not only occur within approaches but also divide approaches from each other as well. They are at the heart of the diversity that is so characteristic of the field.

Underlying Assumptions

The conflicts that pervade out-of-school education are real and demand further explanation. One hypothesis is that a number of the approaches proceed from very different assumptions and values about education. If two groups hold different beliefs, assumptions, and values about the nature of the educational venture and how and why it occurs, then the existence of a high level of disagreement is easily understood. The purpose of this section is to explore differing assumptions on two key issues in order to see if those differences have the power of suggesting explanations for these conflicts.

Two major theoretical categories have been explored here as relevant to this discussion. Both derive from the definition of education used here: any overt, organized effort to influence individuals or groups that improves the quality of life. In general, when one explores how one influences an individual person, one gets involved with learning theories. If, on the other hand, one's purpose is to influence a group, one is involved in social change.

Each of these two bodies of theory in turn suggest interesting questions. If one wants to know how a person learns, one gets into issues such as: Do people learn a given topic holistically (as Gestalt) or in carefully sequenced steps? Do people learn a particular topic more effectively when motivated by extrinsic rewards or are they more likely to learn if they pursue inner interests? If, on the other hand, one is interested in how groups change, one asks such questions as: Does change best start at the top of the organization or society or at the bottom? Is it more effective if it is evolutionary or radical in nature? Is change more likely to occur if it is aimed at individuals in the group or at the group as a collective?

Clearly these are not the only questions one could ask on these topics nor the only bodies of theory that have relevance for nonschool education, but they represent a beginning. What follows is an exploration of the potential implications one might derive from grouping our ten approaches or, more specifically, their twenty subparts on any one of these questions.

Learning Theory

The first question concerning how people learn deals with whether people learn most effectively all at once, intuitively, as a whole, or whether the topic to be learned must be first broken down into its component parts and taught separately. A related question is whether learning is largely a cognitive process or is equally a physical and emotional process as well. Table 3 presents the results.

Table 3

Learning Theory: Incremental or Gestalt

Incremental Emphasis	Gestalt Emphasis
Adult Basic Education	Adult Noncredit
Adult Credit Education	Appropriate Technology—Hardware
Community Education	Appropriate Technology—Software
Human Services—Medical	Community Development—Local
	Community Development—National
	Community Legal Education
	Human Services—Social Change
	Human Services—Welfare
	Museum—Cultural Preservation
	Museum—Public Service
	Nonformal Education—Process
	Nonformal Education—Maintenance
	Nonformal Education—Social Change
	Quality of Worklife
	Self-Help—Inner
	Self-Help—Outer

Incremental or Gestalt. The quite overwhelming emphasis on gestalt learning seems close enough to be considered a major characteristic of out-of-school educational approaches. It is interesting to look at the exceptions. Two of them, adult education and community education are so closely connected to schools that it is hard to categorize them properly as non-school approaches. Both typically have classes and are held in schools. Likewise, it takes only a small extension to go from the school model to the medical model. Doctors, like teachers, are experts dispensing information or prescriptions from their hospitals or offices. The parallels are notable.

In contrast, the vast majority of nonschool approaches rarely resemble a school or classroom and seldom prefer the step-by-step learning processes so typical of graded schools. Learning after graduation is assumed to be a very holistic process. A two week on-the-job training experience immerses the trainee in the job; he or she either makes it or leaves. A community group learns how to construct a solar greenhouse or heating system in a day-long workshop. Total involvement in the process is the basic learning theory.

Sources of Authority. When one turns to the question of whether nonschool approaches emphasize external or internal authority, however, the picture is less clear. On the one hand, there are a number of nonschool approaches which see learning as largely an unfolding of internally directed aspirations. Table 4 below summarizes the results on this issue. Examples would include visiting a museum, joining a support group, or living in a community-based, halfway house. The individual makes a decision to spend a certain amount of time in an enriched environment in order to allow his/her understanding of a work of art or a personal problem to grow and change.

On the other hand, there are just as many examples of nonschool learning in which the individual either volunteers or occasionally is coerced to accept learning from an external source. Going to the doctor, seeing a welfare caseworker, attending a real estate licensing course or GED course are examples. The learners either believe or are forced to act as if they believe that a given expert has the needed knowledge and can teach it using relatively familiar schooling methods.

Theory conflicts. Interestingly enough, there is also a third group of approaches which are involved in considerable internal conflict on these issues. Most typically the people operating the program believe in the power of internal learning, but also believe just as strongly that the specific message they have to teach is important for the learners to accept. Examples would include a local appropriate technology group which believes equally in self-reliance and the need to install better insulation. A local community development or nonformal educational project is similar in its belief in community action and the power of better agricultural techniques, basic literacy, cleaner water, innoculation of children and so on. Quality of worklife experts hired by management get into a similar dilemma with their belief in the importance of increasing worker autonomy and their inability to understand why unions would oppose the effort.

The table that follows summarizes the results of this sample on this question. In making the choice, approaches that largely rely in practice on external authority are placed in that column, and those that used a wide variety of techniques to foster internalization of learning are placed in that column.

Implications. There are some interesting implications for understanding nonschool education which emerge from this listing. The first is that there is certainly a greater interest in exploring internal learning mechanisms by nonschool approaches. The lack of a captive audience makes the greater time and effort involved necessary. In addition, nonschool approaches tend to use external authorities more selectively. Two reasons for the choice emerge from this list: the first is a clear need for a specific form of expertise (e.g., a doctor) and the second is a desire to make a national level change (e.g., in energy policy). The wide scope of a national level change and a need for speed seem to be reasons for the selection here.

An explanation of the two basic questions about how learning best occurs yields some interesting propositions about major characteristics of out-of-school education. The first is that the majority of approaches make different assumptions about how learning most effectively occurs than do schools.

Table 4
Learning Theory: Authority Sources

External	Internal
Adult Basic Education	Adult Noncredit
Adult Credit	Appropriate Technology—Software
Appropriate Technology—Hardware	Community Development—Local
Community Development—National	Community Legal Education
Community Education	Human Services—Social Change
Human Services—Medical	Museum Education—Cultural
Human Services—Welfare	Preservation
	Museum Education—Public Service
	Nonformal Education—Process
	Nonformal Education—Maintenance
	Nonformal Education—Social Change
	Quality of Worklife
	Self-Help—Inner
	Self-Help—Outer

They are much more likely to see learning as physical and emotional as well as cognitive and rarely spend much effort in carefully sequencing the process. In addition, they are more likely to put energy into methods which rely largely on internal unfolding or acceptance in contrast to schools which rely largely on external, expert authority. The fact that the three approaches studied here that are most closely identified with schools or resemble schools make the same assumptions about learning as do schools, merely reinforces the point.

However, just as important is the finding that different beliefs and assumptions about learning are at the sources of some major conflicts in the field. Whether or not effective use of expertise can develop an economy or bring about change in a nation's technological base divides the national and local functions of the community development and appropriate technology approaches. Similar disagreements divide quality of worklife proponents from such approaches as worker co-ops or workplace democratization. Even the medical field, which has a firm base in the use of expertise, is challenged by holistic health groups and social change human service proponents who contest the notion that illness is a physical and individual phenomenon. Learning when it is investigated in nonschool settings seems to occur in some fundamentally different ways and is at the heart of some very basic conflicts in beliefs about how individuals and societies change.

Social Change

The phenomenon of social change is only of peripheral concern to schools. For the most part, schools serve to preserve the culture by inculcating the young in the basic skills, knowledge, and structures of society. While there is frequent theoretical discussion of schools as a force for change, in practice schools tend to adopt a change only after that change has wide acceptance in the society.

In contrast, many out-of-school educational approaches frequently are conceived of and supported because they are potential vehicles for social change. Nonformal literacy projects in Cuba and Mainland China, for instance, were supported not just because of a desire to teach literacy skills, but because of their power in supporting the major social changes of the revolutions in those respective countries. Many of the less revolutionary movements have an equal interest in changing society though in somewhat less inclusive ways.

However, the way these movements see change occuring, as well as the object and nature of change, is quite different from one approach to another and has a profound effect on the way education is delivered by the approach. Even more than was the case with learning theory, differing assumptions about change lead to major conflicts within and between fields and lead to very differing practices.

Objects of change. The first question asked relevant to the social change theory of a given approach concerns the object of change: Does the approach aim its change at individuals within the community or society, or at the society as a whole?

Table 5 summarizes the results.

Table 5

Social Change Theory: Individual or Collective

Individual	Collective
Adult Basic Education	Appropriate Technology—Software
Adult Credit	Community Development—Local
Adult Noncredit	Community Development—National
Appropriate Technology—Hardware	Community Legal Education
Community Education	Human Services—Social Change
Human Services—Medical	Nonformal Education—Social Change
Human Services—Welfare	Quality of Worklife
Museum Education—Cultural	Self-Help—Outer
Preservation	
Museum Education—Public Service	
Nonformal Education—Process	
Nonformal Education—Maintenance	
Self-Help—Inner	

The first reaction one has in looking at this list is that more approaches seek to change individuals rather than collectives. A probable cause of this result is the North American cultural bias of this volume. Western culture as a whole is highly individualistic. Both causes of problems and their solutions are conceived as being within the scope of individual action. If one can change individuals' energy use patterns, provide them with good medical care, provide a minimum subsistence, provide access to aesthetic and personal growth opportunities, etc., then society as a whole will have evolved or changed for the better.

In contrast, the smaller number of approaches advocating collective change have a larger number of alternative life-style or Third World groups, and/or the group's definition of the collective unit to be changed is very small (e.g., a women's consciousness raising group or an autonomous work group). For instance, appropriate technology projects in this country are staffed largely by young "alternative life-style" people. Many of the other approaches on the list are more important in the Third World or minority cultures than in the developed countries.

Evolutionary or basic change. Is the change aimed at evolutionary modifications in the major structures of society, or is it more radical, aimed at basic social change? The results on this question correlate very highly with the question asked above.

Table 6

Social Change Theory: Evolutionary or Basic Change

Evolutionary	Basic Change
Adult Basic Education	Appropriate Technology—Software
Adult Noncredit	Community Development—Local
Adult Credit	Community Development—National
Appropriate Technology—Hardware	Community Legal Education
Community Education	Human Services—Social Change
Human Services—Medical	Nonformal Education—Social Change
Human Services—Welfare	Self-Help—Outer
Museum Education—Cultural Preservation	
Museum Education—Public Service	
Nonformal Education—Process	
Nonformal Education—Maintenance	
Quality of Worklife	
Self-Help—Inner	

Only the quality of worklife approach has changed sides. Again, it seems less a matter of the question being the same and more a case that a fundamental aspect of Western social structures is their individualized bias. If one is interested in changing a Western structure in a very profound way, it is often difficult to avoid shifting to a more collective emphasis. In any case, the two questions, taken together, serve to identify a major subgroup within out-of-school approaches which can then be investigated to see if they resemble each other in additional significant ways.

Top-Down or bottom-up. The last question about social change concerns the most effective direction of change. Will a change spread more easily if it is first adopted by the central government or the top levels of an organization or society before an effort is made to spread the change to the periphery or the bottom? Or is the reverse more effective? The results on the question are in Table 7.

Table 7

Social Change Theory: Top-Down or Bottom-Up?

Top-Down	Bottom-Up
Adult Basic Education	Appropriate Technology—Software
Adult Noncredit	Community Development—Local
Adult Credit	Community Legal Education
Appropriate Technology—Hardware	Human Services—Social Change
Community Development—National	Nonformal Education—Process
Community Education	Self-Help—Inner
Human Services—Medical	Self-Help—Outer
Human Services—Welfare	
Museum Education—Cultural Preservation	
Museum Education—Public Service	
Nonformal Education—Maintenance	
Nonformal Education—Social Change	
Quality of Worklife	

This table shows a clear preference for top-down or center-periphery change strategies. Virtually all approaches with a national or management level focus prefer these strategies together with those that resemble schools and/or see learning as depending on external authority. On the other hand there is a reasonably strong correlation between bottom-up strategies and those with collective, structure changing tendencies.

Additionally, there are some rather clear contradictions which in turn are a major source of conflict between those approaches which on the one hand are top-down in practice and on the other hand see empowerment as a major goal and put a strong emphasis on learning from internal authority. The national levels of the appropriate technology, community development and nonformal education movements experience this contradiction, as do management-initiated quality of worklife projects. This group forms another interesting subgroup which may be explored for similarities on other variables.

In Summary

This exploration of some important theoretical issues facing out-of-school education approaches not only suggests some specific insights into these issues, but, together with the earlier definitional work, begins to suggest some bases for forming groupings of approaches. Four groups which share a number of central purposes and assumptions are as follows:

1. **School-like approaches:** Adult basic education; adult education (credit); community education; and human services (the medical model).

The first three of these approaches actually are tied very strongly to schools and the latter to hospitals which resemble schools in their basic assumptions. These approaches share a reliance on experts, are basically conservative in nature, are top-down models and see learning as more of an incremental rather than gestalt process.

2. **Leisure-time, individualistic approaches:** museums, adult noncredit, self-help (inner focus).

A number of approaches share very similar assumptions which seem to stem from their similar purpose. In contrast to the groups above, museums, noncredit courses, and probably such institutions as libraries and national parks see learning as a holistic, internal process, but share the above group's very minor interests in social change.

3. **Bottom-up change movements:** local community development and alternative technology projects, consciousness raising groups and social change human service groups, community legal education.

These groups share a number of similarities. They put a strong emphasis on such social issues as empowerment and equity; they see a need for structural change in society, and their changes tend to be aimed at society as a collective rather than an aggregation of individuals. Additionally they tend to operate with a more local or regional focus.

4. **Top-down national level change movements:** National level appropriate technology, nonformal educational and community development, quality of worklife.

This group shares some similarities in emphasis on gestalt learning and the shared conflict concerning the relative importance of internal versus external authorities for learning. They also share a common desire for gradual improvement rather than radical restructuring of social structures.

In defining these groups, there is no intention to suggest that these are the only groupings that might be usefully investigated. The selection of approaches is too small for such an inclusive statement. Rather the purpose is to highlight the types of groupings that occur as one explores the wide variety of purposes and belief systems underlying nonschool education.

It is also important to note again the broad support this brief investigation provides for viewing nonschool education as highly diverse in nature.

Schools in all parts of the world share quite similar profiles on these issues, while out-of-school approaches, in contrast, are noted more for the number of issues they disagree on than on any high level of uniformity. It is true they share an emphasis on attaining basic human aspirations, but they disagree sharply on how these aspirations should be pursued. Since education out-of-school is largely a means rather than an end in itself, one can expect great variety in the actual delivery of services.

Delivery Variables

Like so many other fields, education is subject to wide discrepancies between theory and practice. So far this chapter has discussed issues of goals, definitions and beliefs, all of which are quite theoretical in nature. This section describes the practice of each approach, concentrating on each approach's delivery systems.

The Lifelong Learning Scale used to analyze each approach's delivery was described in Chapter 2. In general the scale makes it possible to compare very different approaches by breaking every delivery system down into eleven components and measuring how each varies on a continuum going from formal (1) to nonformal (5). Results from this analysis on the twenty subapproaches are displayed in Table 8.

Diversity of Delivery

The first conclusion that emerges simply from glancing at the data again reinforces the idea that out-of-school education is a highly diverse phenomenon. There is a substantial group of approaches that can be characterized as almost completely nonformal. Self-help groups fall in this category as do many approaches that seek change in small local groups using collective, bottom-up strategies. On the other hand, there are highly formal approaches as well. Art museums and many of the courses adults take for credit are examples. In between are numerous other combinations of variables. While there are significant groupings which might possibly be investigated as delivery patterns, nonetheless the fact remains that there are many patterns, each of which has a record of effectiveness for implementing out-of-school education.

Clusters of variables. However, the fact that the field is characterized by its diversity does not mean that there aren't some very significant clusters on some variables and some strong correlations among others. The field is diverse but not totally random. For instance, there are no examples in this sample of learners being selected according to very precise, predictable criteria and carefully graded according to age. Instead, by far the majority of learners are selected by very nonformal criteria, age being unimportant and other criteria very unpredictable. A smaller number have some criteria (e.g., all the people in a given work group or specific job); however, it is rare to find the issue of gaining admission to a nonschool approach having as much importance as it has for schools.

There are two other significant groupings of items that are largely non-

Table 8

Lifelong Learning Scale Data: The Approaches
and Their Delivery Variables
(1 = formal - 5 = nonformal)

Delivery Variables

Approaches	Objectives	Content and Sequence	Time	Learners	Staff	Teaching-Learning Methods	Rewards and Evaluation	Materials	Finances	Buildings	Power, Control, Organization
Adult Basic Education	1	1	3	5	1	3	3	1	1	3	1
—Noncredit	5	5	5	5	3	5	5	5	3	3	1
—Credit	1	1	3	3	1	1	1	1	1	1	1
Appropriate Technology—Hardware	3	3	3	3	1	3	3	1	1	1	1
—Software	5	5	5	5	3	5	5	5	5	5	5
Community Development—Local	5	5	5	5	5	5	5	5	5	5	5
—National	5	3	5	5	3	3	5	3	3	5	1
Community Education	5	5	5	5	3	3	5	3	3	1	1
Community Legal Education	5	3	5	5	1	5	5	5	1	3	3
Human Service—Medical	5	3	5	5	1	1	3	1	1	1	1
—Welfare	5	5	3	3	1	1	1	3	1	1	1
—Social Change	5	5	3	5	3	5	5	5	3	5	3
Museum Education—Public Service	5	3	5	5	1	5	5	3	3	3	3
—Cultural Preservation	1	1	5	5	1	5	5	1	1	1	1
Nonformal Education—Process	5	5	5	5	5	5	5	5	5	5	5
—Maintenance	3	3	3	5	3	5	3	3	5	5	3
—Social Change	5	5	3	5	3	5	3	5	3	5	1
Quality of Worklife	5	5	3	3	3	5	3	3	3	3	1
Self-Help—Inner	5	5	5	5	5	5	5	5	5	5	5
—Outer	5	5	5	5	5	5	5	5	5	5	5

formal as well. For the most part, out-of-school approaches have nonformal objectives. They seek to apply knowledge to immediate problems which have psychological and physical dimensions as well as cognitive ones. Not surprisingly the content or curriculum of these approaches tend towards the nonformal as well.

Secondly, by far the majority of approaches use more nonformal methodologies including treating time as a fairly flexible commodity and relying on more nonformal intrinsic reward systems as well. The learner is assumed to be quite responsible, and methods foster activity rather than passivity. Even some of the approaches with quite formal objectives such as adult basic education or art museums tend to use more nonformal teaching-learning techniques.

Thus, out-of-school educational approaches tend to be, for the most part, significantly more nonformal than schools in some important areas: the goals and objectives of the approach, the content, the methods, the use of time, the nature of the rewards and the characteristics of the learners. Just as interestingly, this tendency towards nonformality is not as strongly carried over in many equally important areas.

Mixed approaches. For instance, staffing of out-of-school approaches is as likely to be formal as nonformal. Many staff people are full-time and experts in their fields while an equal number are neither. Similarly many of the organizations running out-of-school educational approaches are as bureaucratic as schools — and another significant group are not. In like fashion, some approaches are just as costly as are schools, using sophisticated materials and taking place in elaborate physical facilities; many, in contrast, are not.

It is interesting to speculate why out-of-school educational approaches favor the nonformal end of the continuum on one group of variables and are so mixed on others. One tempting proposition is to look at the latter group of mixed variables (staff, control, finances, etc.) as being much more crucial to the basic social system of the society which generated most of the approaches chosen here. Certainly, the notion of professionalism is deeply embedded in Western culture as are capital intensive approaches. Bureaucracy is also dominant, not just in the West, but worldwide. In other words, the "softer" components of education such as aims and methods vary from the norm of schooling much more frequently than do variables which are crucial to the overall social fabric.

Possible relationships. In addition to looking at individual variables, it is also interesting to look at various correlations among the delivery variables. For instance, there is a very strong tendency for approaches to have similar ratings on the variables of staffing, resources, and organization. If an approach is nonformal on one, it is likely to be nonformal on all of them; a similar strong connection is found at the formal end of the continuum.

An equally strong correlation is found between methodology and reward systems. Formal methods are accompanied by letter grades or a similar system; less formal methods seem to require intrinsic motivational systems.

Lack of correlations also has a certain amount of interest. While one might predict a certain amount of connection between the objectives of an approach and the organizational forms used to carry them out, in fact there are few strong connections. While it is true that approaches with formal objectives have formal organizational structures, the reverse is not as likely. National level community development and nonformal education social change projects have nonformal objectives, but are often administered by heavily bureaucratic organizations. What remains to be judged is whether this lack of correlation derives from the power of bureaucracies in the society, whether bureaucracies are a more effective form of organization no matter what the objectives, or whether the correlation results from some other cause. In any case, the lack of a strong connection on these variables is a source of interest.

In Summary

A close analysis of a number of nonschool educational delivery systems on the one hand suggests that there are many quite distinct ways of delivering out-of-school education, and on the other hand that there are a number of definite patterns which occur widely in the field. Prime among the latter include the tendency of nonschool approaches to have nonformal goals, methods, and reward systems and to be relatively open in selecting learners. People seeking educational experiences out-of-school tend to have immediate needs which quite frequently are not highly intellectual. They prefer active, participatory methods and would rather not be subjected to letter grades. Just as interesting, however, is the fact that this tendency of nonschool approaches to be less formal than schools is not supported on other variables, specifically on organizational, staffing and resource variables. While the sample of approaches analyzed here is too small to extrapolate these findings, they nonetheless have strong enough support to warrant more thorough investigation.

Conclusion

The basic image that is reinforced over and over again, as education beyond schools is explored through a number of lenses, is the idea of a field that is highly diverse but not random. All of the various analytic modes used here highlight both of these characteristics equally. Only very infrequently is there enough uniformity on any particular issue for it to be considered definitional. Even those that emerged in this study must be considered tentative because of the limited nature of the sample. Education beyond schools is characterized by its immense variety. On the other hand, each of the lenses employed here uncovered some generalizations that were strongly enough supported to warrant further study. These generalizations are equally characteristic of the field as a whole.

The generalizations that received strong support from a number of approaches include the following:

- Out-of-school education is a very common organizational function which is usually highly integrated with other purposes and functions.

- Differences that divide an educational approach into a variety of subapproaches can be due to differences in purposes and/or means to obtain various ends.
- Pervasive themes that can be found in a wide variety of approaches most often concern very basic human aspirations.
- Most approaches see learning as a holistic rather than incremental approach and the majority rely on internal sources of authority for learning. However the latter position is a frequent source of conflict within approaches.
- The majority of approaches studied here use typical Western modes of social change (individual, evolutionary and top-down). However, the group of approaches that held opposite assumptions represented one of the more cohesive subgroupings discussed in the study.
- Out-of-school educational approaches tended to be nonformal in their selection of objectives, content, learners, methods, rewards and use of time. However they were very mixed in their choice of organizational, staffing, and funding patterns. These latter three variables tended to be highly correlated to each other but to show little relationship with other delivery variables.

The fact that out-of-school education is diverse and varied needs little further demonstration. Though the selection of examples is small here, common experience easily extends the conclusion. The generalizations, however, are tentative. There are, no doubt, other generalizations to be constructed, and some of the ones suggested above might not hold up under more rigorous research. There is a clear role for much more detailed investigation in the field.

There are, though, enough initial ideas that can be of immediate interest to practitioners. The enormous range in the delivery variables among out-of-school approaches suggests that for any given approach, the practitioners should explore ideas and techniques of other approaches. If educational aspects of an approach are not highly effective, practitioners should be alert to the educational potentials of other approaches.

Some of the broad generalizations also have implications for practice. The importance of purpose suggests that out-of-school educators should spend adequate time in forming and clarifying purposes. Tying that purpose to a basic life function also seems effective. The more frequent choice of nonformal objectives and experiential holistic methodologies suggest that practitioners would benefit from thorough exposure to these techniques as an alternative to abstract, segmented, formal school approaches. The fact that three variables (taken together they can be seen as organizational or structural variables such as type of staffing, source of funding, and use of power) range so widely and do not seem to have any consistent connection to the purpose and methodologies used suggests, at the very least, that practitioners should pay attention to these issues. Issues of how the organization is structured and funded and who is qualified to be staff are as influential a part of education as the more traditional issues of content and methods. Initial findings here suggest that these variables in fact are the source of great differences among approaches.

Perhaps most importantly, however, practitioners should acquaint themselves with their counterparts in other fields. There is a rich potential for cross-fertilization which has barely been tapped in the few studies available. The ten essays that follow offer one opportunity to explore some alternatives, to see how others have struggled with some of the same underlying issues, and to discover some new ideas. These approaches and the many others that could not be included here contain innumerable specific and general suggestions for the out-of-school practitioner.

PART II

4
NONFORMAL EDUCATION

Horace B. Reed

Early evening in a slightly smoky tea shop of a small village in a remote mountainous zone of Nepal, three government workers and a multinational employee are chatting over their evening meal of rice, puree and tea. Conversation inevitably drifts towards sharing impressions, happenings and issues about their daily village work. The young man from the Water Resource Agency, newly arrived out of Katmandu, is full of anxious questions about local conditions, villager attitudes, how to personally survive during his tour of duty here. He is especially concerned with the problems of communicating with village leaders and opinion-makers. A quiet, austere Nepalese gentleman, with years of worldwide experience as a Gurkha soldier, now in an agricultural extension program, offers bits of useful advice. A personable and articulate woman employed by the UNICEF organization adds her insights gained from 20 years of varied Third World assignments dealing with nutritional problems. The fourth member of the group, the local district Panchayat representative of Nepal's political structure, says little at first, but becomes highly voluble as the evening progresses and the tea shop grows darker in the flickering kerosene lantern light.

The conversation soon focuses on the water supply problems for the homes and fields of the village people. Each day the girls and women must walk several miles over the difficult Himalayan terrain to carry back water for household use. The crops are often seriously reduced due to inadequate rainfall. It is this water problem that has drawn together the three agency facilitators coming out of Katmandu and the local political representative.

Throughout the world, in backyards, fields, marketplaces, or meeting rooms, for thousands of such situations, vital information is shared in out-of-school settings. And when trainers from agencies such as government ministries and UNESCO interact with individuals and groups of villagers, nonformal education is being practiced.

Nonformal education is a practical, rather than abstract, approach to learning (Frith and Reed, 1982). Psychological and physical objectives, as well as cognitive, are important and of equivalent worth. The content of nonformal education tends to focus on every day concerns and is specific and close to sensory levels. Learning experiences are short-term with easily altered sequences. The learners are of widely varied ages with few selection criteria being used. Staff are often lay people with minimal formal training. Teaching-learning approaches favor interaction among learners, using a wide range of experiential techniques. Learning may take place in many settings: homes, a field, an available community building.

Definitions and Distinctions

Formal and Nonformal Education

Nonformal education (NFE) is any organized, intentional and explicit effort to promote learning to enhance the quality of life through out-of-school approaches. Compared with formal schooling, NFE has these characteristics: learner-centered, community-oriented content, nonhierarchical relationship of facilitator and learner, use of local resources, present time focus, age inclusive for learners. It takes place through the daily operations of self-help groups, human and social service agencies, religious groups, the media, clubs, etc. It is no accident that the formal school system and nonformal education units of a nation may be at variance as to both means and ends, as well as complementary.

One vast area of learning which is not addressed here is called informal and is distinguished from nonformal and formal education. Informal learning is not education; it is unorganized, often unintended and often less consciously aimed at identified objectives. Yet much of the most crucial learnings for individuals and for the conservation of cultures is carried out informally. Prime examples are the learning of one's native language, inculcating the values of family and community, and the coordination of complex muscle control.

Formal education and nonformal education represent a range of concepts and practices along a continuum. Within formal education, from one classroom and school to another, there is some variation in the degree of formality of structure. There is variation also with nonformal approaches, although the variation is far greater between, than within, each of them.

Practitioners assume that NFE makes a diverse, useful, and more pervasive influence on most individuals, and on community development, than does formal education. Documentation of this assumption is meager, but given the wide range of agencies and organizations that deliver NFE compared with schooling, it is safe to claim that the quantity of learning is much larger and more diverse. Whether it is more useful may be a fruitless question given that the objectives are often not comparable.

Origins of NFE

Background information on NFE can be viewed from differing perspectives: individual theorists, international organizations, national ministries, and specific projects.

While NFE activities have been a part of all cultures throughout human history, special attention to it as an examined educational approach started in the early 1960's (Coombs, 1968). The origins for this recent attention stem from several sources. Practitioners of education working out of cooperative extension services, adult education programs, youth clubs, religious groups, etc., have constructed a vast amount of useful information about alternative learning activities and strategies. Long-range planners of educational systems in such organizations as UNESCO, ICED, World Bank, and National Ministries have found it necessary to promote learning through many NFE agencies, in addition to schooling, in order to make realistic budgets to achieve national educational goals. Another source is the widespread criticism of formal schooling as a sufficient vehicle to attain the diverse and complex development goals of Third World countries. A similar level of unease concerning schooling is expressed in modernized nations. The major impetus continues to be provided by such international agencies as world regional organizations, foreign missions of industrialized nations, private foundations, and educational and religious organizations with international goals (Paulston, 1974; Reed, 1982). The impact of UNESCO is especially strong in arousing concern over the long-range difficulties of depending upon only formal education for rapid national development in the Third World.

National Level Emphasis

During the late 1960's and into the present, a large number of nations, especially in the Third World, have developed national programs to explicitly promote NFE. Some of these have been tied to existing adult education efforts; others have been organized as separate units. In most cases, an NFE unit is seen as being a subdivision of a nation's ministry of education. These ministries are largely concerned with formal schooling. There is a concern that the characteristics of formal education will tend to blunt the distinctive qualities of nonformal education. Some countries have tried to deal with this concern by establishing an overarching NFE national policy board or committee, with representation from a wide range of governmental and other agencies. These boards are also seen as a way to encourage collaboration in NFE efforts among the varied related groups in the nation. In Thailand, Nepal, Indonesia, South Korea, and several other countries, there are national governmental commissions or committees that have been formed to promote nonformal education as an explicit goal. Appointments to such national committees are made so as to represent a broad spectrum of organizations and agencies that have an educational function: human services, agricultural extension, family planning, formal schooling, libraries, and cooperative credit are examples. In Nepal, this group is headed through the office of the King, thus signaling its potential importance. There does not appear to be much success as yet in finding ways for these national boards to exert significant influence.

In all countries of the world, much NFE implementation is carried out at the national level through government ministries such as agriculture, health, commerce, and internal affairs. Operating independently of the education ministry, they tend to be only indirectly influenced by formal education traditions. The NFE units connected to the ministries of education are in some instances making an effort to be a resource for the educational activities of the other government agencies (DeJene, 1980).

Linkage Efforts

No national level, generalized, multi-agency model for NFE fits all countries. There is, however, a commonality in the complex of restraining forces that NFE leaders face in efforts to create effective linkages among relevant agencies (Ahmed and Coombs, 1975). First is the fact that those who deliver services through nonschool agencies (human services, agriculture, etc.) do not see themselves as educators. Education is seen as the exclusive role of school systems, while other agencies see themselves as counselors, facilitators, trainers, consultants, or public relations people. Another constraint is confusion over the purposes and tasks of an NFE national, multi-agency linkage. Information sharing can be carried out with relatively low levels of involvement by each agency. But resource sharing of materials, time, personnel, funds, ideas, and facilities require major adjustments in the leadership styles and organizational structures of an interagency NFE linkage. Such adjustments may require skills that many agency personnel either do not have or do not believe are useful. A third constraint is the tendency for each agency to see other agencies as competitors for financial support, power and status in the national arena. A fourth hindrance can be traced to clashes among personalities, where personal rivalries between agency representatives interfere with linkage tasks. Very little information is yet available that can be directly turned to, as guides for minimizing such constraints and maximizing the supporting forces.

Programs and Projects

Within each nation, there are large numbers of NFE projects and programs. These include diverse features such as piping spring water to a central village location; helping farmers improve rice production through new varieties of seeds, irrigation and soil improvements; encouraging kitchen gardens to enhance nutrition; constructing low-cost newspaper reading centers; establishing planned parenthood facilities; organizing local problem solving discussion groups; building year-round serviceable roads; and skill training for wayside mechanics. The range of projects matches the varied richness of life functions in cross-cultural contexts (Ahmed and Coombs, 1975). The water supply project in Nepal represents a multifaceted approach by various agencies to address a complex village problem.

Accounts of a single program provide detailed information on a range of delivery variables, as well as on underlying major issues relevant to NFE. It is through examination of many specific projects, both on site and written accounts, that one obtains the full and distinctive flavor of nonformal education.

Sponsorship of these NFE projects comes from many sources, both from within and from without national boundaries. In developing nations, foreign sponsors' motives may range from benign to domination. Some sponsorships have an international basis, such as UNESCO, UNICEF, ILO, World Health, World Bank and Colombo. Many are government missions of the industrialized nations, private foundations, philanthropic and religious organizations, and issue-oriented, voluntary groups.

Urban Efforts

Background information for rural, village-level projects is readily available, but much less so for urban NFE efforts. This is because so much of the Third World is predominately agriculturally based. But it may also be that the characteristics of NFE tend to be most readily relevant to the more cohesive, smaller community characteristics of rural patterns. It may also be that NFE agency efforts are much less easily traced in the mobile, complex urban settings—there probably are significant and numerous NFE urban programs that have yet to be thoroughly examined and recorded in the literature. In fact, much of the literature seems to assume that NFE and rural life have some sort of exclusive affinity. As urban populations continue to grow in the cities, and as formal education continues to fail those populations, it is predictable that NFE's relevance to urban life will occupy much more attention by planners and practitioners.

Delivery Variables

The clearest, most significant qualities of nonformal education are apparent through examination of commonalities among program variables. These variables are germane to any organized educational endeavor, formal and nonformal. NFE is distinctive in the descriptors that are associated with these NFE variables. Some of the most prolific and potentially useful literature in the field is focused on these characteristics (Frith and Reed, 1982).

Learners

A basic characteristic of NFE is that the target populations of learners may be any age. In the Nepalese water supply problem nearly all membes of the community are the potential learners. The lack of readily accessible water supply affects everyone in the village in a variety of ways. The solutions to the problem especially affect members of the older youth and adult populations, both male and female.

The phrase *lifelong learning* is central to NFE. Any given project may focus on specific categories of people such as early childhood, out-of-school youth, older adolescents, adults, senior citizens, women, rural poor, villagers, urban workers, minorities, occupation groups. The particular characteristics of the learners are important factors in the decisions made concerning other educational variables discussed in the following sections.

Objectives

There is considerable discussion and technical material in the literature about constructing NFE objectives. Purposes and goals associated with NFE have both a community, as well as an individual, development emphasis. The water problem in the Nepalese village implies several educational objectives. An inadequate supply, plus unclean storage facilities, results in serious health concerns. The energy and time required to transport water in heavy containers on the backs and heads of the girls and women takes its toll. The low crop yield due to unpredictable rainfall from year to year produces near starvation diets for some, and pressures for outward migration for others. This migration may draw off from the village those with the most energy, imagination and daring, resulting in reduced psychic resources for quality of village life.

The objectives in the above examples are clearly community-oriented. Yet, they also require that selected individuals gain specific skills, attitudes and information in order to work with one another in finding and carrying out solutions to the community development problem. NFE objectives are characterized as functional, daily-life centered, immediate, concrete, holistic. This is in contrast to schooling objectives which favor the symbol systems of the culture, are long-range and delayed, and have more indirect relationships to daily living.

Accounts of some NFE projects suggest that their objectives are very much like those of formal schooling. Many projects have a mixture of objectives for subunits of a project, with more or less emphasis on non-formal qualities. It would be strange if this ambiguity did not appear in the implementation of NFE plans. Given that both formal and nonformal objectives may have high value for a culture, one would expect that specific projects might well incorporate a mix of both.

To achieve purposes with such features as employment, sanitation, governance, and housing, there are complementary features of other educational variables that ensure a means and end relationship. That is, the objectives that are selected will strongly influence the teaching-learning approaches used as well as the resources, the facilities, the organization, and other variables that make up the total educational endeavor.

Methods and Materials

When the villagers in Nepal get together with one of the agency facilitators out of Katmandu, to question and comment and discuss and argue and share information about the causes and possible solutions of the water problem, typical NFE methods and materials are illustrated. When hands-on techniques relevant to laying of pipe, safe storage of water, and construction of irrigation ditches are demonstrated and practiced by villagers, NFE methods and materials are utilized. While pictures and reading matter will be used, occasional lectures given, and abstract theoretical explanations offered, these school-like approaches may not be emphasized and certainly are not the dominant mode.

Illustrations of the flexibility and innovations of NFE materials and resources are techniques such as simulation games, fotonovelas, the "Fun Bus," puppets, theater and other folk media, educational radio and TV, village-level discussion/study action groups, use of tape cassettes, records, learning activity packages, programmed instruction, peer learning, and role playing (Evans, 1976). Russell (1977) describes the use of a creative mix of methods and materials in the "Fun Bus," where community development issues are addressed through the performing arts using local participation, workshops to prepare skits, grass roots level public relations and advertising, a public facility for performances, local audiences, and post-performance discussions of the community issues used in skits. This specific example is also of interest since it is one of the few detailed accounts of an NFE project that was based in a modern, industrialized nation.

The tangible, readily observable qualities of teaching-learning approaches (methods) and of learning resource materials may help explain why these NFE variables are treated so extensively in written sources (CIE, 1972). Nonformal education characteristics of learners, objectives, and content require correlated methods and materials. Considerable invention and field testing has resulted. These explorations have borrowed heavily on two precedents: progressive education practices and indigenous traditions of Third World countries. Nonformal education funding sources in the industrialized countries are attracted toward supporting efforts that will result in protocols of methods and materials. These can be generalized and disseminated worldwide. At any rate, there is now interrelated, detailed information available for out-of-school educational programs. Methods and materials that work for a village development project in Asia may be modified and found useful for nonformal education agencies throughout the world.

Content

What do the Nepalese villagers need to know in order to understand the nature of the water problem and to decide among alternative solutions? This knowledge provides the "curricula," the messages, the contents of NFE. There is information needed about sanitation; health issues; space and size and measurement facts; gravity and pressure concerns; agricultural ideas relating water, soil, manure, seed and sun; socio-political patterns of resource sharing and distribution. (It is intentional that the local Panchayat representative is one of the facilitators.)

The logical sequence of what content must be learned first is much less an issue in NFE as contrasted to schooling. It is in this sense that NFE content is organized around the situation-specifics of the group of people. Thus, in each instance a unique ordering of knowledge is required where a learner's basic life functions provide much of the source of authority for what is learned. In schooling, the source of authority for what is learned is largely derived from sources outside the learners. Further, the Nepalese villagers may not always need to know how to read or write in order to be involved in highly complex, problem solving operations in village and personal life.

The information, messages, and meanings conveyed through NFE cover significant areas of the knowledge base of any given culture. The important exception is that body of complex, highly abstract knowledge that comprises the curricula of the formal school system, especially the highly theoretical knowledge systems and their corresponding symbol systems. Such knowledge is not readily conveyed through NFE. What is relevant is the *application* of more abstract theories to the daily lives of people and their communities. Government extension agencies, museums, human services, and occupational groups all may have different content to convey, yet all can make use of the low structured, flexible, concrete characteristics of NFE.

Content Across Agencies

Our Nepal village story provides an example of a common failing in many NFE projects. While thoughtful and highly valuable interagency linkages have been developed among the several facilitators, there is the failure to consider just how far reaching village water supply development innovation can be. The introduction of new appropriate technology, such as a water supply system, will have implications for the land tenure system. In this Nepalese village, much of the land is owned by a few and tenured out to many. The financial rewards of an improved water supply, that allows for controlled irrigation, will largely go to the few land owners. Why then should the villagers as a whole pitch in and provide many weeks, perhaps months, of hard labor (including many new learnings) to enrich the few? One answer is that this project may not ever get beyond the discussion and arguing stage, because crucial related issues have not been included, in this case land reform. Many problems and concerns of a community require information that crosses the message boundaries inherent in each agency's operations. There is a strong tendency for agency personnel to mistakenly assume that village learners can readily integrate separate content packages, in solving problems of poverty, malnutrition, family planning, agricultural and land reform, environmental pollution, water supply, etc. What is required is the cooperative efforts of other agencies in addition to the government workers we first met in the tea shop. These additional agencies will surely modify the overall nonformal educational design.

Personnel and Staff Development

Village-level workers such as the young Water Resource Agency man or the ex-Gurkha soldier probably do not perceive themselves as performing an educational role (education being seen as the exclusive role of schooling). Yet, the characteristics of nonformal education personnel are well exemplified by the four participants sharing their supper of dahl-baht and tea. They may have had no formal training in pedagogy as it is taught in teachers' colleges and will not have taught in a formal school setting. In the Nepal illustration, the four will select several men and women from the village who will provide to the rest of the villagers leadership and facilitating roles specific to the varied objectives and content arising out of the water supply problem. NFE staff are required to have more information, skills and desired attitudes than their learners, but this can often be gained through daily life experiences and through short-term training workshops. Some of the most effective NFE educators have had little or no formal schooling experience. They do have to have close touch with the complex culture of the learners; be flexible in use of methods and materials; be quick to pick up new ideas, facts, attitudes, understandings; have the respect of their learners; and be interested in both the processes and the outcomes of the project. None of these requirements necessarily involve a high school or college degree or a teaching certificate.

Advantages of NFE personnel. Two powerful arguments for the attention to NFE relate to personnel and staff development delivery variables. One is that relatively untrained people have lifestyles and qualities that are closely similar to those of the learners. The advantage is that given learners' impoverished backgrounds, including inadequate previous schooling experiences, their fears or negative attitudes towards schooling may be significantly reduced by learning from people with whom they can identify (Etling, 1975).

In several Third World nations, there are national level staff development programs to train NFE personnel. Such training requires innovative organizational and administrative leadership. One good example of a long-term staff development planning and implementation design is fully operational in Thailand's Department of Nonformal Education. Supported by the Thai government, with help from World Bank, World Education, the University of Massachusetts, and other organizations, staff development is being carefully nurtured on a local, provincial, regional and national level. The underlying premise is that NFE programs require training of personnel that has many features distinctive of formal schooling. Since most of those hired to work in these NFE projects are only familiar with formal pedagogy, there is urgent need for helping NFE administrators and facilitators acquire the new skills consistent with NFE variables.

The techniques used in the training of many NFE personnel are designed to model the actual ways the facilitators will work with the grass roots target populations. For example, training may take place where there are opportunities to field test the skills in village situations. A high degree of trainee participation during staff development workshops is explicitly provided.

The methods and materials used in the workshops are similar to ones the trainees would be using with village populations. Needs analysis of trainees' beliefs, expectations and wants are used to help design the staff development program. Evaluations of training include qualitative techniques that can be adapted by trainees to their own evaluation efforts at ongoing, NFE village-level projects.

The second argument attracting worldwide interest in the efficiency of NFE relates to issues of economics. Since the cost of sustaining formal education is largely in personnel, there can be major savings from NFE facilitators who cannot and do not expect high wages. In some cases, their services may be voluntary with little or no cash involved. Not all NFE objectives can be implemented using low wage deliveries. Examples of high-cost facilitators would include personnel in human services, governmental extension, libraries, and museums. Nonformal education projects that approximate schooling objectives, such as programs for the General Equivalency Diploma (GED) and Adult Basic Education (ABE), will also often have higher wage costs. Personnel for these programs are frequently highly trained school professionals working at a second job. It can be argued that characteristics of such programs are too close to those of formal education to be labeled as NFE. For example, GED and ABE have almost no direct concern for community development, and the curriculum is largely school-oriented.

A useful body of information on preservice training and staff development for NFE personnel is available (Etling, 1975; Heredero, 1979). The designs of these training programs are constructed around the theoretical assumptions about the distinctive aspects of NFE: participatory mode, learner-centered, collaborative, functional, community development oriented, experiential, humanistic values.

Facilities

Instruction in building a water storage and pipe laying system in the Nepalese village is carried out on-site in field and forest. Discussions and debate at the planning and decision stages take place around the banyan tree that serves as the village common.

Nonformal education can take place in a family kitchen, under a tree in a village or field, at a bazaar, on a porch, in a school building in the evening, at an unused store. The diversity of possible uses of space for NFE is so large as to make it pointless to catalogue and describe them. About all that can be said is that any need for expensive, complex facilities connected with the delivery of NFE may be more a reflection of personnel who are still locked into formal traditions.

Finance

The financial aspects for the Nepalese village's water supply project are modest. Resources come in part from the national government in Katmandu, from the zonal and district offices, and from the village. Compared with the financial outlay required to support a schooling system, the nonformal educational investment is minimal. Major savings are due to very low costs for personnel, facilities and materials. Much of what is needed for delivery of nonformal education is already present in the indigenous social structures of village and district life.

Efforts to provide precise cost estimates for NFE are not well documented. There is a need for more accurate information that would be helpful to planners, staff and learners regarding appropriate sources of funds, allocation of resources, and simple record keeping (IO-ETS, 1979; Mannon, 1975).

Organization

There is a tendency for NFE projects to borrow the organizational structures and practices of formal education, resulting in hierarchies and bureaucracies which may not be very conducive to decentralization and cooperation. Much of NFE is delivered by established agencies and organizations (cooperative extensions, human services, etc.) and these tend to have corporate characteristics, reflecting neither a participatory mode nor collaborative principles. Obvious contradictions between the flexible, low-structured, inclusive objectives and methods of NFE are contrasted to hierarchical, bureaucratic organizations. These tensions suggest the need for governmental and other established agencies to explore the field of organizational development. The principles and practices of organizational development might be a way to bring flexible, more responsive qualities into these organizations.

Thailand offers an example of a large NFE department that is making a major attempt to address the problems of centralization versus participation, competition versus cooperation. Leadership in this department has gradually developed policies that place much decision making at five NFE Regional Centers (instead of centralized in Bangkok) and Lifelong Learning Centers at the Provincial levels. Personnel at all levels are being introduced to organizational development approaches to such issues as problem solving, conflict resolution, group decision making, and communication techniques that enhance participation and shared control.

Evaluation

The Nepalese villages and the NFE facilitators from Katmandu will have a deep investment in the quality of the construction of the water supply project and in the final product of a readily available supply of water for homes and fields. Evaluation of nonformal education focuses on how knowledge is implemented, rather than on how knowledge is memorized. The assessments of NFE processes are made continuously by participants and staff through how well daily decisions are working out in tangible tasks. The final products are readily judged by those who use them.

An encouraging and reinforcing merger is occurring between NFE project needs for evaluation and innovations by behavioral science evaluation theorists who are exploring ways of dealing with complex educational settings. NFE projects have many inclusive objectives that fuse the cognitive, psychological and physical domains in complex environments in home, field, place of work, and community life. Development of a producers' co-operative for leather tanning in Morocco, for example, involves cognitive understandings regarding dyes, sources of supplies, and marketing. The psychological domain involves the complex nature of varied staff personalities, of motivation, of dealing with uncertainty and tensions, of the mix of failure and success. The daily physical skills are equally complicated in starting and carrying out the tanning cooperative. Evaluation of processes and outcomes of NFE efforts to encourage such learnings cannot be usefully carried out with only the quantitative tools of behavioral science evaluation techniques.

There are several highly competent evaluation researchers working to invent techniques for addressing the complex nature of educational settings, formal and nonformal (Kinsey, 1978). Very little is yet available on detailed case accounts of the application of these more appropriate evaluation approaches to ongoing projects. In general, this expansion of techniques may be described as a concern with the meaning or significance of what is being evaluated. This implies that quantitative information may sometimes be less useful for the meaningful evaluation of a project than what more qualitative techniques can provide. Such techniques include interviews, case studies, written records of the history of a project's processes, and on-the-spot observation. There is a growing interest in finding applications of evaluation in other fields, such as law, anthropology and political science, to NFE situations.

Research

Research in NFE is mostly focused on gathering data about the where, what, when, why, and how of ongoing NFE projects around the world by nations and regions. There are several research reports of this type in the literature sources. Most of these have been carried out by national governments and international organizations. Additional research reports are available on facilitator models, needs analysis, appropriate methods and materials, collaboration, participation, cultural context, and learner characteristics. Many of these studies are the result of doctoral dissertations. A vast resource of research studies relevant to NFE must be available, but is not yet widely shared, because literature from agencies such as human services, government extension, health sciences, businesses, libraries and museums are not usually catalogued under NFE headings (Bock and Papagiannis, 1976).

Summary

The foregoing descriptions of NFE variables highlight several characteristics that distinguish nonformal education from formal schooling. The most pervasive are such qualities as flexible, indigenous, functional, concrete, low structure, immediate, participatory, community-centered, accessible.

Theory of Nonformal Education

Social Change Issues

A pivotal issue among practitioners is this dialogue: Is NFE largely perceived as a nearly value-free process, characterized by low-structured, interrelated educational variables (objectives, learners, teaching-learning approaches, resources, etc.), or is it also seen as a way to promote socioeconomic-political reform? The dialogue can be viewed as a difference in emphasis between the epistemological and the axiological.

Process theory. As a set of interrelated educational process variables, the focus in NFE is on developing and implementing ways of learning that are congruent with the target population's interests and their unique environmental and social settings. The emphasis is on the how, somewhat independent of social value. This perception of NFE is seen as contrasting in varying degrees from formal education by being flexible, immediate in results, inexpensive, less abstract, less structured and with functional objectives. The value of NFE is seen in its more effective, less expensive ways of achieving the objectives of an established social system (Hansen, 1977).

Social reform theory. Those emphasizing the reform potentials of NFE are especially interested in its possibilities as a participation mode, involving consciousness raising for disenfranchised groups. Long-range purposes often converge around interpretations of socialist principles and/or decentralized socio-economic control. These schools of thought perceive formal schooling as elitist, as hand-in-glove with maintaining established social structures that ensure power, wealth and status for the elite minority. Practitioners of this reform view fear that NFE, unless it is tied to an explicit value emphasis, could be used as a band aid to cover up and make bearable the injustices seen as characteristic of many cultures. There is deep concern that the benefits from outside resources for NFE projects may have too many negative strings attached, intended and unintended, to be worth the risk. The issue may be summed up as the fear of victimization through cultural colonialism and may be expressed by both host and donor nations. Those who are especially interested in the social reform potentials of NFE see much of the NFE activity in the Third World as dominated by industrialized nations' beliefs about what modern development means. These critics suggest there is a need to adopt other development models that take into account the cultural-contextual variables of the NFE target population's origins (Hall, 1975; Heredero, 1979; Labelle, 1976).

Many practitioners do not take an explicit position on the issue of NFE being process and value-free versus social reform. Instead, they assume that the implementation of NFE implicitly means there will be a forwarding of egalitarian and empowerment goals. It seems doubtful that such an assumption is warranted without taking into account the overall, controlling, philosophical-political-economic context of a culture within which each NFE program operates.

The process-reform dialogue. Sources emphasizing NFE as a reform approach are concerned with the ways in which socio-economic forces in a nation's culture can make even the most participatory local NFE approach end up by conserving authoritarian social structures in a nation (Bock and Papagiannis, 1976; Hall, 1975; Labelle, 1976). Several sources have explored this seeming contradiction. Their analyses point out that NFE, seen largely as a process, can be used to buttress a benevolent, paternalistic or authoritarian social structure. Through NFE processes, injustices to the impoverished masses of people may be sufficiently alleviated to mute any revolt, thus maintaining the wider context of a nation's discriminatory socio-political structures.

The reformists (who attack those who see NFE as mainly a value-free process) are countered by others who believe that local projects carried out in a participatory, community-centered mode will establish seedbeds of increased social awareness among grass roots populations (Brembecks and Thompson, 1973). These small local efforts are seen as a significant evolutionary force for gradual reform at the national levels. The "process" versus "reform" dialogue, along with disagreements as to the social reform significance of the local NFE projects to wider authoritarian cultural contexts, remains unresolved. There are positive aspects by both sides, as there are to those who focus largely on "getting the job done."

Those working from a position that NFE is designed to promote social reform are often also interested in theories about social change. As with psychological theory, there is little in-depth treatment of relevant theory in the NFE literature. The discussions are largely around generalizations about such concepts as socialization, social action, consciousness raising, community interaction, collaboration, indigenous, social strategies, reform and revolution, empowerment, self-reliance.

Learning Theory

There is little available in NFE literature that deals in-depth with psychological theories of learning. Instead, there is a level of discourse that appeals to the reader's common sense beliefs about learning. Frequent mention is made of learning-related terms such as experiential, participatory, intrinsic, functional, concrete, active, sensory (Ahmed and Coombs, 1975). These terms are seen as serving a psychological description of NFE processes of learning and teaching. There are implicit premises that these terms somehow explain and provide theory bases for why NFE can be predicted to be effective in given settings. There is not much evidence that these premises would be accepted as givens among major learning theorists. Those familiar with John Dewey's work and the early Progressive education movement will recognize many similarities with this stance of NFE. In fact, there is a blending here, as with Dewey, of both psychological and philosophical beliefs.

Pervasive Themes

In this section, a number of additional themes will be explored. The concept of development is especially pervasive for NFE adherents. Equally of interest is the distribution of wealth and power. A related topic involves the ideals of lay participation and self-reliance. Most recently, attention has been given to the relevance of agency linkages to NFE and community development and to cost-effectiveness issues.

Development: Local and National

Development is a frequent concept referred to by NFE practitioners. The term is seldom used in reference to individual development or growth, as it is in formal schooling. In NFE usage, development refers to community, village, regional and national development. Much of the earlier literature focused on economic development, using indicators such as gross national product, employment, economic infrastructure, modern industrial and agricultural production (Mannon, 1975). More recently, discussion revolves around development as measured by evidences of quality of life in a community or culture. The emphasis is on a much broader range of life functions, beyond those of an economic nature, such as play, affiliation, meaning, creating, understanding, and empowering (Ariyaratne, 1979).

There is a tendency to identify the economic emphasis with the influence of modern industrialized nations. NFE programs sponsored by modernized nations and hosted by less developed nations are criticized by some as an example of cultural colonialism (Buchanan, 1975). Such criticisms are made even though the host countries' power elites may eagerly welcome the economic development emphasis. It is evident that NFE efforts in any country, modern or Third World, will differ markedly depending upon whether the nature of developmental goals are seen narrowly as economic, or broadly as quality of life.

The Disenfranchised and Empowerment

There is almost universal agreement in NFE circles that the target populations are the disenfranchised: illiterates, the poor, racial-ethnic minorities, women, rural villagers and other excluded populations. These populations are sometimes identified as adults and out-of-school youth. The common denominator here is that there are populations who are not served well by formal schooling. Learner characteristics profoundly influence the what, how and why of education. There is a logical match between the variable of disenfranchised learners and other educational variables associated with NFE. The variable of educational objectives has to do with the NFE emphasis on functional implementation of knowledge and theory, as contrasted to formal schooling's emphasis on abstractions and symbol systems required to understand and build theory (Hoxeng, 1973).

A few critics have hinted at the possibility of NFE being "second rate." Their point is that those in a culture who develop and control highly abstract theory are in a special position to hold ultimate power. No careful study is available that demonstrates how the NFE approaches to learning can be used to build new knowledge of a highly theoretical nature. Implementing knowledge is useful, in fact essential, for the building of theory, but it is not sufficient. For example, the practical implementation of modern communications, transportation, administration, agriculture, industry, distribution, etc., can be learned through NFE. But the ways these modern systems are built into the basic economic-political-social structures of any culture are controlled by those who understand and build the theories that underlie these everyday practices, not by those who learn the day-by-day implementation through NFE.

Thus, there is a quandary buried in NFE sources that has yet to be more fully articulated and discussed. On the one hand NFE is seen as a viable educational alternative to help empower the masses of people throughout the world. On the other hand, formal schooling is seen as having the capacity to construct abstract theory which in the long run empowers theory users with control over the basic social structures of a culture. Many NFE critics of formal schooling, with its tendencies toward meritocracy, exclusion and elitism, have overlooked the fact that formal education has been highly successful in building useful theory. Efforts to modify formal schooling approaches so as to empower the masses of people, such as Progressivism in the United States, have apparently failed. Such modifications are seen as interfering with the cultural conservation and theory building functions of formal schools. The dilemma may be managed, but NFE sources have yet to seriously address the issue.

Participation and Self-Reliance

The concepts of self-help, grass roots involement, and local control are integral to what makes NFE most meaningful for many practitioners. Participation is seen as both a motivating force in learning and as an empowering force, through addressing the needs of learners. Self-reliance is an important outcome of NFE, being viewed as central to empowering the disenfranchised by developing skills in awareness, problem solving, and decision making (Hoxeng, 1973).

Examples of the emphasis on grass roots participation are seen in the special ways that NFE community-centered projects are identified, designed and implemented. Efforts are made by NFE facilitators to tap the thoughts and feelings of the learners (often villagers) concerning what villagers see is needed to improve the quality of their lives. Information and resources for projects such as water supply, sanitation, food production, cooperative distribution, and small industries may come from agencies outside a village context. But NFE processes have the flexibility to foster learner control over the how, what, when, where, and why of information and resource implementation. Literally hundreds of thousands of specific village-level projects have attempted to implement the concepts of self-reliance and grass roots control.

One example is the Sarvodaya Movement in Sri Lanka, where large numbers of village projects have been successfully carried out with maximum village learner involvement leading to the enrichment of community life (Ariyaratne, 1979). Aimed at integrated village development (including individual personality awakening) with the philosophy of Buddhism as the basic premise, this movement has made a major impact on over three thousand villages over a period of twenty years. NFE approaches are used such as voluntary sharing between urban youth and village participants, local resources and leadership, functional needs of the village, and grass roots control. A Sri Lankean village may decide to work on developing basic health care facilities, improved housing, a supply of safe water, the organizational strength of the community, cooperative production of agricultural products or more attention to cultural and spiritual needs. Training of community workers as leaders, training of youth in special skills, helping locate grants and credit, and providing access to technological information are all parts of the movement's processes. Through a complex of interrelated variables, education for personal and community development is carried out in nonformal (out-of-school) ways.

Networking

The late evening tea shop scene in the Nepal village illustrates the need for linkage activities among the several agencies that come together to work on a common problem. Unlike schooling, NFE is delivered through a multitude of agencies — human services, government ministries, community interest groups, libraries and museums, unions and businesses. The possibilities for interagency cooperation are, therefore, more obvious. The need for networking is also more apparent since the educational objectives of NFE are often aimed at multiple life functions (food, health, housing, literacy, etc.). Achievement of these physical-psychological-cognitive learnings may require the reinforcing, interrelated efforts of two or more NFE agencies. This is especially the case where community development is involved (Frith and Reed, 1982).

A community having, for example, distressing employment problems for out-of-school youth may find that the educational issues involved in possible solutions require the cooperation of the competencies and resources of several organizations. In Nepal, as in other countries, the regional representatives of the Small Business and Industries Agency have access to basic resources and know-how. The Nonformal Adult Education unit of the Ministry of Education has nontraditional functional ways to promote relevant vocational skill building. The local religious organizations have powerful connections to parents and youth, essential for motivation and commitment purposes. The Ministry of Cooperative Credit, Production and Distribution can provide essential economic structures. These and other agencies or groups usually operate in relative isolation, but their separate effectiveness can be multiplied dramatically when their staffs have learned the skills required for collaboration. It is also possible that from a national perspective, significant financial savings may be made through sharing of human and material resources among agencies, each having relevance to a complex community problem.

A network of organizations cooperated around the skill training of wayside mechanics in Ghana (McLaughlin, 1979). The NFE education program was supported by Ghana's Institute of Adult Education, the People's Educational Association, the University of Massachusetts and USAID. The complex, often delicate interactions among these agencies characterize the difficult, but highly rewarding, tasks of developing and implementing networks.

In practice, networking is more talked about than implemented. NFE personnel run into problems with interagency efforts, just as others do who may be attempting networking for other reasons. It seems very likely that much more attention will be paid in the future to this facet of NFE, given the inherent characteristic of multiple agencies practicing NFE in the same community.

Resources and Cost-Effectiveness

Early writings of the 1960's on NFE played up the cost-effectiveness aspect of this approach. This is especially the case for literature of the Third World or developing nations. The financial impossibility of providing formal schooling for all the populations of these countries has forced development planners to seek alternative ways of achieving the educational goals of national long-range plans. It was assumed there would be cost-effective characteristics in NFE such as much less expensive teaching personnel, low cost facilities, short-term learning sequences, and inexpensive learning materials (Ahmed, 1975).

A few sources have tried to address this issue of costs through traditional economic analysis. As yet, there is only scattered data as to whether there really are major savings (Coombs, 1974; Green, 1979). It seems likely that comparisons of cost-effectiveness between formal and nonformal education are inappropriate since their objectives in many instances are very different. If NFE could achieve formal education's objectives at an appreciably lower cost, there would be no need for formal education. But there is no sign at this time that NFE can achieve both formal and out-of-school objectives without losing most of the distinctive characteristics of the NFE variables.

Even with NFE objectives, there is some question as to its cost-effectiveness. Thus, there will undoubtedly be much more attention paid in the future to the complex, difficult problems of gathering data on this theme.

A World Movement

Most of the sources of NFE are concerned with Third World countries. The very high cost per learner for formal schooling and the low level of wealth in most of these countries, both now and for the coming decades, has focused attention on the assumed lower cost per learner inherent in NFE. NFE is especially applicable where the content and objectives of massive formal schooling are not seen as essential for some degree of modernization (Brembecks and Thompson, 1973).

In recent years, there is also growing attention to NFE as it has been and is practiced in modern industrialized nations. Growing recognition that much education occurs in agencies and organizations other than schools in all cultures, has led to some examination of the characteristics of the educational variables used by these groups in industrialized nations.

It still remains that most documented NFE efforts are coming from such institutions as UNESCO, World Bank, international missions of the wealthier nations, and world-oriented private groups. These organizations focus much of their attention on the developing nations. As more is learned from such efforts, there will be many significant applications that can be applied to internal educational problems of the sponsoring industrialized nations, who also have significant groups of people that are not served well by the formal system.

Conclusion

Nonformal education is characterized by its efforts to closely relate learning to ongoing, practical individual and community concerns. The daily life functions of home, field, business, and community affairs provide the context for the educational means and ends. Learning experiences are short-term, occur in simple settings, use locally developed materials, and involve varied age groups. The teaching-learning methods are highly interactive and experientially oriented. Sponsors of NFE include such agencies and organizations as human services, self-help groups, government agencies, libraries and museums, businesses and unions.

Much of the worldwide impetus for NFE activities comes through international organizations: UNESCO, World Bank, foreign missions of industrialized nations, foundations, and national ministries. The major focus has been on rural village development in Third World countries. Increasing interest is being expressed in urban applications and in the relevance to community development concerns in the industrialized nations.

Pivotal issues for nonformal practitioners include the value-free versus reform positions; economic versus total community development; maintaining the power structure versus empowerment of the disenfranchised. Those who see NFE as relatively value-free are less interested in the goals and more concerned with the means. This position emphasizes the usefulness of the NFE delivery system to provide low cost learning experiences, in part as a substitute for formal schooling, and in part as a way to meet minimum survival needs of village populations. The reform position envisions the impact NFE can make towards changing the underlying socio-economic structures of a nation.

Supporters of economic development are interested in encouraging Third World countries to adopt modern corporate principles of production and consumption. In contrast, total community development is concerned with the enhancement of all life functions, the economic aspects as no more central than interpersonal relations, play, health, education, safety, etc.

The dialogue over maintaining society's power structure versus empowerment of the masses gets played out in the ways that nonformal education variables are implemented. A top-down process of goal setting and decision making is possible in NFE, if empowerment and self-reliance are not an objective. But those who favor grass roots participation at all stages of an NFE project, see such a position as contradicting the inherent nature of NFE. All three of these pivotal issues are closely related; taking a position on one of them usually predicts where one will stand on the other two.

Suggested Resources
Nonformal Education

Bibliography

Ariyaratne, A.T. *Sarvodaya and development.* Moratuna, Sri Lanka: Sarvodaya Shramadana Movement, 1979.

Ahmed, M. *The economics of nonformal education resources, costs and benefits.* New York: Praeger, 1975.

Ahmed, M. and Coombs, P.H. *Education for rural development: Case studies for planners.* New York: Praeger, 1975.

Bock, C. and Papagiannis, G.J. *The demystification of nonformal education: A critique and suggestions for a new research direction.* Amherst, MA: Center for International Education, University of Massachusetts, 1976.

Brembecks, C.S. and Thompson, T.J. (Eds.). *New strategies for educational development: Cross-cultural search for nonformal alternatives.* Toronto, Canada: Lexington Books, 1973.

Buchanan, K. *Reflections on education in the Third World.* Nottingham, England: Bertrand Russell Peace Foundation, 1975.

Center for International Education. *Nonformal alternatives to schooling: A glossary of educational methods.* Amherst, MA: Center for International Education, University of Massachusetts, 1972.

Clark, M. Meeting the needs of the adult learners using nonformal education for social action. *Convergence,* 1978, *11,* (No. 3-4), 44-53.

Coombs, P.H. *Attacking rural poverty: How nonformal education can help.* Baltimore: Johns Hopkins Press, 1974.

Coombs, P.H. *The world educational crisis.* New York: Oxford University Press, 1968.

DeJene, A. *Nonformal education as a strategy in development: Comparative analysis of rural development projects.* Lanham, Maryland: University Press of America, 1980.

Etling, A. *Characteristics of facilitators: The Ecuador project and beyond.* Amherst, MA: Center for International Education, University of Massachusetts, 1975.

Evans, D.R. *Technology in nonformal education: A critical appraisal.* Amherst, MA: Center for International Education, University of Massachusetts, 1976.

Frith, M. and Reed, H.B. *Lifelong learning manual: Training for effective education in organizations.* Amherst, MA: Community Education Resource Center, School of Education, University of Massachusetts, 1982.

Green, R.H. Organization and finance of nonformal education. *Convergence,* 1979, *12,* (No. 3), 42-54.

Hall, B.L. *Nonformal education: Redistribution of wealth and production.* Lusaka, Zambia: African Adult Education Association, 1975.

Hansen, K.H. (Ed.) *Beyond the school what else educates.* Lansing, Michigan: Department of Education, Michigan State University, 1977.

Heredero, J.M. *Rural development and social change: An experiment in nonformal education.* New Delhi, India: Manahor, 1979.

Hoxeng, J. *Let Jorge do it: An approach to rural nonformal education.* Amherst, MA:

Center for International Education, University of Massachusetts, 1973.

International Office — Educational Testing Service. *A manual for the analysis of costs and outcomes in nonformal education.* Princeton, NJ: Educational Testing Service, 1979.

Kinsey, D.C. *Evaluation in nonformal education.* Amherst, MA: Center for International Education, University of Massachusetts, 1978.

Labelle, T.J. *Nonformal education and social change in Latin America.* Los Angeles, CA: UCLA Latin America Center Publications, University of California, 1976.

McLaughlin, S.D. *The wayside mechanic: An analysis of skill acquisition in Ghana.* Amherst, MA: Center for International Education, University of Massachusetts, 1979.

Mannon, M.A. *The economic aspects of nonformal education.* East Lansing, MI: Institute for International Studies in Education, Michigan State University, 1975.

Paulston, R.G. *Nonformal education: An annotated international bibliography.* New York: Praeger, 1974.

Reed, H.B. and Associates. *Lifelong learning in the community: An annotated, cross-referenced bibliography.* Amherst, MA: Community Education Resource Center, School of Education, University of Massachusetts, 1982.

Russell, R. *The fun bus: An experiment in nonformal education through the arts.* Amherst, MA: Center for International Education, School of Education, University of Massachusetts, 1977.

Journals

Adult Education and Development: Journal for Adult Education in Africa, Asia and Latin America

Convergence: An International Journal of Adult Education

Indian Journal of Adult Education

Resource Centers

Center for International Education
School of Education
University of Massachusetts
Amherst, MA 01003

Nonformal Education Information Center
Michigan State University
East Lansing, Michigan 48824

United Nations Educational, Scientific and Cultural Organization
UNESCO
7 Place de Fontenoy
75700 Paris, France

5
EDUCATION FOR COMMUNITY DEVELOPMENT

Stanley Gajanayake

A.T. Ariyaratne, President of the Sarvodaya Shramadana movement of Sri Lanka, gives this account:

> Once in a village in Sri Lanka I happened to meet a group of villagers who were in great need to get their tank bund [reservoir embankment] repaired. There were about sixty people gathered at the meeting. I asked them what the problem was. They said they needed their tank bund in the village to be completely repaired, to conserve water to irrigate their paddy fields. They said that the bund would also serve as a motorable road to the village. Then they showed me a thick file full of correspondence with the government. They had been trying to get this job done for fifteen years.
>
> I got the people to analyze their problem themselves assuring that there was nobody except themselves able to solve this problem. What do you need to construct the tank bund? Earth. How many cubes of earth? 200. Where can you get this earth to make the bund? From the tank bed. What implements do you need to dig this earth and make the bund? Some mammoties, earth pans, pick axes, etc. Where can you get them? Except for the earth pans, the other equipment could be found in the village. Can you suggest a substitute for earth pans? Yes, sheaves of arecanut leaves and gunny bags. Who can find these? (One offered to find them.) How

many people have to work for how many days to get this job done? Two hundred people working for four days. Now tell me, each one of you, how many volunteers can you organize for this work? One, two five, ten, fifteen... All right, who is going to feed these two hundred people? (A rich land owner gets up.) I will feed all of them for two days. Thank you. But let me see, who can feed one man by sharing his meal with another. Several hands went up. Who can feed two?, three?, five?. .... Well, now we have enough food without the first offer, for all four days. But let us accept the first offer also and organize a Shramadana Camp because I am sure two hundred more will join when they hear we started work on Shramadana. When shall we start the work? During the next weekend. So why do you need to petition the government? All right, let us burn your file containing fifteen years of correspondence and start afresh with our own self-reliance written in.

A working committee was formed to make the preparations. I myself joined the villagers, and the job was finished by tea time in the afternoon of the very first day of the camp. In this instance, what I did was to remove the constraint, the file which stood between the people's problem and the solution which was well within their reach. That is a classic example of breaking down the self-made barriers of 'Dependence'. (Ratnapala, Ed., undated, pp. 77-78.)

The episode described above illustrates some of the main ingredients of community development. A community, whether urban or rural, has a built-in potential to solve its own problems. Given the proper guidance and motivation, the community will be able to identify and articulate its problems in the proper perspective, come up with simple and instant solutions without resorting to the advice of "experts," and plan and implement activities to achieve its goals by relying on its own resources and initiative.

A Worldwide Movement

The term *community development* is a widely used one and has taken on an increasingly specific meaning during the past few decades. Associated with the British and American experience in local government and social welfare, it is basically an Anglo-Saxon concept that emerged as a strategy for development at the grass roots level. In Asian countries, such as India and Sri Lanka, the concept is based on a "respect for all life" and the "dignity of the human being" rooted in Buddhist and Gandhian philosophies. The values of community development in the Western countries are also firmly rooted in the Judaeo-Christian teachings of the worth of human beings and respect for the individual. Community development is based on the belief that the initiative, imagination, capacities, and energies of the people can be used to improve their own lives using democratic processes and voluntary efforts. It is assumed that through a process of consciousness raising, the people at the grass roots level can be awakened and motivated to realize their own potentials. This will in turn promote community involvement, democratic dialogue and participation on the part of each individual, leading to social action.

In the Third World countries, the concept of community development came into prominence after the Second World War with the coming of independence of British, and later other countries', colonies. The community development strategy was selected as a means of helping colonies make a peaceful transition to independence. In a sense, it was used as a strategy to win over the hearts and minds of the people of the new emerging nations by the Western powers in their global struggle against the growing power and influences of the Soviet Union and the Socialist camp.

Animation Rurale

Animation rurale is the French equivalent of the British and American conceived community development programs. After 1958, the French colonies in Africa gained independence, and the leaders of these countries sought ways to alleviate poverty, to reduce disparities, and to raise the quality of life of these countries. The French wanted to promote rural modernization to prepare for the transfer of power to these newly independent countries. Animation rurale was a strategy that came into existence in this attempt to activate and mobilize the rural areas for development.

Alliance for Progress

The Alliance for Progress—a progam with similar intentions—was promoted by the U.S. in Latin American countries in the 1960's. It was a formula for gradual evolution and reform in housing, education, and other sectors, with the participation of the people at the grass roots level. However, the strategic aims of the West and the maintenance of the balance of power within these countries figured more prominently in this strategy than the alleviation of poverty and hunger.

Assumptions of Community Development

Community development is based on the idea that development should start at the grass roots level, and if people are helped to realize their own potentials, they can solve their own problems through self-help programs using their own imagination and initiative. In India the concept of community development was introduced from Britain. The movement, however, was chiefly inspired by the ideas of Mahatma Gandhi, who aimed to bring about a "Sarvodaya Samaj" (a confederation of self-reliant, self-sufficient villages based on agriculture, handicrafts, and small industries) and by Archarya Vinoba Bhave, who started the Bhoodan (donation of land) Movement.

Both in the West and East, the philosophies on which community development programs are based emphasize the worth of human beings, respect for the individual, nonviolence, the common good of the people, altruism, peaceful resolution of conflicts, and basic needs satisfaction. Biddle (1965), using as a basis his experiences in several case studies, sets forth a number of assumptions on which community development programs proceed. His assumptions include the following:

- Each person is valuable, unique and capable of growth towards greater moral sensitivity and responsibility. Each person has underdeveloped abilities in initiative, originality and leadership. These qualities can be cultivated and strengthened.
- Human beings and groups have both good and bad impulses. Under wise encouragement, they can strengthen the better in themselves and help others to do likewise. When people are free of coercive pressure, and can then examine a wide range of alternatives, they tend to choose the ethically better and the intelligently wiser course of action.
- There is satisfaction in serving the common welfare, even as in serving self-interest . . . . Sense of responsibility and belonging can be strengthened even for those to whom community is least meaningful.
- Satisfaction and self-confidence gained from small accomplishments can lead to the contending with more and more difficult problems, in a process of continuing growth. (Biddle, 1965, pp. 61-62.)

Most community development programs throughout the world are based on the above assumptions. Community development movements attempt to draw out to the surface what is good in human beings and try to reinforce and strengthen these elements and make use of them creatively for the common good of the community. Attempts are made to resolve conflicts between individuals and groups by promotion of discussion, cooperation, tolerance, and compromise.

Definitions

There is no unanimously accepted definition of community development. In a literature survey, the writer came across more than twenty-five definitions of community development. A dissertation entitled "Community Development: A Concept Analysis" (Hanberry, 1972) deals mainly with definitions and concepts related to community development. There are a few definitions which stand out among others because they emphasize the most important aspects of community development. Huey B. Long and others writing on community development point out that:

Change is what community development is all about, and there are three basic types of change (1) evolutionary change; (2) accidental change; and (3) planned change . . . Planned change may be seen as the result of an organized direct intervention in a human system in order to achieve known and specific goals ... It is assumed that planned change of community development can and does occur. (Long and others, 1973, p. 5.)

The U.S. International Cooperation Administration (USICA) formulated guidelines in 1956 for overseas missions and defined community development as follows:

A process of social action in which the people of a community organize themselves for planning and action; define their common and individual needs and problems; make group and individual plans to meet their needs and solve their problems; execute these plans with maximum reliance upon community resources; and supplement these resources when necessary with services and materials from government and nongovernmental agencies outside the community. (I.C.A.M.O. #27109.1, 1957.)

The United Nations Bureau of Social Affairs has defined community development as "a process designed to create conditions of economic and social progress for the whole community with its active participation and the fullest possible reliance upon the communities' initiative" (U.N.B.S.A., 1955, p. 6).

These and other definitions of community development, while revealing distinguishing characteristics, differ in the emphasis on this or that facet and the vantage point, perspective and content from which one looks at community development. However, there is a common thread running through all these definitions which emphasizes planned change, common good, community involvement, participation of the community, and reliance on its own initiative.

Distinctions

Besides community development, there may be a number of strategies and movements within a community aimed at bringing about change or improvement in the community. Some of these are community schools, community education, and rural development. Very often these terms are used interchangeably with community development and thus need clarification.

Community schools. Sources dealing with community schools show that the concept is rooted in the progressivist philosophy of John Dewey. The community schools came into prominence during the depression of the 1930's. These were formal schools offering K-12 curriculum but more concerned with such subject areas as nutrition, improved agricultural processes, health education, and vocational training. These schools were oriented towards out-of-school populations, and various mechanisms such as advisory councils and networks of community resources were established to involve the community.

Community education. This later development focused on

> identifying a process through which any community group could provide for its own educational needs. Process concerns are, for example, attention to things like accurate needs assessment that identify real community problems, measures to increase participation at all levels, techniques of empowering and linking with many community agencies, action research, participatory evaluation and so forth. (Loughran, 1981.)

This process called community education also made use of the facilities of formal schools but was more community-oriented than the community schools.

The community concept. A comparative analysis of the outstanding characteristics and dimensions of community schools, community education, and community development reveals that there are many overlapping elements as well as differences. The foci of all three concepts are the problems and the needs of the community, but they differ in the degree of community orientation and participation. If one is to arrange these in a continuum, ranging from less to more community orientation and involvement, community schools and community development will lie at the two extremes, while community education will be in the center. Community schools and community education are educational strategies operating through the formal school apparatus and are inherently top-down in the nature of approach. Community development assumes that members of community themselves should organize "informally or formally for democratic planning and action: define their common and group goals, needs and problems; make group and individual plans to meet their needs and solve their problems; execute these plans with maximum reliance upon community resources" (Green, 1961, p. 3). Education is only one component of community development. It may or may not use the apparatus of the formal school system for its educational and training purposes.

Rural development. Another strategy that has many common features with community development is rural development. One of the most recent publications of the United Nations Development Program (UNDP) has defined rural development as follows:

> a process of socio-economic change involving the transformation of agrarian society in order to reach a common set of development goals based on the capacities and the needs of the people. These goals include a rationally determined growth process that gives priority to the reduction of poverty, unemployment, and inequality, and the satisfaction of minimum human needs, and stress self-reliance and participation of all the people, particularly those with the lowest standard of living. (UNDP, 1979, p. 1.)

Both community development and rural development have many common concerns. Both stress planned socio-economic change, people's participation, self-reliance, self-help, and improving the quality of life. However, the main focus of rural development is on rural areas, especially the rural areas in less developed countries, and the target population comprises the rural poor, disenfranchised and disadvantaged. Community development, at least in theory, is concerned with the development of communities, whether urban or rural, and the target population includes both rich and poor. In practice, of course, community development too focuses on the disadvantaged sections of the population. There are more similarities in these two strategies than there are differences.

Historical Perspective of Community Development

Western origins. The ideas implied in the concept of community development date back to people's early efforts of working jointly for the common good. But the emergence of community development in the present sense of the term is of recent origin. In Anglo-Saxon countries, the first efforts in community development were made in urban areas and were oriented towards social welfare. Its early beginnings can be traced back to the charity organization movement which started in England in the 1870's and later spread to New York and elsewhere. This was followed by the Social Betterment Movement in England in the 1880's and the School Community Center Movement in New York in the 1900's, in which people of a community were to be given access to school buildings during the evenings. Following these beginnings in urban areas, two developments were seen in rural areas. One was the emergence of special interest organizations (e.g., farmer's organizations), and the other was the spread to rural areas of social welfare-oriented urban organizations such as the YMCA and the Boy Scouts. The development of Land Grant Colleges and the community council idea in the United States were also important aspects in the evolution of the community development concept.

Third World origins. In the Third World countries, activities of a mutual, communal nature have been in existence for centuries. However, community development in the present sense of the term was imported from the West. In Africa, Asia, and the Middle East, the beginning of community development efforts can be traced back to the colonial period—the mass education programs in Ghana, Kenya, and Uganda; rural reconstruction in India and the Middle East; and rural development in Sri Lanka. This process accelerated after the Second World War when the British, French, and other colonies began achieving independence. The need at that time was to encourage independence and development of the colonies without disturbing the global status quo. Community development and *animation rurale* are strategies that were used by the British and French for this purpose. Political leaders of the newly independent countries also favored this strategy because many of them feared the spread of socialism in their strongholds (Taylor, 1961).

The community development movement gained momentum with the beginning of community development efforts in India and the Philippines. It spread to about sixty countries in Asia, Africa, and Latin America by the

1960's. During the 1950's and the first part of the 1960's, besides the European colonial powers, the United States was a supplier of funds to community development programs in less developed countries, choosing countries that were significant to Western interests (Uphoff, 1979). A special community development division was created in United States Aid to International Development (USAID) to channel funds to community development programs. Many international conferences were held on community development during this period and special ministries and departments were created both at the national level and state level in the Third World countries to implement community development programs. However, by the end of the 1960's, community development efforts receded to the background, while other strategies were given prominence. One of the major reasons for this trend was the precedence given to urban industrial development over rural agricultural development by the 1960's, and the failure of community development to show tangible achievements in the context of cost-benefits analysis.

Community Development Process

Most authorities on community development tend to perceive it as a process characterized by a series of steps, stages or activities through which the individuals in a community are expected to pass to achieve desired goals. Generally, the responsibility for the process rests upon the facilitator or the nucleus group that takes initiative in community development. No matter who takes the initiative, the involvement of the people in the locality to be served is considered essential.

The process adapted may vary from community to community, and it may be unique to each situation. However, sequential stages common to nearly every process can be identified through a review of literature and by observing some of the ongoing community development activities in various countries in the world. Wileden (1970) observes eight sequential stages: motivation; data collection; group decision making; planning; organization formation; training community leadership; action or goals; and evaluation. Biddle and Biddle, whose study in 1965 was specifically focused on community development processes, outlined a somewhat similar sequence.

Sarvodaya process sequence. At this juncture, it is interesting to observe the process adopted by the Sarvodaya Shramadana Movement, an ongoing indigenous community development in the Third World (Sri Lanka) presently involving 3,000 villages. This process involves the following seven steps: identification and exploration of the situation; raising consciouness and creating psychological-sociological infrastructures (Shramadana Camp Stage); survey stage; formulation of plans; setting up organizational structures (children's group, farmers' group and village reawakening council); implementation of plans; and evaluation.

One of the features that distinguishes that Sarvodaya Process from the Western process is the consciousness raising strategy (the Shramadana Camp Technique). The Shramadana Camp is the Sarvodaya revolutionary strategy for consciousness raising about the people's indigenuous strengths and traditions. It is one of the most outstanding contributions of the Sarvodaya Shramadana movement to the social development of Sri Lanka. It enables the people in the community to think, plan, and work together, and then, to evaluate their efforts.

Developed and Developing Countries

The foci, nature, and the methods used in community development differ in developed and developing countries. In developed countries, the majority of the population lives in urban areas, and the focus of community development is urban-oriented, attempting to involve all sections of the population irrespective of social class distinctions. Most community development programs are nongovernmental and voluntary in nature. Private and local initiatives play a major role. Community development is looked upon as a method of carrying out specific projects evolved by the community, rather than as a part of some national plan. Involvement of local residents in planning and decision making is considered important, and nonmaterial benefits to the people are thought to be as valuable as the material goals achieved.

In developing countries, community development is viewed as a rural phenomenon and as a strategy to improve the conditions of the poor and disadvantaged in rural areas. The tendency in these countries is to set up community development programs on a national scale. With some exceptions, there is less opportunity for involvement and participation on the part of the local populations, and there is a relatively high degree of governmental involvement and centralized decision making.

Theoretical Dimensions

Social Change

Sources dealing with community development and observation of ongoing community development programs, reveal that the community development movement assumes social change takes place mostly in an evolutionary or status quo context. Use of coersion, violence or physical force, class antagonism, and class war are not supported by any of the approaches of community development. Instead, it promotes local initiative, popular participation, democratic discussion, self-help, and nonviolence.

The idea of community development emerged in England at a time when the *laissez-faire* theory was losing its credibility and the concept of the welfare state was gaining ground. *Laissez-faire,* which aimed at bringing about minimum government intervention in the affairs of the individual, in practice led to the poverty of significant numbers and the affluence of the rich minority. As a result, the theory of the welfare state, which believes in state intervention to bridge the gap between rich and poor, emerged. These trends had other ramifications (i.e., the birth of the Trade Union Movement and Cooperative Movement). The community development movement had its beginnings at a time when these changes were taking place; it is embedded in the idea of community welfare.

As discussed above, community development in Third World countries was introduced by the ex-colonial powers as a strategy to prevent these countries from drifting toward the socialist camp and to maintain the global status quo. There are community development movements in the Third World which attempt to avoid the present global, ideological struggle between capitalism and communism and which advocate an independent path of development. Yet, most of these tend to favor evolutionary social change.

Top-down, bottom-up approaches. Literature on community development shows that community development movements tend to adopt both top-down and bottom-up change strategies. In the United States and developed countries, the stress has been on local initiative, usually sponsored by private groups, organizations, youth clubs, women's clubs, Junior Chambers of Commerce, etc., with occasional assistance from government agencies. Decisions are made, development plans are formulated and carried out at the local level with little or no guidance from the central or state governments. The community development programs are not wedded to national development plans or programs. There is a high degree of voluntary group involvement and initiative at the local level.

In many Third World countries, community development programs are national in scale and are a part of an overall development plan conducted as an arm of the government. This is because major financial help comes from the government or philanthropic foundations funnelled through the government. In countries like India and the Philippines, the government treats community development as a national strategy designed to transform the social and economic life of the villages. In several countries, special ministries, departments or groups of interrelated ministries have been set up to implement community development programs.

In India, during Prime Minister Nehru's time, a new ministry of community development was created for planning and executing community development actions at the national level, and ministries were also created at the state level. (The national ministry declined in effectiveness due to bureaucratic conflict and was later absorbed by the Ministry of Agriculture.) Nevertheless, community development in India remains a top-down strategy, although it must not be assumed that all community development programs in the Third World countries are governmental and top-down in nature. There are a number of exceptions. The Sarvodaya Shramadana Movement in Sri Lanka is a rare example of a community development movement which views that development should start from the grass roots level and proceed upward, with a more horizontal power structure.

Available evidence shows that the top-down approach, in most cases, leads to more bureaucratic control and dependency, while the bottom-up approach promotes participation, self-reliance, self-help, and local initiative. Collantes, 1980, studies two community development programs in the

Philippines, one sponsored by the government (top-down approach) and one sponsored by a voluntary church organization (bottom-up approach). Collantes concluded that the effects of the voluntary church effort

> were to stress internal aspects, to provide a focus on process and human relations, and were relatively empowering, at least in terms of attitudes. The effects of the government effort were to stress external aspects, to focus on material elements, and tended to reinforce passive attitudes and postures. (Collantes, 1980, p. 103.)

Theory of Learning

There are hardly any references in the community development literature that deal directly with an explicit theory of learning in community development. Nevertheless, casual references on the subject show that learning in community development is a two-way process: you teach while you learn. The people in the community learn from the instructors/facilitators about modern knowledge and new methods that can be used to solve their problems. At the same time, the instructors/facilitators can learn from the people about their lives and problems. A two-way communication line is established, and it becomes an educational process for both groups. Learning in community development is self-oriented, experiential, and participatory.

Pervasive Themes

Importance of the Community

One of the pervasive themes in community development is the emphasis it places on the importance of the community as a unit (Malassis, 1976). Community development assumes that to bring about development, the focus should not be on individuals or separate groups but on the community as a whole. Most community problems are not limited to individuals or groups but permeate the entire community. What affects one member of the community, naturally affects all. And for many purposes, corrective measures must be aimed at changing the whole community, because it is the social, cultural, economic and political structure of the whole community that breeds particular kinds of problems peculiar to that community.

Given these circumstances, the type of intervention by an outside agency on a group within the community has to take into consideration the needs of the various groups in the community, the religion and cultural values, the attitudes, the power structure, and other realities in the community life. Any attempt without these considerations is liable to fail, even if the intention may be good (Miniclier, 1961).

Need-Orientation and Self-Help

Need-orientation. Community development is essentially a grass roots level, need-oriented development strategy based on two basic beliefs: (a) Any development program should start from the attempt to fulfill the basic needs of people, as identified by the people themselves; (b) Development should proceed on the basis of mutual self-help. Nerfin has defined need-oriented as "geared to meeting human needs, both material and non-material. It begins with the satisfaction of needs of those dominated and exploited, who constitute the majority of the world's inhabitants, and ensures at the same time, the humanization of all human beings by the satisfaction of their needs" (Nerfin, 1977, p. 10). Most community development programs in developed and developing countries start their activities with a survey of the basic needs of their target population. The Sarvodaya Shramadana Movement in Sri Lanka has identified ten basic needs: environment, water, clothing, food, housing, health services, communication, fuel, education, and spiritual and cultural environment. The Movement's village development plans are formulated with the objectives of fulfilling these needs. Need-orientation of community development activities has been one of the crucial factors that generates participation and cooperation of the people at the grass roots level.

Self-help emphasis. Another important factor in community development is self-help. The concept of self-help implies aiding one another in the community without depending on the aid of outsiders. This idea has its roots in most religious philosophies in both Western and Eastern countries. During the time of the first European settlement in the United States, and for a long time since then, mutual self-help played a very important role in community activities. In developing countries too self-help has been one of the most important ingredients in the community life in villages. With the emergence of capitalism and the emphasis on individualism, the concept of self-help receded to the background in both developed and developing countries.

The emergence of the community development movement was partly due to the re-emergence of the concept of self-help. A survey of community development movements shows that most movements or projects start in the community with the formation of basic nuclei in the community. Often these basic nuclei are composed of members who have grouped together for mutual self-help. Self-help is a common idea promoted by community development movements all over the world. Most central governments in developing countries also emphasize self-help; government treasuries simply cannot marshall sufficient resources to totally finance community development activities.

Participation

All community development programs put a heavy emphasis on participation. For example, the Sarvodaya Shramadana Movement in Sri Lanka, with its concern with human dignity and human worth, believes in popular participation in all aspects of development. In order for the people to control and shape their own destiny, they should realize their own worth and strength. This realization can only be achieved by popular participation in all matters that pertain to the village or community in which one lives.

The issue of participation is centered around who participates, what is participation, and how participation takes place. In analyzing these dimensions of participation in the context of rural development, the Rural Development Committee of Cornell University (1977) points out that the participants can be local residents, local leaders, government personnel and foreign personnel. They may be participating in decision making, implementation, benefit sharing, and evaluation. The "how" dimension of participation is concerned with the way in which participation occurs—where the initiative for participation comes from (below or above); what inducements for participation are involved; the structure and channels; duration and scope of participation; and whether participation leads to empowerment (Cohen and Uphoff, 1977).

Participation as a continuum. The intent in this paper is not to discuss participation in the context of these criteria. The experience of community development in developing and developed countries shows that the members of the community, community leaders, government officials, and sometimes foreign personnel have participated in community development movements. Since community development puts heavy emphasis on the role of community, it is especially interesting to see to what extent and what ways the members of the community participate in community develop-ment projects. Experience in community development shows that general-izations cannot be made regarding this aspect. In practice, participation lies on a continuum, from nominal participation (one way communication officials get a chance to deliver the message) to consultative paticipation (people are consulted, but decisions are made elsewhere) to responsible participation (active involvement in all stages of the process).

Erosion of Participation. Though community development is based on the assumption that initiative should come from the people at the grass roots level, in actual practice in most Third World countries, decisions are imposed through ministries or departments at the national level through a bureaucratic hierarchy. The village level workers become agents of the government rather than change agents working at the village level. In most Third World countries, the bureaucrats' mode of operation itself leads to a reduced level of participation. Experience in India shows that participation in sharing benefits has been one of the weakest links in the process. After several evaluations, it became evident that "the better off, mainly the dominant land-owning groups, benefitted from the extension work and other projects, rather than the majority of the poor peasants in the community" (Narayan Das, 1978, p. 12).

Self-Reliance

Sources on community development show that one of the major pervasive themes emphasized by community development movements throughout the world is self-reliance. This theme has many dimensions, and there are numerous types and degrees of self-reliance ranging across a wide spectrum. Self-reliance in manpower, resources, capital, technology, and expertise are some of the major dimensions encompassed in the concept of self-reliance. In the People's Republic of China, self-reliance was seen as relying on local manpower and resources without depending on either the United States or the Soviet Union. For some other Third World countries, self-reliance in community development means making full use of local manpower and resources while depending for financial aid, technological help and expertise from developed countries. Though community development programs in most countries aspire to self-reliance in all aspects involving development, complete self-reliance is not possible in the modern day world where developing countries are dependent on developed countries and rural areas are dependent on the cities.

Delivery

The delivery system in education programs pertinent to community development depends on the nature of learners, their training needs, the background of the staff, content and nature of the curriculum, teaching-learning approaches, various resources available and organizational patterns. The delivery system also varies according to the cultural background of the country or the community in which it takes place.

Learners

A basic characteristic of community development programs is that the target population of learners may be of any age. It may include all types of functionaries—local leaders, voluntary leaders, community organizers (village level workers), subject matter specialists (agriculturalists, sanitarians, literacy experts), and persons responsible for keeping the administrative machinery of a national or local program in running order.

Objectives

The objectives of the delivery system vary according to the target population of learners. The field level workers in community development need skills in working with the people, grounding in the relevant subject matter, and training in extension-type ways of facilitating learning. The people at the local level need help in overcoming their differences, working together for a common purpose, and raising their level of consciousness to make better use of local resources.

Staff

The staff serving these distinct groups of the target population may range from professional instructors to relatively untrained village level workers. In India, there were instructors (trained by the Ministry of

Community Development) to train professional workers. These trainers were highly skilled in the subject areas relevant to their fields and methods of working with the people. Besides these trainers, university professors, school teachers, and employees from various government departments and Ministries were often invited to training programs for professional workers as well as nonprofessional workers. The education conducted for members of the community in villages was often done by the village level workers.

Curriculum

The curriculum content in community development is determined, for the most part, according to the type of learners and their needs. Areas of operation of village level workers cover such diverse fields as agriculture, animal husbandry, health, home economics, irrigation cooperatives, public works, social education, youth welfare, and history and culture of the country. In many cases, the aim is to train the village level worker as a generalist in these subject areas. These workers also need training in working with the people, a knowledge of data gathering techniques, skills in formulating plans, and techniques of motivating people and eliciting their participation. These skills are an indispensable part of the curriculum. For nonprofessional workers and all others associated with community development, the curriculum should be centered around changing attitudes. The curriculum content for the people at the local level may range from subjects such as scientific agriculture, home economics, and health to the use of local resources, training for self-employement, and education for liberation and empowerment. The emphasis in different subject areas may vary from situation to situation.

Teaching-Learning Approaches

In countries such as India and the Philippines where community programs have been in existence for some time, the training programs consist of in-service and pre-service components for professional workers, orientation training programs for nonprofessionals and ad hoc training programs for the people in the community. Most training programs for field workers contain an institutional component (classroom activities) and field component (practical experience in the field). In the institutional component, lectures have often been used as a principal method of delivery, but experience has shown that they have not been very effective in training field workers. Therefore, the trend has changed in favor of other methods considered to be more effective—role play, demonstrations, workshops, observations, discussions and the use of audio-visual techniques. For the field component of the training, methods most often used are case studies, survey methods and formulating and implementing short-term development plans with the participation of the people. The discussion method is one of the major techniques used for orientation to programs for nonprofessional workers. A wide variety of methods, including demonstrations, lectures, discussions, audio-visual techniques and films are used for education programs for the people at the local level. Use of mass-media on a national or local level is one of the principle ways which community development organizations try to reach the people at the grass roots level.

Resources and Organization

Most community development programs use the resources in the community, often schools or other government buildings, for their education and training programs. But certain community development organizations have built their own development education centers with well-equipped classrooms, media centers and community centers. In countries where community development programs are affiliated to religious groups, religious buildings are widely used. In areas where none of these facilities are available, classes may be conducted under trees or in other convenient places. Human and material resources in the surrounding villages were generally made use of for the field component of the training program in most Third World countries. Handbooks, manuals, and the audio-visual materials used are often locally produced. The funding comes from local sources in the case of developed countries, and a large part comes from government sources in developing countries.

The administration of community development projects in developed countries, especially in the United States, is often done by voluntary organizations. In the case of larger organizations, there may be a paid staff in charge of various aspects of the project. In the cases of projects of a smaller scale, the responsibility for the management of the project is generally undertaken by the basic nucleus (which may consist of a President, Secretary, and other office bearers). The funding for most projects comes from local contributions, philanthropic foundations, and grants from state and federal governments.

In Third World countries where the top-down approach is prevalent, in most cases the administration of community-developed projects is a responsibility of the central government or the local authorities. In countries like Thailand, the Philippines and Korea, community projects are formulated and implemented by the central government and are a part of an overall national development plan. The responsible department or ministry sets up structures in the regional areas, implements, and manages community development projects. The village level workers act in the capacity of agents of the government. The funding mainly comes from the government or other funding sources (philanthropic foundations, USAID, etc.) which are funnelled through the government.

Sarvodaya Education: A Short Case Study

The Sarvodaya Shramadana Movement has a built-in education component—Sarvodaya Development Education—in its community development program. Development Education is an integrated approach to awaken rural and urban groups, so that people themselves can take creative actions toward development based on self-reliance. With this broad perspective, the Sarvodaya Movement attempts to satisfy the needs of individuals and groups by providing opportunities:

- To understand their problems and uncover potentialities to solve them;
- To develop community leadership skills;
- To develop economically useful skills and organizational patterns;
- To facilitate planning of program and finding resources;
- To coordinate all self-development programs into a coherent whole.

Target Populations

The main target populations of the Sarvodaya Development Education Program are: (a) The rural community that the movement is committed to develop: (b) Sarvodaya volunteers; and, (c) Buddhist monks who are selected for community leadership roles. Special attempts are made to secure the participation of government officials, officials of local government institutions, members of other voluntary organizations, and other interested persons in the community.

Development Education Institutes

To facilitate the organization of education and training activities in the country, the movement has set up six Development Education Institutes. The Institute, located in Pathakada in Sri Lanka, was begun with the idea of utilizing the services of Buddhist monks who are still the traditional leaders in villages for village development. Below the Development Education Institutes are the Sarvodaya Extension Centers, about 52 in number, spread throughout the country to coordinate the education and training activities of 20 to 30 villages within a radius of about 10 miles.

The education and training programs offered by these Development Education Institutes and extension centers are: (a) Pre-school training; (b) Training in community kitchen and nutrition; (c) Community development and leadership training; (d) Training in librarianship; (e) Scientific land development; (f) Scientific irrigation; (g) Scientific farming; (h) Dairy farming; (i) Training in carpentry, masonry and handicraft; (j) Experiments in the evolution of technology in development (appropriate technology); (k) Aesthetic education; and, (l) Collective patterns of living.

Leadership

The instructors in these training programs consist of two groups: the trained instructors employed and paid by the movement and volunteers from among school teachers, university professors or government officials. At the village level, a university faculty member or a school teacher going to serve the village in a voluntary capacity is "required to live with the people, share the cooking arrangements and food, plan development projects and implement them with the villagers, and learn from the villagers while working with them" (S.R.C., 1975-76, p. 33).

Methods

The Sarvodaya Delivery System consists of various types of methods such as lectures, discussions, demonstrations, use of audio-visual materials, learning by doing. One of the main instruments used by the movement at the village level for reawakening and motivating villagers is the Shramadana Camp, where people at the village level and Sarvodaya volunteers participate in lectures, discussions, singing, folk dance, and dialogue.

Objectives

The broad objectives of a Shramadana Camp are:
- To experience the traditional social living based on the principles of sharing, pleasant speech, constructive activity and equality (which are the fundamentals of Sarvodaya philosophy), and
- To share their labor in completing a physical task that satisfies a long felt need of the community.

A Shramadana Camp normally is inaugerated in the evening with the traditional ceremonies. This is followed by a meeting of the villagers, called the "family gathering," the idea being that all the people gathered consider themselves members of one family, and in that spirit, discuss problems facing the village and lay down plans for the camp. In these camps each day, six to eight hours of labor are given by the people, both young and old. This labor is used for satisfying a common need of the community, such as the construction of an access road to the village or an irrigation channel. But the actual purpose of the Shramadana Camp is not confined only to this physical task. Precedence is given to:
- Creating the necessary awareness and community spirit,
- Preparing the psychological infrastructure necessary for development through mutual self-help and cooperation,
- Evolving a sociological and organizational infrastructure to generate a sense of unity and harmony and prepare the ground for reconstructional activities in the villages.

Organization

Another somewhat unique feature in the Sarvodaya Process is the attempt at local village mobilization by organizing peer/interest groups. No successful community development program based on the people's participation can be implemented without a sound organization of the community. Sarvodaya advocates organizing the community into various functional groups by age and occupation. The creation of such peer groups encourages the people to plan and implement their own program.

Conclusion

Community Development in Industrialized Countries

In most developed and developing countries, community development programs have helped to create an awareness and interest among the rural and urban populations about their own problems. In developed countries, communities have been able to solve some of the problems facing the community and attend to their community needs through community development programs, mostly on a voluntary basis. They also have been able to get things done through community development organizations, from local government institutions, from state governments, business organizations, and the central government. Still it is difficult to pass a conclusive judgment about the accomplishments and failures.

Third World Community Development

In the Third World countries, on the other hand, the outcomes of community development have not been very promising, though there are a few exceptions, such as the Sarvodaya Shramadana Movement in Sri Lanka which has some positive accomplishments to its credit. Even in this case, the movement is not mature enough to pass any final judgment. On the whole, in less developed countries community development programs, except for the provision of infrastructual facilities in the villages (roads, school buildings, houses, wells, opening up of cottage industries) have not been able to make a major change in rural communities. As a strategy, it has failed to solve the basic problems of urban and rural areas—poverty, hunger, disease, and inequalities.

Most Third World countries started implementing community development programs in the post war period, and at the initial stages, the national governments took a keen interest in the community development programs. Assistance also flowed into the rural areas in these countries in the form of experts, money, and machinery. But with national governments getting more involved in industrialization, urbanization, and modernization with the aim of increasing the national income of the countries and catching up with advanced countries, the interest fizzled out. There were no follow-up programs to complete the work started by the self-help groups at the village levels. At the present juncture, the Sarvodaya Shramadana Movement in Sri Lanka is facing a similar situation. While the Sarvodaya Movement advocates a basic needs, bottom-up approach based on people's participation and self-reliance, the policy of the national government in Sri Lanka in recent years has been to follow an urban oriented, capital intensive mode of development which is diametrically opposed to the ideology of the Sarvodaya Movement.

Another development taking place in Third World countries and detrimental to the self-help concept is the assistance flowing into these countries from funding agencies. Due to this, the "emphasis on self-help declined and government extension workers increasingly displaced local people as 'change agents' " (Uphoff, 1979, p. 18).

Questioning Some Assumptions

There are many other shortcomings, built-in defects, and questionable assumptions on which community development approaches are based. In Asian countries, especially in India, community development programs are based on the assumption that the village is the ideal unit on which this community development program should be based. This thinking has been partly influenced by the romantic descriptions of the villages by individuals like Charles Metcalf who, in his report to the British House of Commons in 1832, stated as follows:

> The village communities are little republics, having nearly everything they want within themselves, and almost independent of any foreign relations. They seem to last where nothing else lasts. Dynasty after dynasty tumbles down; revolution succeeds revolution, but the village communities remain the same. This union of village communities, each one forming a separate little state itself has, I conceive, contributed more than any other cause to the preservation of the people of India, through all the revolutions and changes they had suffered, and is in a high degree conducive to their happiness, and to the enjoyment of a great portion of freedom and independence. (Metcalf cited in Kantowsky, 1980, p. 87.)

This description may have been relevant regarding a few villages in India where the people organized themselves against gangs of robbers at a time when the central authority was declining (prior to the establishment of the authority by the British East India Company), but this type of generalization is not relevant to most villages in India or any other part of the world. Dr. Ambedkar (a leader of the untouchables in India), on the other hand, refers to the villages as "a sink of localism, a den of ignorance, narrow-mindedness and communalism" (Ambedkar cited in op cit, p. 90). Karl Marx, referring to the villages in India, confirms this idea in the following words:

> We must not forget that these idyllic village communities, inoffensive though they may appear, had always been the solid foundation of Oriental despotism, that they restrained the human mind within the smallest possible compass, making it the unresisting tool of superstition, enslaving it beneath traditional rules, depriving it of all grandeur and historical energies. We must not forget that these little communities were contaminated by distinction of caste and by slavery, that they subjugated man to external circumstances instead of elevating man to be the sovereign of circumstances, that they transformed a self-developing social state into never changing natural destiny, and thus brought about a brutalizing worship of nature, exhibiting its degradation in the fact that man, the sovereign of nature, fell down on his knees in adoration of Hanuman, the monkey, and Sabbala, the cow. (Marx

cited in op cit, p. 90-91.)

Arvind Narayan Das of the National Labor Institute, New Delhi, has expressed the following opinions on the community development movement in India:

> The Community Development Movement implicitly accepted the assumption that individuals, groups and classes in the village have common interests which are sufficiently strong to bind them together. it also assumed that interests were sufficiently common to generate enthusiasm and further that conflict of interests were sufficiently reconcileable. These assumptions proved to be unrealistic. In fact, the better off benefitted the most from programs and a growing disparity and inequality became visible in rural areas. (Asian South Pacific Bureau of Adult Education, 1978, Number 13, p. 12.)

In most countries where community development programs were implemented, it was generally considered that working with the traditional leaders at the village level would benefit the whole community.

Unfulfilled Expectations

Although community development was based on the assumption that initiative should come from the people at the grass roots level, in actual practice decisions were imposed from above through ministries at the national level. The bureaucrats in Third World countries, who are accountable to their respective ministries and not to the people, did not respect the ideas coming from below. Village level workers soon became agents of the government more than the change agents working at the village level. As agents of the central government, they were overburdened with many responsibilities. Moreover, they were outsiders who had no interest in the villages and their training was not appropriate for the work they were expected to do.

At the initial stages, people in the Third World countries expected that community development programs would help to generate employment, increase incomes, and alleviate poverty. But when put into operation, the results were limited to providing certain community services and were not concerned with activities that led to the betterment of the rural poor as a whole. Due to these and other reasons, the community development approach in less developed countries has been subjected to severe criticism, and many questions have been raised regarding its ability to bring about desired change.

Suggested Resources
Education for Community Development

Bibliography

Ariyaratne, A.T. *Sarvodaya and development.* Moratuwa, Sri Lanka: Sarvodaya Shramadana Movement, 1979.

Asian South Pacific Bureau of Adult Education. *People's participation in rural development.* December 1978, 13.

Batten, T.R. *Training for community development: A critical study of method.* London: Oxford University Press, 1962.

Biddle, W.W., and Biddle, L. *The community development process: The rediscovery of local initiative.* New York: Holt, Rinehart and Winston, 1965.

Chambers, R. *Managing rural development: Ideas and experiences from East Africa.* Uppsala, Sweden: The Scandanavian Institute of African Studies, 1974.

Cohen, J.M., and Uphoff, N.T. *Rural development participation: Concepts for project design, implementation and evaluation.* Ithaca, NY: Cornell University Rural Development Committee, 1977.

Collantes, M.F. *A tale of two barrios: Education implications of community liberation development.* Unpublished doctoral dissertation. University of Massachusetts, 1980.

Das, A.N. Role of worker organization in rural development. *People's participation in rural development.* Asian South Pacific Bureau of Adult Education, December 1978, 13.

Green, J.W. Community development as economic development: The role of value orientation. Background Paper III. *Economic Implications of Community Development.* Inter-Regional Community Development Conference. Seoul, Korea: May 6-12, 1961.

Hanberry, G.C. *Community development: A concept analysis.* Florida State University, 1972.

International corporation administration manual. Order No. 27109.1, July 2, 1957.

Kindervatter, S. *Learner-centered training for learner centered programs.* Amherst, MA: Center for International Education, University of Massachusetts, 1977.

Long, H.B. (Ed.) and others. *Approaches to community development.* Iowa: American City Testing Program and Minnesota: National American University Extension Association, 1973.

Loughran, E. *Community education in context.* Unpublished manuscript, Amherst, MA: School of Education, University of Massachusetts, 1981.

Malassis, L. *The rural world: Education and development,* Paris: UNESCO, 1976.

Metcalf, S.C., *Report of the selected committee of the House of Commons,* 1832, Vol. III, Appendix 84. Cited in Kantowsky, *Sarvodaya: The other development.* New Delhi, India: Visaka Publishing House, PVT LBD., 1980.

Miniclier, L. Values and principles of community development. In *Community development: Concept and definition.* Inter-Regional Community Development Conference, Seoul, Korea: May 6-12, 1961.

Nerfin, M. *Another development: Approaches and strategies.* Uppasala, Sweden: Dag Hammarskjold Foundation, 1977.

Ratnapala, N. (Ed.), *A.T. Ariyaratne collected works Vol. 1.* Printed in Netherlands. Undated.

Sarvodaya Development Education Institute. *Basic Human needs and their fulfillment.* Moratuwa, Sri Lanka: Sarvodaya Press, 1978.

Sarvodaya Shramadana Movement in Sri Lanka. Sri Lanka: Sarvodaya Press, 1977.

Sarvodaya Shramadana Movement of Sri Lanka: Ethos and work plan. Moratuwa, Sri Lanka: Sarvodaya Press, 1976.

Sarvodaya Research Center. *Sarvodaya study service in Sri Lanka 1975-1976.* Columbo, Sri Lanka: Sarvodaya Research Center.

Shields, J. *Education in community development: Its function in technical assistance.* New York: Praeger Publishers, 1967.

Stavis, B. *People's communes and rural development in China.* Ithaca, New York: Center for International Studies, Cornell University, 1974.

Taylor, P.S. Community development. In *Community development concepts and descriptions.* Inter-Regional Conference. Seoul, Korea: May 6-12, 1961.

United Nations Bureau of Social Affairs. *Social progress through community development,* 1953.

United Nations Development Program. *Rural Development Evaluation Study No. 2.* Issues and approaches to technical cooperation. New York: 1979.

Uphoff, N.T., Cohen, J.M., and Goldsmith, A.A. *Flexibility and application of rural development participation: A state-of-the-art paper.* Ithaca, New York: Cornell University, Rural Development Committee, 1979.

Wileden, A.F. *Community development: Dynamics of planned change.* Totowa, NJ: The Bedminster Press, 1970.

Journals

Community Development Society Journal

Community Planning Review

Community Development Journal

Resource Centers

ACCION International (Community Development) (AI)
10-C Mt. Auburn Street
Cambridge, MA 02138

American Research Institute for Community Development (ARICD),
P.O. Box 292 A
St. Louis, Missouri 63166

Center for Community Economic Development (CCED),
1320 19th Street, N.W.
Washington, D.C. 20036

Center for International Education (CIE)
Hills House South
University of Massachusetts
Amherst, MA 01003

Community Development Society (CDS)
27 Kellogg Center
Michigan State University
East Lansing, Michigan 48824

Community Education Resource Center and
    Citizen Involvement Training Program (CERC-CITP)
School of Education
University of Massachusetts
Amherst, MA 01003

Community Fellows Program (Community Development) (CFP)
Massachusetts Institute of Technology
77 Massachusetts Ave.
Cambridge, MA 02139

International Society for Community Development (ISCD)
777 United Nations Plaza
New York, NY 10017

National Association for Community Development (NACD)
161 W. Wisconsin Ave., Suite 7156
Milwaukee, WI 53203

National Community Development Association (NCDA)
1620 Eye Street, N.W., Suite 503
Washington, D.C. 20006

National Self-Help Resource Center (Community Development) (NSHRC)
2000 S Street, N.W.
Washington, D.C. 20009

Sarvodaya Shramadana Movement of Sri Lanka
Methmedure, Moratuwa, Sri Lanka

6
APPROPRIATE TECHNOLOGY

James E. Masker

The appropriate technology movement is a global phenomenon which provides a theoretical and practical alternative to the prevailing capital-intensive, industrial economic paradigm. From its origins in England less than twenty years ago, the appropriate technology movement has captured the imagination and loyalty of a diverse group of development specialists. In fact, its adherents include such a wide range of engineers and scientists, political leaders, community educators, and social reformers that little agreement exists among those who call themselves appropriate technologists as to what the proper goals and implementation strategies should be. This is not uncommon, however, for a movement which has as its basis a critique of our contemporary world.

This essay attempts to analyze the appropriate technology movement from the perspective of community-based appropriate technology groups and organizations in the United States. While this perspective is admittedly a narrow segment of the appropriate technology spectrum, an effort will be made to place it in the context of the global movement so that the reader will gain an understanding of one perspective while, at the same time, being introduced to the origins and diversity of the movement. The first section will briefly describe the major aspects of the appropriate technology movement's critique of our contemporary world. The next section, Definitions, will attempt to develop the ends of a continuum which will be helpful in understanding the various theoretical and practical aspects of the movement. The third section, Distinctions, will analyze the continuum in the context of community-based appropriate technology groups and organizations in the United States. The following two sections, Social Change Theory and Learning Theory, will examine the extreme ends of the continuum in order to provide a perspective on the two major camps within the movement. The Pervasive Themes and Delivery Variables sections will again focus on the community-based programs in the United States. The final section, Resources, will provide the reader with an extensive list of printed material for further examination of the appropriate technology movement in the United States and throughout the world.

Origins

The appropriate technology movement in the United States emerged in the mid-Seventies from a critique of contemporary society which had intensified in the late Fifties and Sixties. This critique focused on the impact of the prevailing economic paradigm on the environment, the socio-political structure, and the ethical values of the nation and its impact on the global community. This section of the essay will briefly describe six major themes of the critique. An understanding of the breadth of the critique is essential for interpretation of the various distinctions within the movement which will be discussed in later sections.

Resource Limits

First, a major premise behind a growth-oriented economic model is the inexhaustable availability of natural resources. The experience of the last quarter century has seriously challenged this assumption. M. King Hubbert, an oil company geologist, forecast in the Fifties that the world's crude oil production would peak and decline in the last quarter of this century. By the time his projections became a reality in the mid-Seventies, the "limits to growth" debate was well underway. The combination of increased industrial output and a rapidly expanding population base had created a situation where the irreplaceable natural resources that took hundreds of millions of years to form were being depleted in a matter of a few decades.

While this trend had obvious ramifications for the future of the American economy, the fact that the United States with six percent of the world's population consumed over thirty percent of the world's yearly resource output had serious international implications. One writer estimated that if the developing nations of the world were to increase their resource use to only half what the United States consumed, they would need approximately three hundred percent of the world's annual resource output (Diwan and Lingston, 1979). This is an obvious impossibility. Such global inequities in the use of rapidly depleting natural resources suggest increased international tensions in the coming years.

Environmental Limits

Second, it became apparent that serious environmental consequences resulted from our economic system. Research indicated that the air, water and soil were approaching, if not already surpassing, natural tolerance margins. Every biological organism produces wastes. These wastes are usually absorbed back into the environment as nutrients for other organisms. Many of the wastes produced by our nation are not reabsorbable into the biosphere, but remain as deadly toxins in the environment. The combustion of fossil fuels, for example, has serious consequences for the environment. Sulphuric acid is carried in the air and precipitates to the earth in rain and snow. Studies have shown that in some lakes, plant and animal life are disappearing, concrete buildings are prematurely eroding, and water is being polluted. Similarly, fossil fuels release significant amounts of carbon dioxide into the air, causing a trend toward global temperature increases, which could mean the melting of the polar ice caps and glaciers. Deadly chemical toxins and nuclear wastes which remain active for upwards of 50,000 years are being produced. These materials cause cancer and other serious physical ailments as they seep into the air and water.

Millions of acres of precious topsoil are eroded annually from farmland. This occurs because of the trends towards large, corporate farms emphasizing monoculture development which leaves the soil bare and unprotected for lengthy periods of the year. Irrigation in areas where little surface water exists produces salts which decrease the land's fertility. Massive applications of petroleum-based fertilizers and pesticides cause toxic chemicals in the water runoff.

Social Limits

Third, appropriate technology writers see the technocratic and elitist nature of our economic system as another socio-political shortcoming. Modern technology, they propose, is highly sophisticated, requiring years of formal schooling and a trained, specialized elite to design, fabricate, and operate the computers, robots, and organizational infrastructure. These specialists function at the behest of those who provide the initiative and capital. Hence, an ownership elite also exists whose interests are closely aligned with profits and further capital formation.

The impact of capital, technology, and managerial elites on political decision making from the local to international levels is profound. One writer proposes that the average citizen is isolated from the political process which affects his life because political decisions are presented as complex technical ones assessible only to experts (Dickson, 1979). Because of their special position, those experts have preferential access to elected or imposed representatives and national communication media. Financial interests of the elite, therefore, tend to receive greater attention in the final anaysis than the interests of community stability, environmental quality, and natural resource stewardship.

Economic Limits

Fourth, recent investigations have disclosed that a capital-intensive, high technology based economy actually creates unemployment rather than expanding job availability. For years it was assumed that a positive correlation existed between the level of employment and increased resource consumption. The intermediate factor was the strength of the economy as measured by the gross national product (GNP). However, while GNP's increased in both industrialized nations and developing countries, the number of workers in existing industries decreased and the number of unemployed increased. This trend occurs because capital-intensive technologies are substituted for human labor.

For example, since 1920, energy use in agriculture has quadrupled, while employment has been cut in half. In the twenty-year period ending in 1969, the American steel industry's productivity rose 45 percent, while its labor force was cut by 20 percent. Productivity in combined manufacturing and agricultural sectors rose 250 percent between 1959 and 1971, while half a million jobs were lost (Quammen, 1980).

The situation is even more severe in developing countries where technologies are usually imported from industrial nations. One author vividly describes how 5,000 leather shoemakers were forced out of work when two plastic-molding injection machines were imported into a North African country. These machines cost $100,000 and employed only 40 machine operators. Furthermore, where leather products were once purchased from local cattlemen, the plastic needed for the machines had to be imported from abroad and the local owners did not have indigenous expertise to repair the machines when they broke down (Dunn, 1979).

Profits increase when capital replaces human labor because machines can work faster and cause less labor unrest, but employment decreases. This situation places severe strains on social services and governmental income maintenance programs.

Dependency Limits

A fifth critique often articulated by appropriate technology writers is the various forms of dependency that develop in industrial societies due to the trend towards centralized production, distribution and decision making. Such dependencies are viewed as the result of the trend towards centralized infrastructures which must be reversed if citizens and communities are to have control over their basic needs and futures (Design Alternatives, 1978). For instance, skyrocketing fuel prices have made industrial powers all too aware of their vulnerability to economic and political decisions made outside their territorial borders.

A city like Detroit is so dependent upon the automobile industry that threatened shut-downs or lay-offs find immediate labor union support for the federal government's intervention to shore up failing companies in the name of job protection. A few years ago, the mayor of a large city in the United States was forced to make a public plea to residents to reduce water consumption. Days later, he was back in the media asking citizens to start using more water. The problem was that residents had conserved a large amount of water, and the water company faced the possibility of not receiving their mandated profit unless consumption was increased. The company had so much capital invested in water technology, engineers, and support staff that, even though the city proved it could use less water, the company's and citizen's dependency upon the technology required more water to be consumed than was needed.

A pickers' and haulers' strike in California means no fruit or vegetables in New England. A garbage or police strike in a major city means no essential services until political and economic matters are settled.

American agriculture is wholly dependent on fossil fuels. Monoculture farming practices require excessive amounts of fertilizers and pesticides to achieve the productivity levels of recent years. For example, since the end of World War II, Illionis farms have nearly doubled their corn production levels. However, achieving this increase has required a forty-fold increase in the use of chemical fertilizers. Insecticide use has increased ten-fold, while crop loss to insects has doubled. What these figures mean is that the land cannot produce today's food levels without massive fossil fuel inputs. Any decrease in fossil fuel availability or increase in price will drastically affect the cost and availability of food.

Psychological and Community Limits

The sixth area of concern for appropriate technologists relates to the breakdown of community and increased personal alienation that occurs because of our economic system. While Buckminster Fuller's "spaceship earth" metaphor provides a useful vision of the fragility of the environment and the unity of humankind on this planet, it also describes the reality of an interdependent global economy. The impact of a global economy on individual communities is to break down those community institutions which once provided the basic needs of local residents.

National food chains push small local grocery store owners out of business, which means that small local producers no longer have access to local markets. Citizens have little control over fuel costs or availability in a system where producers and consumers are separated by thousands of miles of oceans and business infrastructures. Recent attempts in this country for community energy management are often futile and have little impact because the resources and decision making are outside their political jurisdictions.

A highly centralized, technological society leaves individuals as isolated units exchanging labor for wages to purchase basic needs. Individuals and families become dependent consumers no longer capable or knowledgeable in the skills of supplying their own food, clothing, shelter, and energy requirements. Most workers do not have the satisfaction of seeing a task completed or having direct, day-to-day involvement in their survival.

Many writers see the increase in numerous societal ills (crime, mental illness, drug addiction, broken homes, etc.) as concrete indications of the breakdown of a sense of community and increased personal alienation (Clinton, 1977).

While there are numerous themes often described by appropriate technology writers, the six described here are the most consistently examined ones. These will provide the reader with an overview of the nature and breadth of the critique of our contemporary economic and social systems which will help in understanding the definitions and distinctions within the appropriate technology movement.

Definitions

What is appropriate technology? It
depends on what we are trying to do.
—Schumacher, 1973

It is difficult to arrive at a single definition that would apply to all individuals, organizations, and programs involved in the appropriate technology movement. For the most part, this stems from wide disagreement among the movement's proponents about the emphasis to be placed on various aspects of the critique, the proper goals for development of appropriate technologies, and the relevancy of various implementation strategies for technology dissemination. These discrepancies become acute when attempting to scrutinize the profusion of educational programs that are the essence of a number of appropriate technology programs and organizations.

An Appropriate Technology Continuum

While there is a divergence of opinion among the movement adherents about the goals, development, and diffusion of appropriate technologies, it is possible to develop a continuum to aid in sorting out the various participants within the movement. This section of the essay will consider the significant elements of the extreme ends of the continuum. The reader must understand in advance that the archetypes described here are drawn from the literature. Very few individuals, programs or organizations actually practicing the principles of appropriate technology would fall completely into one or the other end of the continuum. In the following section, Distinctions, a selection of existing community-based appropriate technology programs in the United States will be described in the context of the continuum in order to demonstrate the breadth and subtleties of the movement's educational implementation and dissemination strategies. Two writers, Rybczynski (1980) and Dickson (1979), provide the clearest descriptions of the two primary camps within the appropriate technology movement. The former uses the terms evolutionary and revolutionary, while the latter develops a similar dichotomy using the concepts of reform and change.

An Evolutionary Emphasis

At one end of the continuum are the evolutionary/reform-oriented proponents of the movement. These individuals would agree that our economic system, both nationally and internationally, is facing resource and environmental constraints, placing strains on a harmonious, inter-dependent world. Such constraints are the result of technologies which waste natural resources and create unnecessary pollution of the environment. They would perceive unemployment to be the key social problem from which most other social ills arise. Unemployment is caused not only by economic growth unable to keep pace with a rapidly expanding population base, but also from the replacement of human labor with capital-intensive technologies.

The evolutionary/reform proponents would see increasing a nation's gross national product, increasing the number of jobs, and diversifying the benefits of affluence to an ever expanding number of people to be the primary goals of economic activity. While there would be concern about the need to increase the number of small businesses and limit the growth of multinational corporations, traditional ownership and management structures would prevail.

The primary concern of the evolutionary/reform perspective would not be with the goals of the traditional economic paradigm, for these would be upheld as valid; rather the concern would be with the need to evolve or reform the technologies which achieve these goals. To this group, therefore, **appropriate technology is concerned primarily with engineering and** hardware research, development, and dissemination of specific technologies which conserve scarce resources, minimize environmental impact, and create jobs.

This end of the continuum originates with E. F. Schumacher and what was first called Intermediate Technology. Schumacher and his colleagues in England were principally concerned with the problems inherent in tech-nology transfer to the Third World; the principles of the Intermediate Technology movement remained intact when the term *appropriate* replaced *intermediate,* and the movement spread to the United States in the early Seventies. Schumacher's world was a technologically deterministic one. Since technology shaped values and the form the world took, resource, environmental, and social problems stemming from technology could be solved by designing and disseminating new and more appropriate tech-nologies. The basic foundations of a society and the economy need not be questioned or altered to improve the conditions of a nation and its citizens. This theme will be explored more thoroughly in the section Social Change.

Dunn provides a popular example of appropriate technology from the evolutionary/reform perspective (Dunn, 1979). Entrepreneurs in Zambia needed an egg tray producing machine which could produce twelve million trays a year and cost £150,000. This machine was too productive and too expensive for the Zambians. A graduate student at the Royal School of Art in England took on the project as part of his master's program. He succeeded in designing and developing a smaller, cheaper egg tray machine which produced 300,000 trays a year and cost £8,000. More Zambians were employed with this machine supplying the country's one million egg tray need than with the twelve million tray machine for about one-twentieth of the cost. The machine was exported to other countries who needed the smaller machines.

In the United States, efforts to promote energy conservation and renewable energy resources have been undertaken as a means to conserve dwindling fossil fuels, minimize their harmful environmental impact, and to stabilize the cost of food, space heating, and hot water for families. Numerous studies have been conducted which demonstrate that investment in conservation and renewable energies has a greater beneficial impact on resources, environment, and job creation than does investment in other capital-intensive, energy production technologies. Subsequently, many entrepreneurs have begun researching, developing and marketing conservation and solar technologies. While large corporations such as Exxon and Grumman have invested in solar air and water heating technologies, a much larger number of small businesses have begun as the vehicle for disseminating these appropriate technologies to local communities.

The definition of appropriate technology promoted by the United States Department of Energy would be a good representation of the evolutionary/reform end of the continuum. DOE states that appropriate technology is a "technology that is small scale, simple to install, operate and maintain; low cost and durable; employs novel applications of existing technologies; is environmentally sound; satisfies local needs."

A Revolutionary Emphasis

At the other end of the continuum are the revolutionary/change proponents of appropriate technology. These individuals would emphasize all aspects of the critique, particularly those dealing with social, political, and ethical considerations. They would challenge the economic goals of maximizing production and consumption and place human welfare and community self-reliance as the primary goals of any economic system. Quality of life, rather than productive quality, should be an essential measure of economic success.

Rather than having private corporations determine human needs and technological solutions to those needs, the revolutionary/change proponents would see individual participation in community problem diagnosis and planning efforts as being essential. Once communities have determined the direction of their own development, natural resources, technologies, and human labor would be fashioned to achieve those goals. Community harmony and long-term stability are vital objectives. Development should emphasize local human needs not private accumulation of wealth. Production is for local and regional needs not national or international, consumer-oriented products.

The revolutionary/change proponents would reject the technologically deterministic attitudes of the evolutionary/reform perspective. The former would claim that the problems facing today's world are caused primarily by the economic, political, and social structure which direct the form technology takes. Technology in and of itself is neutral; a direct manifestation of a society's values. Evolving or reforming technology will not appreciably affect a society, except to further solidify the prevailing economic paradigm which maintains existing patterns of dominance, control, and the dichotomy of interests between workers and owners.

The revolutionary/change perspective, therefore, purports that any technology has two aspects: hardware/technical and software/process. The software/process component deals with the ways in which the socio-political structure is organized to produce, distribute and consume technologies or the by-products of technologies which are consumer goods. A food cooperative, for example, is a software/process technology developed to further a particular philosophy about the ways in which people should interact with each other while meeting their basic needs. Appropriate technologies at this end of the continuum, therefore, emphasize both hardware and software components.

Revolutionary/change appropriate technologists would reject the Zambian egg carton machine as an example of appropriate technology for two reasons. First, the machine was designed and fabricated in an industrial country for sale to a developing country. Scientific, engineering, and technical expertise was not transferred, only the final hardware product. Therefore, no indigenous research and development capabilities were enhanced. Secondly, the machine was owned by entrepreneurs, not by the community where the displaced jobs occurred. Therefore, not only were people put out of work, but the profits from the machine's productivity went to private owners and not to improve the quality of life for the affected community.

The definition of appropriate technology devised by Tom Bender (*RAIN*, 1975) should be a good representation of the revolutionary/change end of the continuum. He states that appropriate technology is:

> A technology that operates capably within the levels and patterns of activities sustainable with renewable energy sources and material recycling; . . . permits easy control of political, economic, and social systems; . . . promotes equity, independence, soundness, stability, and other values appropriate to a sound and enduring society; . . . and permits ownership of the means of production by those who do the work.

Distinctions

The previous section examined the major definitional differences within the appropriate technology movement by developing the ends of a continuum. This section will describe the subtle variations along the continuum in the context of community-based appropriate technology programs and organizations in the United States that seek to disseminate technical information to the public through community education strategies. The purpose of these descriptions will be to demonstrate that, while there may exist a wide range among theoreticians and writers about the proper goals of appropriate technology, a much narrower range exists when practitioners attempt to disseminate information and skills in the socio-political climate of this country.

Evolutionary Nature of Appropriate Technology in the United States

There is little room for community-based education in the evolutionary/reform end of the continuum. Appropriate technology from this perspective is primarily concerned with researching, developing, and marketing technologies. The only role for education is in the context of consumer sales information. Even when a community-scale technology is developed, such as a cogeneration facility or methane production plant from garbage dumps, little community-wide education occurs. Usually, an engineering firm determines the size of the population base needed to support the technology and contacts governmental or planning officials to sell them on the idea of purchasing the technology for their community.

Community-based education, on the other hand, is an essential component of the revolutionary/change end of the continuum. From this perspective, community residents continually educate themselves about the social, political, economic, environmental and resource conditions in which they live. Residents continually seek values and lifestyle changes which alleviate poverty, class distinctions, environmental damage, and resource depletion in their community. Coincident with this software/process educational activity is the education involved in researching, developing and disseminating technologies throughout the community which will provide the hardware essential to bring about the values and lifestyles previously determined by the community. From this perspective, therefore, there is as much organizational education as there is technological education.

Conserving Forces

In spite of the wide variety of ways in which community-based, appropriate technology education is practiced throughout the United States, nearly all would fall far short of the ideal of the revolutionary/change perspective. There are several reasons for this. First, the shortcoming of our society shapes the direction of dissemination by the appropriate technology movement. Individuals and families are interested in lowering domestic operating expenses, not with challenging the economic, political, or social foundations of our society. Most see the foundations as valuable forces which help to shape our nation's technological and economic prowess. Second, many appropriate technology advocates in this country are primarily concerned with resource conservation, environmental health, and self-reliance. While self-reliance is often phrased in the context of a social vision of community self-reliance, the actual implementation of the concept is usually conducted by targeting programs to individuals or families. Consequently, appropriate technology organizations usually concern themselves with developing programs for individuals and families which provide information and construction skills for specific technologies that will conserve resources, improve the environment, and lower family expenses. Third, the common funding sources for appropriate technology programs in this country—federal, state and local governments—do not place a high priority on radical economic or political change. They tend to act as a conservative force, moving away from the revolutionary/change end of the continuum. Also, homeowners and renters want specific technical information for their money, not political or ethical theory. Businesses which supply components and products essential for the fabrication and installation of site-built technologies would not promote community ownership of resources. Fourth, a vast majority of those involved in the appropriate technology movement in this country come from middle- and upper-class families. To many of these highly educated and mobile individuals, appropriate technology is a means to pursue a livelihood. While a large number of these individuals raise social, political and ethical issues when discussing the goals and values for appropriate technology, most would adhere more closely to the evolutionary/reform end of the continuum. In general they would agree that the technologies we use need to be designed or reformed with resource and environmental considerations in mind.

While most appropriate technology programs and organizations fall short of the extreme revolutionary/change ideal, they are decidedly more interested and involved in community education than the extreme evolutionary/reform perspective. Nearly all community-based, appropriate technology educational activities in the United States are concerned with developing regional and local domestic technologies and disseminating information and skills about those technologies to interested citizens. The various educational programs do not differ greatly in their ethical and political positions. Differences appear more in their research, development policy and dissemination activities.

Examples of Community-Based Programs

The remainder of this section will briefly describe four major categories of community-based, educational programs and organizations in the United States. The programs and organizations mentioned here are by no means all-inclusive, but they do serve as good examples of the range of activities existing along the continuum.

Research and Dissemination

One category of community-based, educational organizations is the research/dissemination center. Among the organizations in this category are the New Alchemy Institute in Massachusetts, the New Mexico Solar Energy Association in New Mexico, and the urban and rural centers of the Farallones Institute in California. These private, nonprofit centers are concerned with researching and demonstrating optimal agricultural and/or energy technologies. They do not focus on developing technologies for individual communities; rather they provide viable technologies applicable to particular climatic or regional conditions. Scientists and researchers delineate projects and conduct research programs to better understand resource-conserving and environment-enhancing technologies.

While most of their efforts are directed toward research and development activities, all the centers offer a variety of educational programs to the public. Most conduct tours of their facilities during weekends. Individuals are led on a guided tour by a member of the staff who explains the various projects and answers questions. Very often these centers offer longer, more intensive courses which focus on a particular aspect of the research, such as cold frame construction or the use of "breadbox" hot water heater design and installation. Another form of education dissemination is through publications. Some centers offer periodicals, while others publish reports about specific research projects. These are often written with the do-it-yourselfer in mind, offering specific information and construction details needed to replicate the technology.

Generally, community organizing is not conducted by these centers. Their primary goals are research, development, and dissemination of appropriate technologies. Working demonstrations of these technologies are built and displayed at the centers and described in the workshops and publications. Information from research/dissemination centers diffuses into communities in two ways: (a) Interested individuals will attempt to replicate a particular project in their homes, and (b) Community organizers visit the center to learn about the projects and then organize educational programs in their communities to teach local residents.

Formal Education Approaches

A second category of community-based educational organizations is adult education and continuing education programs. These programs, conducted through local universities and high schools, offer a wide variety of self-improvement and recreational courses to adults. In the last few years, courses have been incorporated into the curriculum about agricultural and/or renewable energy technologies. Members of the community who are interested in learning practical subject matter register for courses and pay a fee for the instructor's time and course materials. While some continuing education programs at universities employ energy professionals, most of these courses are taught by local residents who are either professionally trained in the field or experienced through previous self-help endeavors.

As with the research centers, little attention is paid to community organizing activities. While the focus is on disseminating practical information about appropriate technologies to the public, the educational techniques and goals are fairly traditional.

Action-Oriented Programs

A third category of community-based appropriate technology programs is the Community Action Agency (CAA). These local or county anti-poverty agencies are funded by state and federal monies and are concerned primarily with low-income individuals and families. Their goal is to irradicate poverty by educating and organizing low-income families in self-help projects. These agencies have developed two types of appropriate technology programs. The first has little educational context, while the second not only has an information dissemination focus, but also a community organizing emphasis. The latter would be closer to the revolutionary/change end of the continuum than the research/dissemination center and the adult/continuing education categories.

First, for a number of years, Community Action Agencies have conducted weatherization programs where income-eligible people receive free energy audits, weatherization materials, and retrofits by workcrews of the agency. In recent years, many CAA's have received funds to incorporate solar retrofit programs into their weatherization activities. Greenhouses, air heaters, and water heaters have been installed in low-income homes by CAA's throughout the country. While some CAA's may require recipient homeowners to monitor their systems or allow tours of their retrofitted homes, very little involvement is required of the homeowner. Consequently, not much community education value is derived from such projects. In fact, these solar retrofit programs would be much closer to the evolutionary/reform end of the continuum since little emphasis is placed on education or organizing.

The second type of CAA program, however, is much closer to the community-based education/organizing ideal of the revolutionary/change perspective. These programs seek to organize interested low-income families into cooperative self-help projects, such as community gardens, community greenhouses, food co-ops, and self-help housing retrofit projects. Their goal is to use the self-reliance potential of appropriate technologies to organize people. In this way, both the hardware and software aspects of technology are incorporated into programs that train people.

The Appropriate Technology Program of the Hampshire Community Action Commission in Massachusetts is but one example of this type of CAA community-based educational project. An organizer, hired to work with families in low-income apartment complexes, conducted a number of educational sessions in various apartments. Interested families learned about heat loss and potential energy saving technologies. The families then determined how best to stop the heat loss and redesigned technologies to fit their particular apartments. Bulk purchasing of materials was made possible through a state grant, and cooperative work sessions were organized to build and install thermal shades in the apartments. The success of this project led this CAA to offer community workshops around the county, teaching other residents about the economic benefits of thermal shades and the fabrication techniques. Because of this project, a CAA in an adjacent county became interested in thermal shades and started a worker-owned business to manufacture and sell the shades.

Grass Roots Efforts

The fourth category of community-based, appropriate technology educational programs is the local solar energy association, two of the more successful being the Urban Solar Energy Association in Massachusetts and the San Luis Valley Solar Energy Association in Colorado. These solar energy associations are usually composed of unpaid or minimally paid volunteers who are dedicated to community initiative and information and skills dissemination. Their purpose is to generate community interest and involvement in residential appropriate technologies by teaching community residents how to build and install various technologies for their homes and apartments. Dues are usually collected to assist in publishing newsletters and organizing community workshops or events. These groups organize numerous kinds of community-based educational programs— weekend, hands-on construction workshops, monthly speakers, bulk purchasing of materials, design consultation services, blueprints for technologies, tours of local installations, technical assistance in upgrading local building codes, etc.

These associations are participatory, community-based organizations and probably come the closest to the revolutionary/change ideal. While they do not tend to involve themselves with challenging larger power structures and corporations, they do provide a community organization that seeks to involve local residents in shaping their own future through mutual, self-help endeavors. Many of these solar energy associations also conduct small scale research projects on individual homes to determine what is the most cost-effective combination of materials and design characteristics for a specific technology. Whereas CAA's focus primarily on low-income families, solar energy associations are open to any interested individual in the community regardless of income level.

Social Change Theory

There are two distinct positions that the appropriate technology movement can play in bringing about social change. The two positions are consistent with the evolutionary/reform and revolutionary/change positions articulated throughout this essay.

Social change, from the evolutionary/reform perspective, is caused by greater numbers of people being employed in industrial or agricultural production in the market economy. Positive social change results from employment, because people who have jobs are more capable of pursuing the goal of material acquisition while contributing to their nation's economic interactions in the global economy. The cycle of job creation, income expenditure, purchase of consumer goods, and further job creation is not only economically sound, but creates a greater number of upwardly mobile people, thus alleviating poverty and other social ills.

Writers and practitioners of the revolutionary/change perspective would deny that any meaningful social change results from making the prevailing economic paradigm more successful. The proponents of this perspective propose that there is an intimate relationship between the form technology takes and the patterns of social, political, and economic domination within and between societies. Truly meaningful social change, therefore, cannot and will not come about by merely reforming technologies. Social change can only come about when social and institutional changes act in harmony with technological change. Rybcyznski, drawing upon his Indian experience, outlines this position:

> Failure of A.T. in India is complex. It resides in the belief that social reform can come about as the result of technological innovations. There is nothing in the Indian experience that supports this view. . . . Better technology can certainly not be a substitute for social reform. Landlordism, powerful rural elites, conservative bankers, and rapacious money lenders all conspire to maintain the poverty of the landless peasants. These social and political problems require social and political solutions; it is both presumptuous and naive to believe that technology alone will have any effect in a situation such as this. (Rybcyznki, 1980, p. 124.)

Proponents of the revolutionary/change perspective claim that individuals, organizations, and governments supporting the evolutionary perspective are seeking to maintain economic and cultural domination. These proponents would flatly reject Jequier's claim that social and political changes could potentially be unleashed by socially minded entrepreneurs investing in appropriate technologies (Jequier, 1979). Their rejection would originate from their belief that the very process of importing technologies or purchasing indigenous machines, borrowing money, and maintaining a cost-effective workforce necessitates the acceptance of the paradigm of modernization and traditional economics. The kinds of social and political reforms that could occur would not have a large impact on the poor and unemployed. Rather, such reforms would seek to further the dichotomy between entrepreneurial and working classes.

Social change from the revolutionary perspective is based on "the belief that human communities can have a hand in deciding what their future will be like, and that the choice of tools and techniques is an important part of this" (Darrow, Keller and Pam, 1981). Technologies are not developed and disseminated to entrepreneurs, because to do so would enhance social and political divisions. Rather, low-income residents in local communities work with research and development groups to articulate their problems and seek local solutions using local skills within each community. Community-based participatory problem solving is preferred by the revolutionists over the traditional top-down, centrally managed planning and project execution.

Both the evolutionary/reform and revolutionary/change perspectives discuss contemporary problems and the role technology has played in enhancing poverty, unemployment, and social and political domination in both the industrial and developing countries. The former pursues a reformist model by developing technologies that will spread the prevailing economic paradigm through the use of traditional research and development practices, capital formation techniques and technological dissemination mechanisms. Social change occurs because a greater number of people participate in material acquisition. The role of technology is to create wealth, thereby irradicating poverty and unemployment. The revolutionary perspective, on the other hand, seeks to link research and development activities directly to community-articulated problems. The economic motivation is not as pressing as the motivation of empowerment, teaching people to use their own resources to solve their own problems. People's participation is key to this perspective about appropriate technology. Social change occurs because community members begin to articulate causes of their poverty and seek solutions to this situation. The role of technology is to provide the tools and techniques to achieve the articulated goals of community members.

While the evolutionary perspective needs to integrate individuals into the national and global market economy, the revolutionary perspective interprets this as furthering the causes of poverty and domination. Therefore the latter seeks to find avenues whereby the poor can become self-reliant and independent of the market economy. While the former considers national and international interests the focus of attention, the latter sees individuals and community as the primary context for research, development, and transfer of appropriate technologies.

Learning Theory

The distinct features of the evolutionary/reform and revolutionary/change perspectives discussed in relation to social change manifest themselves in their respective learning theories. While neither perspective articulates specific cognitive or psychological learning theories, each makes general assertions about the form and content education and training should pursue in relation to appropriate technology.

The evolutionary/reform perspective views learning as the retention of a body of knowledge that is directly linked to the information and skill requirements necessary to maintain a society's viability. As a society changes and evolves, so do its learning needs. The actual school curriculum that students absorb is developed and implemented by knowledgeable experts who understand changing societal needs. Evolutionists believe that educational reform is the appropriate path to follow, not a radical restructuring of the concept of education or a questioning of the validity of formal schooling. Reformation of the university curriculum focuses on recommendations to establish closer links between the university, its students, and local communities.

The key concepts stressed by the writers of the evolutionist perspective are:

- to increase interaction and involvement of university students and faculty with the community (engineering schools might be an A.T. target);

- to have students actively participate in developing technologies that are small-scale and commercially viable;
- to learn by creative problem solving not rote memorization.

The rationale underlying these concepts is that through such behaviors (participation, action, and involvement), the learners will become more aware and committed to applying their knowledge toward the development of appropriate technologies.

Recommendations are also made by the evolutionists that primary and secondary education include technology transfer and locally appropriate sciencing efforts. For example, one writer recommends stressing contemporary topics such as bio-gas and solar energy principles and technologies in the science curriculum of secondary schools.

In summary, the evolutionary/reform perspective views reform of formal schooling as the appropriate course of action. Replace inappropriate engineering and science curriculum with more relevant, appropriate curriculum, but retain the basic information and skills; only the specifics of the information and skills and the scale of application are changed. Rather than sitting in a classroom or laboratory, students will practice their talents in the field. Engineering degrees and school diplomas are still viewed as the primary goal of education. Instructors and teachers are professionals who have attained a level of subject matter competence as documented by their diplomas and degrees.

The revolutionary/change perspective rejects formal education, seeing it as the mechanism by which social, political and economic domination is maintained in society. This despite the reforms outlined by the evolutionists. Degrees, grades, age- or skill-based classroom sorting, and teacher/student relationships all represent hierarchical forms of organization necessary for advanced technocratic societies.

Jua sets the tone for the form and content of education from the revolutionary perspective: "Appropriate Technology is a participatory development strategy" (Jua, 1980, p. 10). Participatory, community-based and user-defined education is a recent and radical departure from the traditional, formal educational system. The principles and techniques of nonformal education have become particularly popular with appropriate technologists of the revolutionary/change end of the continuum. The works of such writers as Freire and Srinivasen figure prominently in the literature.

The basic premise behind this learning theory is that individuals working in collaborative environments, mutually defining their problems and needs, will often have sufficient knowledge and skills to solve effectively their own problems. The role of the educated expert is as a resource person. Structured learning techniques are needed to assist community members in problem definition, preferred-state projection, and action strategy development. Nonformal education provides such a structured experience.

Nonformal education techniques have also been proven effective in short-term, technology transfer programs. Across the United States local solar energy associations have proliferated in recent years. These associations are typically composed of solar energy activists and interested community people. A popular educational strategy is to conduct weekend or evening community education programs that teach local residents basic solar design and construction skills. At such workshops, people are taught to build their own solar air or water heater or greenhouse. Groups such as the Franklin County Energy Office in Massachusetts developed community-based sciencing efforts; local residents who built greenhouses shared information about their experiences with other community members who could benefit from their successes and failures. The National Center for Appropriate Technology in Montana conducted week-long nonformal training programs. At these training sessions, representatives from Community Action Agencies and other anti-poverty organizations were given training in solar design principles and hands-on construction of various solar retrofit technologies.

The objectives of nonformal educational principles, when applied to the revolutionary perspective of appropriate technology are:

- to provide practical information and skills;
- to develop an awareness of the benefits of shared community experiences;
- to solve immediate community-defined problems;
- to stress the importance of participation in the learning process.

The goal is to enhance the ability of local communities to control their future by becoming more self-reliant.

Pervasive Themes

The five themes described in this section represent the major concerns of most community-based appropriate technology organizations in the United States.

Regional Research and Development Activities

Residential technologies are truly appropriate when they are designed for specific climates and indigenous materials. A company, such as Exxon, will design and market one particular type of solar panel throughout the country, but community-based appropriate technologists see this as a classic shortcoming of centralized, industrially produced technologies. In order to design the most cost-effective, easily constructed solar water heater, for example, an appropriate technologist would need to take into account a number of factors including the number of degree days, percent sunshine factor, and the cost and availability of various glazings or absorber plates. The end result might be a triple-glazed collector with insulated night coverings in cold, northern climates and a single-glazed collector with reflectors in a hot, southern climate. Continual research and monitoring of technologies is an important aspect of regional technology development activities.

Self-Reliance

This is one of the major themes of the community-based appropriate technology programs. Most proponents see the dependency that occurs when basic needs are acquired in a cash-based market economy as detrimental to a sense of control over one's life and household economy. If one does not grow even a portion of his/her food, then that individual will remain totally dependent on agri-business, whose concern is profit, not food quality or cost. Similarly, dependency on fossil fuels for air and water heating is precarious in times when shortages and rapidly rising prices predominate.

Appropriate technologists attempt to provide practical demonstrations of various technologies that homeowners or renters can build themselves. In this way, the family can become more self-reliant by stabilizing expenses for basic needs and reducing the need for market-based fuel and food resources. Self-reliance means that one is less dependent on the vagaries of the prevailing economic paradigm for basic needs.

Participation

Participation, in the context of community-based appropriate technology programs, usually means an active involvement by the homeowner or renter in the construction and installation of a technology. Many appropriate technologists feel that our contemporary society removes individuals from an understanding of principles and construction characteristics of the tools and machines we use for our very existence. Items are purchased and plugged into a wall outlet; when they break, they are either thrown away or taken to a specialist for repair. In order to reduce this dependency, appropriate technologists continually seek ways to involve people in building energy saving technologies. Some groups organize special classes for women who traditionally do not have much experience with hand or power tools. The purpose of participation is to involve people in concrete activities that will help them reduce their basic needs costs. Involvement, it is assumed, will lead to a greater sense of control over one's life.

Community

Appropriate technologists propose that the prevailing economic paradigm has been responsible for the breakdown of a sense of community that once prevailed in this country. A sense of community was necessary when activities such as a barn raising and harvesting without modern machinery were common. Individuals depended on each other for survival before the industrialization process isolated people into discrete work tasks. Proponents also claim that the quality of life is enhanced through group sharing in the processes of day-to-day living.

Nearly all community-based appropriate technology programs, therefore, seek to rebuild a sense of community among local residents by structuring their learning activities as community events. Weekend workshops during the construction of a home solar collector or greenhouse are well suited for bringing people together to participate in a practical, hands-on construction activity. Groups and co-ops that seek to organize food procurement or the purchase of energy materials are also attempting to build a sense of community interdependence among local residents. A long-term goal of community-based groups is that of bringing people together to participate in meeting their basic needs. This not only strengthens the community's sense of self-reliance, but also creates a climate whereby citizens work together to shape the future of their community.

Local Job Creation

Building and installing residential energy technologies in a do-it-yourself format will strengthen the local economy. If one buys a solar collector from Exxon or Grumman, money immediately leaves the local economy. If an individual builds a technology, materials are purchased locally and the money that would have paid for increased gas or oil is also available for local use. Skilled craftspeople, such as sheet metal workers and glaziers, can retrain themselves to provide the necessary components for a solar collector. Some local appropriate technology groups have set up small businesses to build systems for people who do not want to build them themselves. All of these efforts act to strengthen the local economy and skill base.

Delivery Variables

In this section, educational delivery variables will be examined in the context of community-based, appropriate technology educational groups in the United Staes that use nonformal educational techniques to disseminate residential technologies throughout local communities. These programs and organizations would include the research/dissemination centers, local solar energy associations, and Community Action Agencies previously described. The community workshop, as an educational technology, offers a unique, innovative approach to technology dissemination which not only incorporates hardware transfer, but also reinforces the software processes of participation and community building.

Objectives

The objectives of these programs are usually to disseminate basic technical information, technology fabrication, and installation skills to the public. Such technologies tend to be related to food production and energy conservation and production for residential use. The emphasis is on immediate acquisition and use of the knowledge and skills to facilitate a family's self-reliance. The programs are participatory and community-building in that people learn these skills by actually building an appropriate technology in workshops open to any interested member of the public.

Content, Sequence and Time

The content of these educational programs tends to be narrowly focused—how to build a solar greenhouse, introduction to wind power, raised-bed gardening, etc. While different levels of subject matter complexity may necessitate introductory and intermediate programs, very rarely is anyone excluded from a workshop. There is usually minimal concern for detailed theoretical understanding of physics, chemistry or biology. The knowledge disseminated takes the most practical information needed and presents it in lay person's terms. For example, rather than detailing the physical principles involved in blade sizing for a wind generator, the participant could be given a simple rule-of-thumb: power triples per foot of blade length. The emphasis is on readily applicable information.

Should the session include a hands-on construction experience, participants' questions about particular design, fabrication, or use issues are incorporated into the construction activity. For example, during a solar hot air panel workshop, a participant may ask why a certain kind of insulation was used. The workshop leader might respond that the materials cannot have an asphalt base glue because of the fumes that would be drawn into the house. Another participant could interject that she is aware of another brand of insulation that has the same properties but costs less money. A discussion could ensue about potential design modifications needed to use the cheaper materials. If the application of the suggested insulation proves cheaper, leaders and participants have learned another design potential. In this way, the content tends, at first, to be directed, but then becomes interactive if the workshop group pursues a direction.

Sequencing of educational offerings is usually not critical since each session tends to be fairly complete in its educational content. What sequencing does occur originates more from the desire to have principles understood before the hands-on component of the workshop takes place. For example, because it takes a few days to build a greenhouse, a program might be offered the evening before the construction phase to describe basic principles and design characteristics of the particular greenhouse. Very often, however, information about principles and design takes place during the hands-on workshop so that participants can ask questions while they are fabricating the technology. Length of workshops tends to be fairly short and is based on the length of time needed to complete the specific objective. Often, an evening session of three or four hours is sufficient to transfer basic principles and design considerations for most residential appropriate technologies. Construction workshops usually take place on weekends when people have free time. Scheduling the activity for the appropriate season is also given consideration. For example, an educational program about energy conservation technologies would not be as well attended in July as in December. Similarly, construction of a greenhouse in

January will not draw as many people as in June because of the weather.

Learners

Learners tend to be older adolescents and adults, both male and female. This is not because young people are excluded by design, but because the interest level or needs perception tends to be characterized by wage earners who are looking for ways to reduce their home's operating costs. It is not uncommon, however, to find a family at a weekend construction workshop since they tend to be relaxed events. Children are often given simpler tasks, such as moving lumber or spray painting an absorber plate.

As mentioned earlier, it sometimes happens that a participant will have a design or material suggestion that enhances the cost-effectiveness of a piece of technology. This fluidity between learners and teachers is one of the hallmarks of the revolutionary/change perspective of appropriate technology.

Staff

Staffing patterns, credentials, and experiences are widely diverse. If the program being offered requires some professional background, a local architect or engineer might teach the workshop. A local Audubon Society or Community Action Program might draw on community residents who have built a hot water heater for their own home. The workshop leader might be a truck driver or a nurse. A nonprofit, community-based appropriate technology organization might have a credentialed staff, but a·volunteer who attended previous workshops may actually lead a construction session.

The point is that each educational group has its own goals and objectives that determine the nature of its staff. Most residential appropriate technologies do not require years of formal schooling. A vast majority of people now conducting workshops across the country have acquired their knowledge by participating in workshops themselves.

Rewards and Evaluation

With these community-based nonformal programs, rewards and evaluation are intrinsic to the learner. The personal satisfaction for many participants of being able to reduce energy bills by building a technology with their own hands is sufficient motiviation for this kind of community education program. Others attend the workshops to be introduced to new ideas. Such persons might conduct follow-up research or attend another workshop before deciding to experiment on their own home.

The workshop process is one of cooperation, information sharing and participation. The emphasis is on group learning and community building, not competition. No evaluation of the participants is done except when tool usage skills are important. Usually, participants are questioned about their skills in using a table saw or drill. The workshop leader will often teach the unfamiliar person how to use the tool or ask another workshop participant who has the skills to teach the less-skilled person. If an evaluation takes place, it is usually done by the workshop leader to assess the participants' feelings about the content and process of the workshop. This is done to increase the workshop's future effectiveness.

Materials and Resources .

Materials and resources usually include audiovisuals, printed handouts, and demonstration models to teach the basic principles and design criteria. Many local groups have their own library or access to the public library where they may develop materials on energy or food self-reliance. Groups acquire their own libraries through grants, local fund raising appeals, or by charging a small fee for the workshop. Construction materials are usually available from local suppliers. Local availability of resources is essential to the appropriate technology movement. If some materials need to be purchased from companies in neighboring states or regions, efforts are usually taken to find a local supplier who can stock the material. Cooperative bulk purchase of materials is stressed by many groups as a way for community members to purchase their construction materials for reduced costs.

Financial Resources

Most programs rely on some combination of government and foundation grants, fund raising events, admission charges to workshops, donations, book sales, and membership fees to remain solvent. Many local appropriate technology groups get skilled local talent to donate their services. Officers of local solar energy associations usually serve without pay. Staff of appropriate technology organizations usually receive pay from the organization's grants or government contracts.

Building Resources

A wide variety of settings are used for these community-based appropriate technology educational programs. Office space for staff, telephone, library and/or mailing address is common. Such space is often donated or rented for a low fee from a sympathetic community member or local government, depending on the group's political position within the community. Groups involved in some form of small-scale research and development activities may have a larger office space, house and land that serve both administrative and educational purposes.

Workshops are held in a wide variety of spaces such as classrooms, local or county governmental offices, church halls, senior centers, and people's homes. The use of any particular space is determined by the nature of the educational activity. A workshop aimed at basic principles or issues of design would be held indoors. Construction workshops could be held in a high school shop or at a family's home where the technology is to be installed.

Conclusion

In conclusion, it is in the revolutionary/change end of the continuum that one sees the most interesting uses of nonformal education as a major facet of the appropriate technology movement. Education is at most an add-on to more evolutionary approaches which stress technological change. However, education is integral in the more revolutionary approaches which stress participatory adaptations by community groups. In this country such groups rarely are revolutionary in the sense of challenging national political and economic institutions, but the challenges to the values of this society at the local level can be quite profound. The integration of learner-centered, noncompetitive, nonformal education techniques are crucial to this appropriate technology approach.

Suggested Resources
Appropriate Technology

Bibliography

Agency for International Development. *Proposal for a program in appropriate technology.* Washington, D.C.: U.S. Government Printing Office, 1976.

Anderson, M.B. Rural development through self-reliance: Implications for appropriate technology. In A.L. Edwards, I.C.A. Oyeka, & T.W. Wagner (Eds.), *New Dimensions of Appropriate Technology.* Ann Arbor, Michigan: University of Michigan, 1980.

Baer, S. Clothesline Paradox. In L. deMoll & G. Coe (Eds), *Stepping stones: Appropriate technology and beyond.* New York: Schocken Books, 1978.

Bender, T. *Sharing smaller pies.* Portland, Oregon: RAIN, 1975.

Bender, T. Why big business loves A.T. In L. deMoll & G. Coe (Eds.), *Stepping stones: Appropriate technology and beyond.* New York: Schocken Books, 1978.

Bhalla, A.S. (Ed.). *Towards a global action for appropriate technology.* New York: Pergamon Press, 1979.

Brown, R.H. Appropriate technology and the grassroots: Towards a development strategy from the bottom up. *Developing Economies,* 1977, *15*(3).

Carr, M. *Economically appropriate technologies for developing countries.* London: Intermediate Technology Development Group, 1977.

Clark, W. It takes energy to get energy. In L. deMoll & G. Coe (Eds.), *Stepping stones: Appropriate technology and beyond.* New York: Schocken Books, 1978.

Clarke, R. The pressing need for alternative technology. *Impact of science on society,* 1973, *23*(4), 257-271.

Clinton, R.L. The never-to-be-developed countries of Latin America. *Bulletin of the Atomic Scientists,* 1977, *33*(9).

Congdon, R.J. (Ed.). *Introduction to appropriate technology: Toward a simpler lifestyle.* Emmaus, Pennsylvania: Rodale Press, 1977.

Darrow, K., Keller, K., & Pam, R. *Appropriate technology sourcebook, Volume II.* Stanford, California: Volunteers in Asia, 1981.

Darrow, K., & Pam, R. *Appropriate technology sourcebook.* Stanford, California: Volunteers in Asia, 1976.

Davis, H.L. Appropriate technology: An explanation and interpretation of its role in Latin America. *Inter-American Economic Affairs,* 1978, *32*(1), 51-56.

deMoll, L., & Coe, G. (Eds.). *Stepping stones: Appropriate technology and beyond.* New York: Schocken Books, 1978.

Design Alternatives, Inc. *Workshop on appropriate technology for the National Science Foundation.* Washington, D.C.: Design Alternatives, 1978.

Dickson, D. *The politics of alternative technology.* New York: Universe Books, 1979.

Diwan, R., & Livingston, D.L. Alternative development strategies and appropriate technology. New York: Pergamon Press, 1979.

Dorf, R.C. and Hunter, Y.L. (Eds.). *Appropriate visions.* San Francisco, CA: Boyd and Frosen Publishing Company, 1978.

Dunn, P.D. *Appropriate technology: Technology with a human face.* New York: Schocken Books, 1979.

Edwards, A.L., Oyeka, I.C.A., & Wagner, T.W., (Eds.). *New dimensions of appropriate technology.* Ann Arbor, Michigan: University of Michigan Press, 1980.

Ellis, W.N. AT: The quiet revolution. *Bulletin of the Atomic Scientists,* 1973, *23*(9), 24-29.

Evans, D.D., & Adler, L.M. (Eds.). *Appropriate technology for development: A discussion and case histories.* Boulder, Colorado: Westview Press, 1979.

Fortner, R.S. Strategies for self-imolation: The third world and the transfer of advanced technology. *Inter-American Economic Affairs,* 1977, *31*(1), 25-50.

Fujimoto, I. *The values of appropriate technology and visions for a saner world.* Butte, Montana: National Center for Appropriate Technology, 1977.

Goulet, D. The paradox of technology transfer. *Bulletin of the Atomic Scientists,* 1975, *31*(6), 39-46.

Hess, K. *Community technology.* New York: Harper and Row Publishers, 1979.

Hoda, M. Development is a two-way street toward survival. *Impact of Science on Society,* 1973, *23*(4), 273-285.

Horvitz, C., & Kahn R. *Tools for a change: Proceedings of the Northeast Regional Appropriate Technology Forum.* Amherst, Massachusetts: School of Business Administration, University of Massachusetts, 1979.

Jequier, N. *Appropriate technology: Problems and promises, Part I, Major policy issues.* Stanford, California: Volunteers in Asia, 1977.

Jequier, N. Appropriate technology: Some criteria. In A.S. Bhalla (Ed.), *Towards global action for appropriate technology.* New York: Pergamon Press, 1979.

Johnson, S.F. Intermediate technology: Appropriate design for developing countries. *Search,* 1976, *15*(1-2), 27-33.

Jua, O. The human development and self-reliance affirmation of appropriate technology. In A.L. Edwards, I.C.A. Oyeka, & T.W. Wagner (Eds.), *New dimensions of appropriate technology.* Ann Arbor, Michigan: University of Michigan Press, 1980.

Lappe, F.M., & Collins, J. More food means more hunger. *The Futurist,* 1977, *11*(2), 90-93.

Livingston, D.L. Little Science Policy: The study of appropriate technology and decentralization. *Policy Studies Journal,* 1976, *5*(2), 185-192.

Love, S. The new look at the future. *The Futurist,* 1977, *11*(2), 78-80.

Lund, M.A. Identifying, developing, and adopting technologies (appropriate) for rural development with applications to Huari Province in Peru (Doctoral Dissertation,

Iowa State University, 1975). (University Microfilms No. 76-91188).

McRobie, G. *Small is possible*. New York: Harper and Row, 1981.

Magee, J. *Down to business: An analysis of small scale enterprise and appropriate technology*. Butte, Montana: National Center for Appropriate Technology, 1978.

Masker, J. and Sesso, J. *Appropriate technology and nonformal education: Training strategies for effective technology transfer in the United States*. Butte: MT: National Center for Appropriate Technology, 1981.

Masker, J. and Smith, D. *Recommended educational programs for the dissemination of energy conservation and renewable energy technologies in the Pacific Islands*. Washington, D.C.: Library of Congress and the House Committee on Insular Affairs, 1983.

Morris, D. *Appropriate technology and community economic development*. Center for Community Economic Development Newsletter, April-May, 1977.

National Center for Appropriate Technology. *Energy and the poor: An imperative for action—a policy proposal*. Butte, Montana: NCAT, 1979.

National Center for Appropriate Technology. *Appropriate technology at work*. Washington, D.C.: Department of Energy, 1983.

Norman, C. *Soft technologies, hard choices*. Washington, D.C.: Worldwatch Institute, 1978.

Office of Technology Assessment. *Technology for local development*. Washington, D.C.: OTA, 1981.

Oyeka, I.C.A. Redirecting education and research to development needs in developing countries. In A.L. Edwards, I.C.A. Oyeka, & T.W. Wagner (Eds.). *New dimensions of appropriate technology*. Ann Arbor, Michigan: University of Michigan Press, 1980.

Ozark Institute. *A special report on appropriate technology*. Eureka Springs, Arkansas: Ozark Institute, 1978.

Quammen, D. *Appropriate jobs: Common goals of labor and appropriate technology*. Butte, Montana: National Center for Appropriate Technology, 1980.

Raman, N.P. Devising and introducing technology to aid the poor. *International Development Review*, 1976, *18(3)*, 8-10.

Reddy, A.K.N. National and regional technology groups and institutions: An assessment. In A.S. Bhalla (Ed.), *Towards global action for appropriate technology*. New York: Pergamon Press, 1979.

Rybczynski, R. *Paper heroes: A review of appropriate technology*. Garden City, New York: Anchor Books, 1980.

Schumacher, E.F. *Small is beautiful: Economics as if people mattered*. New York: Harper and Row Publishers, 1973.

Schumacher, E.F. Technology with a human face. In L. deMoll & G. Coe (Eds.), *Stepping stones: Appropriate technology and beyond*. New York: Schocken Books, 1978.

Smith, F.W. *The relevance of A.T. developments in the U.S. to the Third World*. Washington, D.C.: Agency for International Development, 1979.

Stewart, F. International mechanisms for appropriate technology. In A.S. Bhalla (Ed.), *Towards global action for appropriate technology*. New York: Pergamon Press, 1979.

Tett, C.R. Education systems: Appropriate education and technology for development. In R.J. Congdon (Ed.), *Introduction to appropriate technology: Toward a simpler lifestyle*. Emmaus, Pennsylvania: Rodale Press, 1977.

U.S. Department of Energy. *Appropriate technology: A bibliography*. Oakridge, TN: Technical Information Center, 1981.

Wakefield, R.A., & Stafford, P. Appropriate technology: What it is and where it is going. *The Futurist,* 1977, *11*(2), 72-76.

Westphal, L.E. *Research on appropriate technology.* Washington, D.C.: The World Bank, 1978.

World Future Society. *The Futurist.* Washington, D.C.: Author, 1977, *11*(2).

Journals

Appropriate Technology
Approtech
The Futurist
Resources for Appropriate Technology (RAIN)
Tranet Newsletter
Vita News

Resource Centers

Brace Research Institute
McGill University
Ste. Anne de Bellevue
Quebec HOA ICO

Farollones Institute-Research Center
15290 Coleman Valley Road
Occidental, CA 95465

The Institute for Local Self-Reliance
1717 18th Street, NW
Washington, D.C. 20009

Intermediate Technology Development Group
9 King Street
London, England WC2E 8HN

Modern Energy and Technology Alternatives
P.O. Box 128
Marblemount
Washington, D.C. 98267

National Center for Appropriate Technology
P.O. Box 3838
Butte, Montana 59702

New Alchemy Institute
Box 47
Woods Hole, MA 02543

New Mexico Solar Energy Association
Box 2004
Sante Fe, NM 87501

Volunteers in Technical Assistance
1815 North Lynn St.
Suite 200
Arlington, VA 22209-2079

7
EDUCATIONAL INNOVATION IN THE WORKPLACE

Donald K. Carew and
Elizabeth Loughran

The quality of worklife movement is one of the more innovative segments of an educational effort that extends beyond schools. Precise records of the educational efforts taking place in American businesses and industries do not exist in any one source; however, estimates range from $10 billion (Leepson, 1981) to over $100 billion (Corrigan, 1980) annually invested by business and industry in training their employees.

The scope of educational activities occurring in the workplace is vast. The most familiar activities are the technical training provided for all employees. All jobs require minimal on-the-job training, and the majority involve very organized training in relevant technologies: first aid and CPR for human service workers, basic carpentry for house builders, word processing for secretaries.

Since World War II, however, there has been a steady increase in the activity of trainers and in the importance given to education as a vital component of the workplace. In recent years, many corporations have renamed their training department Human Resource Development in an effort to put it on an equal footing with departments dealing with the development of such key material resources as raw materials, plant machinery and markets. The department has moved higher up in the organizational hierarchy, often becoming the direct responsibility of a vice president; also, the focus has greatly expanded beyond technical training to include personal and professional development, management training, career development, organization development, support for college degrees, planning and implementing change programs, and in some cases, developing organization sponsored, degree-awarding undergraduate and graduate programs. Personnel in the field now have at least a bachelors degree, many have masters degrees, and there is a growing demand for doctoral degrees (Varney, 1981; McQuigg, 1980).

The Quality of Worklife Focus

The quality of worklife movement is one component of this larger field. It has been chosen as a focus for this chapter for two reasons: (a) it is acknowledged as being one of the more innovative approaches to human resource development, and (b) it challenges normal conceptualizations of education by assuming structural change is as essential a component as individual change.

The major aim of most educational efforts in the workplace is to increase productivity. The assumption behind education as technical training is that productivity is increased if workers know how to do their jobs. Quality of workplace educators feel that this assumption is correct but incomplete. Even greater productivity results when workers believe that they are being treated fairly, that pay, benefits, and working conditions are reasonable. Still further increases in productivity result when workers feel valued, that their opinions count in decisions that affect them, that their suggestions on how to improve processes are considered and implemented. Thus, quality of worklife educators (or consultants, to use the prevailing terminology) are involved not just in traditional technical training, but also in restructuring basic aspects of the organization, such as the decision making and communication structures.

The quality of worklife movement, however, is not just an educational approach. It has, in addition to its emphasis on learning, economic, psychological, structural, sociological, ethical, environmental, and technical components. Nor are the educational elements found in easily recognizable forms. Often there are not clearly identified classes or subjects or teachers or grades. Instead, learning is intertwined in complex and organic ways both into individual jobs and into total organizational functioning.

Despite the complexity and difficulty of the task of describing this educational effort, the learning that takes place on the job is crucial to the economic and psychological well-being of both individuals and society. It needs to be studied, not only in readily recognizable places but also in its more hybrid forms. A new vocabulary needs to be used; teaching becomes leadership or supervision; learning becomes problem solving, decision making, or conflict resolution; methodology includes work redesign, job enrichment, and job enlargement; grouping for learning includes autonomous work groups, quality circles, union/management committees, matrix organizations; success is measured in terms of productivity, satisfaction, organization adaptation and innovation. Whatever the differences in terminology, however, the fact remains that the workplace is a major component of the overall eduational system; both traditional educational components such as technical training, and innovative aspects such as quality of worklife deserve the same careful study as do other approaches in the system.

Definitions and Distinctions

Quality of worklife is the name given to a body of theory, commentary, and research aimed at tying a large number of workplace reforms to an ethical position. Quality of life, according to Davis and Cherns (1975), is a macroeconomic factor to be compared with similar factors like a pollution-free environment. Traditionally, responsibility for macroeconomic factors is reserved for government and costs are borne by society as a whole, while microeconomic factors such as profits and wages are the responsibility of individual firms. In practice, macroeconomic factors have usually been neglected by both government and business and their costs ignored.

Quality of worklife theorists believe that the cost of low quality work environments can be measured in both economic and human terms and needs to be taken into account by business organizations as well as government. They believe that improvements made in the social system of the organization are ultimately as important as improvements made in the technical system (Davis and Trist, 1974). These two systems, in fact, are interlocked, and output is a function of both systems operating jointly. The relegation of social issues to government, using such devices as child labor laws, protection of unions, and workman's compensation, ignores the powerful positive effect that high quality work environments can have on the total economic effort.

A Recent Movement

The quality of worklife movement is a very recent movement. The development of the term can be traced to an international conference held at Arden House in New York in 1972. The conference was attended by about 60 people primarily from universities, and topics dealt with the theory and practice of workplace democracy. European and American experiences were shared and the term *Quality of Working Life* was coined. Since then many developments have taken place which have included conceptual and methodological efforts as well as reorganizing and redesigning work. In August, 1981, the International Council in conjunction with the Ontario Quality of Working Life Center sponsored the first open international conference in Toronto which was attended by over 1700 people including 1000 managers and more than 250 union representatives. That conference demonstrated a shift in the field from academia to the workplace (Jenkins, 1981).

Because of its short history, questions of definition are still being discussed and questions of measurement are even more at issue. Theorists are drawing on a wide number of disciplines for theoretical inputs. Davis and Cherns (1975), for instance, list economics, psychology, sociology, industrial relations, systems theory, and industrial engineering as all being relevant. Clearly it is too early to do more than sketch the dimensions that concern theorists.

Some Criteria

Richard Walton (1975) developed a list of criteria for quality of worklife that provides a beginning definition. He sees these criteria as being broader than the issues of safety that concerned people in the early 1900's, broader than the economic and security issues of the 1930's, of the morale and satisfaction issues of the 1950's, and of the equal employment and job enrichment issues of the 1960's. Quality of worklife issues include all these concerns and more. Walton's list includes:

- adequate and fair compensation
- safe and healthy working conditions
- immediate opportunity to use and develop human capacities
- opportunity for continued growth and security
- social integration in work organizations (e.g., freedom from prejudice, supportive primary groups, trust, interpersonal openness, involvement in decision making)
- constitutionalism in work organizations
- a balanced place for work in relationship to total life space
- social relevance of work

This list provides an indication of the comprehensive nature of the concerns of this group, and it indicates why education is such an integral part of the movement. Clearly individual learning and development is essential for the development of human capacities and growth. Just as important is the collective learning and social and organizational change implied in many of the items. Constitutionalism, social integration, balance, and relevance require major collective educational efforts, not just individual training.

An Example

The example of a quality of worklife experiment at the General Motors Plant, Tarrytown, provides an example of the complex interweaving of various types of education involved in a quality of worklife approach. The plant was having major problems in glass breakage and water leaks. The project started out in restructuring the relationships of the 36 people who installed back windows in cars. Workers were trained in goals and objectives, participation, problem solving, communication, decision making, interpersonal skills and organizational structure. Each worker was involved in 24 hours of training. The total plant consisted of 3600 workers, and as other workers became aware of the things happening in the window group (lower grievance rate, higher morale, less salvage, fewer disciplinary actions, higher efficiency), they became interested, and eventually all 3600 received the training which took two years and 24 trainers to complete. In glass breakage alone, the project saved the company $68,000. The overall plant (after all workers were involved) went from seventeenth in quality at

GM to number one (Horner, 1980).

Clearly it is the combination of organizational restructuring and individual training that was at the heart of this quality of worklife project. The group was given training and an opportunity to exercise what traditionally have been seen as management functions (setting goals, problem solving, reorganizing). The organization, in effect, was questioning some very basic assumptions about the capabilities of line workers. Just as importantly, individual workers had to learn an entire range of new skills which are normally taught in MBA courses.

History of the Quality of Worklife Movement

The quality of worklife movement is a more recent effort in a series of educational efforts to improve productivity. A short history of some of these provides insight as to its distinctive contributions.

The notion that managers can intervene in the social as well as technical aspects of work is a very old one. In this century the earliest popularized intervention was Taylor's Scientific Management (1911). He envisioned the human being as another type of machine and believed work should be divided into its smallest component parts with each individual becoming as efficient as a machine in that one operation. The principles of Taylorism are embedded in the assembly line which has been a major form of work organization in the industrialized West. Taylorism sees the principal function of education as being training during the early phases of work; thereafter, education is considered counterproductive for most workers.

Two Approaches

While all educational efforts in Western workplaces are to some degree the inheritors of Taylorism and the assumptions of the early capitalists, nonetheless there are two divergent approaches which are only now beginning to come together in quality of worklife projects as well as in similar workplace democratization efforts. American approaches, in general, have proved more conservative than their European counterparts. During the crucial Depression years, American unions decided to concentrate their efforts on issues of pay, benefits, health and safety. Other issues such as design of work and participation in decision making were left to management. Thus, as theorists began to understand that productivity was not simply a result of know-how but of morale as well, American consultants began to provide opportunity and training for democratic leadership styles and worker participation. The theory was that if workers felt that their bosses were approachable and that they had some input into the decisions that affected them, workers would be more satisfied and more productive. Much of the work of organizational development consultants today is based on these same assumptions.

Meanwhile in Europe, major educational efforts derived from more radical assumptions. Socialist and Marxian analyses are more accepted, and thus educators assumed that greater productivity would result from increased worker control of the workplace rather than, as has been assumed in this country, from just worker participation. Educational efforts ranged from quite small endeavors such as the sociotechnical systems work in England and Scandanavia (Thorsrud, 1976, 1977; Trist, 1977) and quality control circles in Japan (Cole, 1979; Pascale and Athos, 1981) to industry or nationwide efforts in Germany, Israel, and Yugoslavia (Adizes, 1971; Hunnius and Case, 1973).

Coalescence of Influences

Thus, in the late 1960's and early 1970's when the phrase *quality of working life* was being coined, a number of influences were beginning to coalesce. The effort to humanize or democratize management style, a largely American innovation, was beginning to mix with the various types of structural reforms being developed in Europe and Japan. Today, quality of worklife educational efforts continue to combine these two components. In general they involve efforts to restructure relatively small units in the workplace (e.g., a department, not an industry) as well as to include major educational efforts aimed at improving communication, managing conflict, and democratizing management style. Restructuring usually involves a major increase in the autonomy and control of workers within a specific unit as well as considerable training on how to exercise those powers effectively.

Throughout all these theories and experiments is a major concern for and dependence on education. Individual and group development are both goals—or criteria—for a quality worklife, and they are means to that end. Individual training in interpersonal issues as well as relevant skill areas is essential for continued personal growth and advancement. The various structural interventions being attempted with different groupings and different allocations of power represent attempts of the entire organization to learn—to examine fundamental assumptions and ways of operating in order to better adapt to changing influences (Argyris and Schon, 1978). While the terminology and settings for these learnings are very different from the more familiar examples in schools, they nonetheless are extremely influential both to individuals personally and to the society as a whole.

Pervasive Themes
Quality of Life

Clearly the most pervasive theme of the quality of worklife movement is stated in its title. It is this theme that differentiates this approach from various other business training efforts. The title of the movement states the goal of the effort and implies a strong value position as well.

There is a subtle but important distinction between this approach, which explicitly states that improved quality of worklife is its goal, and other educational approaches which may assume such a goal but in fact list more intermediate goals (e.g., to learn to read, to run a computer, to understand history). This emphasis on a value-laden goal forces the question of purpose for every specific objective. If, for instance, the specific reform under consideration is creating autonomous work groups, then the necessary question is the following: How do autonomous work groups contribute to improved quality of worklife?

In other words, the quality of worklife movement puts the greatest emphasis on ends, and it remains quite eclectic and flexible in the choice of means to that end. In contrast, most educational approaches specify means (e.g., formal schools, nonformal education, museum education, adult education) and are less explicit about defining the ultimate purpose of the effort. This rather basic difference explains to some degree why it is difficult to conceptualize the quality of worklife movement as an educational approach. Its total intent is clearly larger than education; rather, education and learning are seen as one possible means to this end.

Because of the broad goal implied in the choice of the term *quality of worklife,* this theme contains within it all other themes that have permeated the movement. In fact, all of the other themes chosen for description here may be seen as specific means towards that end. Personal, organizational, and human resource development describe the learning efforts aimed at enhancing quality of life; individual and small group autonomy and participation are seen as human needs that must be met as an element of a quality life; interdependence and collaboration describe the overall integration of individual and society hypothesized to lead to a quality life. Taken together, these themes are guidelines for choosing strategies which will accomplish the overall purpose of the movement.

Personal, Organizational, and Human Resource Development

Three themes that recur in the quality of worklife literature are the need for personal development, organizational development, and human resource development. Personal development including such things as access to educational opportunities, to challenging work, and to upward career mobility is assumed to be an essential element of a quality worklife for individuals. Organizational development refers to a whole series of efforts that assist the organization in providing a humane and productive environment for workers. Such efforts as improving interpersonal communication, assisting in development of constructive conflict resolution styles, efforts at establishing participatory leadership, supervision, and evaluation styles all contribute towards the organization's evolution towards a quality environment. Human resource development is a term currently used to refer to conscious efforts of the organization to foster both personal and organizational development. The term implies that humans are an important resource, just as are material and energy resources, and need the same level of developmental guidance and effort by the organization.

These three terms will be discussed in more detail below when the theoretical dimensions and delivery systems used in quality of worklife educational efforts are presented. Here the intent is to look at the concepts as overall themes or descriptors of the movement. What, for instance, is implied by the choice of the word development, rather than education, as a term for learning activities? Is there importance in the co-equal status of individual and group growth implied in all three terms?

The thesis here is that the word development as it is currently used (community development; economic development; personal, group, organizational development) is different from the way the word education is commonly used. Development implies an end which is qualitatively better than the starting point. Additionally, while it assumes that external resources and guidance may be helpful, nonetheless the primary motivation, direction, and energy must come from within. In contrast, education, despite the literal meaning of the word (to lead out), commonly refers to many top-down change efforts (e.g., teachers provide lessons and professors provide expertise) as well as internally directed learning efforts. Development implies that while it may be the organization's role to provide opportunities for learning and career mobility, it is the individual's role to choose among alternatives, set the pace, provide the motivation and energy. Similarly, while a consultant may provide opportunities for structured activities and workshops, it is the participant's role to choose to participate, to provide the specific data for the work, and to commit energy to the effort. Development connotes internal progress towards goals, and as such differs from education which frequently emphasizes the role of the teacher or expert.

The equal emphasis on the individual and group aspects of development is also different from the more usual emphasis on the individual aspects of the process. The use of organizational development along with other terms such as organizational learning and organizational change imply that education needs to be aimed at institutions as well as at people. Both developmental concepts are found in quality of worklife writings.

These themes, then, of individual and group development provide important clues about both the theoretical approach to learning and social change that underlie quality of worklife approaches and also to the specific educational delivery systems employed by the movement. Both of these issues will be discussed in more detail below.

Autonomy and Participation

A second set of themes which pervades the quality of worklife movement is the assumption that a basic human need is for individual autonomy over major life functions such as work. A major corollary is that, in order for individuals to achieve autonomy, they must be accorded a high degree of participation in major decisions that affect them. Rosow suggests that the achievement of greater participation and more active involvement of the work force is the most difficult and important challenge of the future (1979).

Despite the pervasive nature of these themes, however, there is, as was demonstrated above, considerable disagreement about how much autonomy is needed and at what level of the organization worker participation is valuable. Typically, American efforts have involved quite small increases in autonomy and increases in participation only at the work group level. In

Europe and Japan, however, more inclusive efforts at reinforcing autonomy have been attempted; in Europe worker participation is frequent at many organizational levels.

Nonetheless the identification of autonomy and participation as human needs are common to a broad range of work reform movements. This common theme in turn has its roots in very powerful assumptions and values about human nature which will be explored below.

Collaboration and Interdependence

It may seem contradictory to say that in the quality of worklife literature collaboration is as powerful a theme as is autonomy, but in fact these terms are complementary rather than contradictory (Loughran, 1981). Quality of worklife theorists assume that just as individuals have the need for both individual control over basic life functions and social interaction, so organizations must foster equally autonomy and interdependence. Collaboration is a term which implies that the intermingling of these two individual needs can be met in the context of the group or organization pursuing its goals.

Collaboration as a theme is found in many different contexts in quality of worklife writing. It is assumed to be an element of a humane workplace, replacing competition and authoritarian processes (Herbst, 1976; Thayer, 1978). It is also effective in increasing productivity (Cole, 1979) and in enabling organizations to adapt effectively in fast changing environments (Emery and Trist, 1978; Toffler, 1980). Additionally interagency and international collaboration are seen as essential to improved quality of life worldwide (Keohane and Nye, 1977).

Productivity

Just as autonomy and interdependence are seen as complementary, so productivity and a humane work environment are co-equal themes in the quality of worklife movement. Theorists assume that meaningful work, challenge, and self-actualization are essential individual needs, and therefore there is no inherent conflict between the organization's need for high productivity and individual desires.

Additionally high productivity is important in maintaining the standard of living that is a part of a quality worklife. While there may be differing interpretations as to the precise standard of living desired, nonetheless, reasonable pay and adequate job security are essential; productivity is the organizational corollary of those needs.

Summary

Pervasive themes in the quality of worklife movement are all related to the broad purpose contained in the title. Personal and organizational development provide the upward sense of movement and goal directed activity that is essential to a sense of meaning, challenge, and fulfillment.

Autonomy over major life functions, including work, is assumed to be a major individual need, and participation is a means to securing that sense of control. Interdependence and collaboration provide both the needed social interaction for individuals and the means of connecting autonomous subunits into a coordinated effective work organization. Economic productivity provides individual satisfaction and an adequate standard of living for all.

A concept that summarizes all of the above themes is synergy. The movement assumes that individual needs can be met at the same time and in the context of work on organizational and societal goals. The energy released by this synergistic effect is part of the human force fueling a highly productive as well as very humane work organization (Loughran, 1981).

Theoretical Dimensions

All of the themes described above contain within them some common theoretical assumptions. They derive from a common set of values, presuppose a theory of how learning takes place, and assume a common emphasis on the relevance and direction of social change. The following section explains those assumptions, describing how various principles and strategies used in quality of worklife approaches embody these common theoretical dimensions.

Values

Values are the differential choices individuals and social groups make in answering basic philosophical questions (Kluckhohn and Stodbeck, 1961). Of these questions, probably the most fundamental is, "What is the nature of human nature?" The answer that underlies the themes and concerns of the quality of worklife movement is the belief in the tremendous potential of human nature. While at any given time an individual's behavior is not necessarily good or productive, nonetheless, these theorists assume the capacity for improvement. There is an optimism about future development that pervades the movement.

A major change from Taylorism is that scientific management tended to assume that thinking on the part of workers was detrimental to efficiency. Thinking was to be done by management, and workers were expected to act. Quality of worklife efforts clearly assume that thinking and involvement on the part of workers is central and to be cultivated (Jahns, 1981).

Clearly, the assumption that human capacity can be further developed is behind the movement's overall goal of improving the quality of working life. Theorists assume that people want quality work situations and are capable of attaining them. They assume that when people are granted autonomy and given opportunities for participation, they are capable of exercising them wisely. They assume the capacity for collaborative behavior and assume that individuals wish to and are capable of being productive.

There are a number of theorists who have advocated this value position within the context of business and industry. It is no accident, for instance, that Abraham Maslow's belief in the drive toward self-actualization has been so influential (1968). The work of Douglas MacGregor (1960) and Frederick Herzberg (1959) are based on this same belief that humans who are provided with basic needs will not simply become lazy, but will further attempt to develop their capacity. More recently the works of Ingalls (1976) and Ferguson (1980) have begun to develop similar views based on what is being discovered about the unused potential of the human brain.

What is interesting to note is that while these theories have been developed and are widely accepted by behavioral scientists in the United States, they have been much more influential in affecting daily practice in industry in Japan (Cole, 1979). This ready adaptation of theory is matched by a more widespread use of some of the techniques supported by quality of worklife theorists in that country than in the United States. The Japanese system of permanent employment (guaranteed employment in the same company until retirement), the quality control circle idea (small groups of workers in charge of improving quality of products), and the more widespread use of consensus decision making are all based on the assumption that human potential is capable of being developed.

In summary, it is important to note not only the fact that the belief in human potential is a basic assumption of the quality of worklife movement, but also that this assumption is supported more by some cultural norms than others. As theorists explore the relative difficulty or ease with which ideas diffuse broadly within the national economy, they need to explore the degree to which the dominant values of the society support or inhibit that diffusion.

Learning Theory

There are two aspects of the learning theory assumed by quality of worklife theorists that are especially important to the current discussion. The first is that the type of learning that interests theorists is not the abstract, often temporary learning typical in many classrooms, but the in-depth learning that results in enduring behavior change. The second is the recognition that learning occurs as much because of the institutions and social structures within which individuals live and work as it does as a result of individual teaching-learning efforts.

While it is true that businesses using quality of worklife techniques have training needs similar to those in other businesses (e.g., learning a specific job related skill), nonetheless much of the learning that is of interest to quality of worklife theorists is more fundamental in nature. As has been stated above, major approaches involve fostering individual autonomy and self-esteem, relying on widespread participation, and responding positively to opportunities for collaboration. The more essential learnings in these situations involve internal motivation, self-direction, and interest in learning, all of which require substantive attitude and behavior change.

Kurt Lewin (1951) is the theorist most influential in developing this more pervasive view of learning. He believed that enduring behavior change involves unlearning old behaviors, learning the new behaviors, and freezing or internalizing the new learning. Implied in unlearning is a willingness to see opposing points of view, a tolerance for ambiguity, and a willingness to risk. He pictured the environment in which the learner exists as a field of forces—driving forces which support the behavior change, and restraining forces which oppose the change. A particularly effective way to cause behavioral change is to convert a restraining force into a driving force.

This more inclusive view of learning leads logically to the second major aspect of learning theory at issue here. The forces that surround the learner are conceptualized not only in the skill of the teacher or the adequacy of the curriculum or methods. Rather, they include a much wider range of factors. Of particular interest to quality of worklife theorists are the institutions within which people work. The assumption is that many traditional work situations and organizations are restraining forces, that is they inhibit the development of human potential essential to a quality worklife. A further assumption is that a change in those institutions, converting a restraining force to a driving force, is a powerful way to effect the desired behavior change. For that reason, a theory of social or institutional change to be discussed below is an integral part of the quality of worklife theory of learning.

Theory of Social Change

Quality of worklife theorists assume that social change is essential if their overall purposes are to be achieved; further, they conceptualize that change as being primarily incremental, evolutionary, structural change.

The evolutionary nature of the change envisioned derives both from the values supported by the movement and from its theory of learning. The development of human potential clearly involves a noncoercive, evolving process. The inherent internal striving towards developing one's capacity is emphasized, not the more Pavlovian learning through response to an external (e.g., coercive, sudden, or revolutionary) stimulus. Similarly, the long-term behavior change envisioned requires internal acceptance, which for the most important learning requires a long-term and gradual process.

The conceptualization of change as requiring substantive structural or institutional modification as well as interpersonal development is the perspective that differentiates quality of worklife theorists from organizational development theorists. Typically the latter have put major emphasis on the need for individuals (particularly high level managers) to change or to evidence more humane and effective leadership and interpersonal styles (Argyris, 1962, 1971). Quality of worklife theorists using the sociotechnical systems perspective have, in contrast, emphasized the need for structural change.

Structural changes include two major classes of changes. The first involves the idea that a structure is a whole with several parts. One can change the nature of the whole and/or the nature of the parts (Homans, 1975). The notion that in order to increase the degree of collaboration in an organization, one must structure an organization with many small, autonomous but interdependent groups would be an example of this type of structural change (Loughran, 1981).

Another type of structural change derives from the notion of structure as involving the relatively permanent relationship between the parts and the whole (Finch, Jones, Litterer, 1976). Generally in organizations this permanent relationship is described in terms of power. Thus, the structural change involved in the autonomous work group or the quality control circle is an increase of power in the subpart. The structural change involved in workplace democratization experiments is increasing the power of the worker over major organizational decisions (e.g., choice of managers or financial decisions).

It is important to note that the emphasis quality of worklife theorists place on structural change is just that. In no way do they deny the desirability of the interpersonal changes involved in improving such processes as leadership and decision making styles, conflict resolution or communication. Rather they see structural change as being essential in reinforcing and shaping these processes in desirable directions. The structure, in their view, has the effect of being the independent variable, while processes are more dependent variables (Goode, 1975). Processes are more liable to improve if they are supported by an effective structure.

Summary

Three major theoretical assumptions of the quality of worklife movement have been explored here. The primary value position supporting the movement is a belief in human capacity. Humans are capable of self-directed productive behavior which serves their own needs and those of the organization simultaneously. The learning theory of the movement is primarily aimed at fostering the basic attitudes and behaviors of internal motivation towards organizational and personal goals, self-direction and initiative. That theory assumes that this type of learning involves not only personal change but institutional change as well. Basic structural change which acts to increase the potential for individual autonomy and control as well as collaborative interaction with other units is essential if individuals are to develop the desired behavior changes.

The Delivery System

Every educational approach has a delivery system which can be seen as consisting of the same major variables. The educational components of the quality of worklife movement are no exception. They have goals and content, learners and staff, teaching-learning approaches, reward systems, a curriculum, a sequence of events, material, building and financial resources, and an organizational pattern. The specific characteristics of these variables serve to distinguish each educational approach from the others and make distinctions within the movement itself as well. Thus, in order to discuss the delivery system with any degree of precision, one must choose an example that can be defended as typical and/or important in the field as a whole.

The example that has been selected for anlaysis here is the quality control circle idea. It has the advantage of being both typical of many quality of worklife approaches and, at the same time, is by far the most widely disseminated approach.

The quality control circle was a concept developed in Japan in the early 1960's (Cole, 1979; Davis and Trist, 1974; Ouiche, 1981; Yager, 1974). Quality control circles are voluntary groups of workers, all working on similar products or tasks who agree to meet together regularly to discuss the quality of their product. Unions are urged to participate. They meet on company time at their place of work and have available to them assistance and training in such matters as measurements, problem solving, and group facilitation. A supervisor meets with the group but in the role of facilitator, not boss. The relative importance of the concept can be seen by the spread of the idea from some 30% of Japanese firms in the early 1970's to use by 50% of Japanese companies in the late 1970's (Cole, 1979).

The quality control circle concept is similar to other quality of worklife approaches in its reliance on the empowered, autonomous small group. It resembles the autonomous work group in many ways, including the fact that it involves a significant, if small, structural change in the organization. Again, quality of worklife theorists support institutional change, but tend to concentrate on small, evolutionary change rather than radical, more inclusive change (Zwerdling, 1980).

Goals, Content, and Sequence

The aim of the collective learning that is at the heart of the quality control circle approach is to devise as many ways as possible to improve the quality of the group's product. Quality can be defined in many ways: fewer rejects, longer lasting, lower cost, and higher effectiveness. Thus, the content of the educational approach is the product along with the process by which it is produced. This content is sequenced in a way that the group mutually agrees is a potentially effective means toward arriving at some specific improvement in the product. The goal can be characterized as immediate and concrete; processes used to arrive at the goal are flexibly determined and eclectic.

It is interesting to note the cultural values embodied in this goal. Japanese workers define quality of worklife as including the production of a high quality product. They identify individually with their company and see the organization's goal as their own. The basic synergy present in the culturally supported value is probably highly involved in the widespread use of the technique.

Organization and Resources

Like other quality of worklife changes, the quality control circle demands a significant structural change in the organization. Management exists not only to make high level decisions and carry out normal administrative processes, but also to make changes in the distribution of power in the organization in order to support desired changes. In this specific case, power to improve product quality is given to a small group of the workers actually involved in the production process. In contrast, this function in most companies is performed by a quality expert who is a manager rather than a worker.

Additionally, the organization agrees to provide the time, meeting place, and technical and material resources requested by the group. Groups usually meet once a month at their place of work and during company time. The company provides the resources the group requests (e.g., technical expertise or training in relevant skills). The organization also is responsible for developing a reward system supportive of the idea.

Learners and Staff

A significant difference in the treatment of learners and staff in this approach is the relative lack of distinction between these two groups. In the technical sense one could see the staff as the supervisor in charge of group facilitation and the outside consultants called in to provide expert advice of some kind. However, in another sense, one could define everyone as learners (the aim of workers and management alike is to learn ways of improving product quality) and as staff (workers and management alike are responsible for providing ideas, structuring work, getting necessary resources, etc.). In effective working groups, the difference between these groups becomes minor as power becomes more widely shared by all group members.

Teaching-Learning Approaches and Rewards

Both the methodology used by the group and the reward system serve to maximize the likelihood that everyone in the group will contribute to the limit of their potential. A frequent technique in use, for instance, is brainstorming—individual members are asked to call out potential solutions to a problem in quick, free-association fashion. No commentary or censoring is used, and this serves to free people to suggest any possible approach. The approach tends to maximize participation as well as to produce a wide variety of possibilities for discussion.

Other types of methods include group problem solving techniques, facilitative leadership styles, consensus decision making, the use of outside consultation, and extensive training in needed skill areas. The common denominator in all these methods is the maximization of each person's contribution through either wide sharing or increasing of power. Group problem solving, facilitative leadership, and consensus decision making all act to share power; brainstorming and skill training tend to increase power.

The reward system tends to reinforce the sharing and/or increasing of power. Rewards are given to the group, not to individuals. Though some firms offer small monetary rewards, the major reward is recognition through successful participation in company-wide or national competitions for the most valuable idea. The rewards, in other words, basically reinforce group effort and such internal motivators as pride in one's contribution to the organization.

Summary

The delivery system used in the quality control circle approach is significantly different from those in many other educational approaches. Its aim contributes to a broad purpose supported by all members of the organization. The content is organized and sequenced around immediate efforts to improve an element viewed as essential to a quality worklife. For that reason, there are fewer distinctions between learners and staff as all see themselves as learners, and all are responsible for some staff functions. Methods used tend to maximize individual contributions through sharing or increasing power; rewards reinforce internal cooperation among members as well as individual pride in accomplishment. Finally, the entire effort is initiated and supported by the organization which makes necessary changes in power relationships in the organization and continues to support the effort with resources, time, and meeting opportunities.

Conclusion

The quality of worklife movement is an important educational approach, particularly in parts of the world where adoption is widespread (Scandinavia, Japan, and, increasingly, Canada and the U.S.). As such it offers some interesting and potentially useful additions to educational thinking in general. The first of these is the importance and the power of articulating the purpose of the approach and ensuring that the purpose meets the needs of both individuals and the organization. The second is the conceptualization of learning as involving important attitudinal and behavioral change (e.g., increasing internal motivation and the capacity to act purposefully, autonomously, and collaboratively). The third is the emphasis on structural change as an essential element both in accomplishing the purpose and supporting individual learning. Last is the evolution of delivery systems which employ a number of strategies that embody the foregoing principles.

The approach is quite different from the more usual, formal school approach where purposes are often not articulated and are often different for staff and learners; where learning and social change are top-down or center-periphery models; and where structures are conceived of as administrative units rather than elements of social change. Thus, the approach is of interest not just because of the important purposes it serves, potentially affecting a major part of adult experience, but also as an alternative educational approach in general. The basic principles are found in several other adult educational approaches described in this book and have the potential of being transferred to others.

Suggested Resources
Educational Innovation in the Workplace

Bibliography

Adizes, I. *Industrial democracy: Yugoslav style: The effect of decentralization on organizational behavior.* New York: The Free Press, 1971.

Adkins, D. *Steven Fuller making people a number one priority at G.M.* Athens: Ohio University Alumni Newsletter, Fall, 1981.

Appley, D.G., & Winder, A.E. (Eds.) Collaboration in work settings. *Journal of Applied Behavioral Sciences,* 1977, 13.

Argyris, C. *Interpersonal competence and organizational effectiveness.* Homewood, IL: The Dorsey Press, Inc., 1962.

Argyris, C. *Management and organization development: The path from XA to YB.* New York: McGraw-Hill Book Company, 1971.

Argyris, C., & Schon, D.A. *Organizational learning: A theory of action perspective.* Reading, MA: Addison-Wesley Publishing Co., 1978.

Blumberg, P. *Industrial democracy: The sociology of participation.* New York: Schocken Books, 1969.

Cole, R.E. *Work, mobility and participation: A comparative study of American and Japanese industry.* Berkeley, CA: University of California Press, 1979.

Conte, M., Tannenbaum, A. & McCulloch, D. *Employee ownership.* Ann Arbor: University of Michigan Survey Research Center, 1981.

Corrigan, G. Corporate training: A career for teachers? *Phi Delta Kappan,* 1980, 16, 328-331.

Davis, L.E., & Cherns, A.B., and Associates (Eds.). *The quality of working life.* Vols. 1 and 2. New York: The Free Press, 1975.

Davis, L.E., & Trist, E.L. Improving the quality of worklife: Sociotechnical case studies. In J. O'Toole (Ed.), *Work and the quality of life: Resource papers for Work in America.* Cambridge: The M.I.T. Press, 1974, 246-78.

Doll, R. (Ed.). Training in business and industry. *Phi Delta Kappan,* 1980, 61.

Emery, F.E., & Trist, E.L. *Towards a social ecology: Contextual appreciation of the future in the present.* London: Plenum Press, 1973.

Ferguson, M. *The acquarian conspiracy: Personal and social transformation in the 1980's.* Los Angeles: F.P. Tarche, Inc., 1980.

Finch, F.E., Jones, H.R., & Litterer, J.A. *Managing for organizational effectiveness: An experiential approach.* New York: McGraw-Hill Book Co., 1976.

General Electric Co. *Quality circle leaders and facilitators manual.* Fairfield, CT: General Electric Company, 1981.

Goode, W.J. Homan's and Merton's structural approach. In P.M. Blau (Ed.), *Approaches to the study of social structure.* New York: The Free Press, 1975, 66-75.

Hackman, J.R., & Oldham, G.R. *Work re-design.* Reading, MA: Addison-Wesley Publishing Company, 1980.

Hackman, F., & Suttle, L.F. (Eds.). *Improving life at work: Behavioral science approaches to organizational change.* Santa Monica, CA: Goodyear Publishing Company, Inc., 1977.

Harman, S. A personal perspective on the quality of working life. *Perspectives on quality of working life.* Ontario: Quality of Working Life Advisory Committee, 1980, 37-50.

Herbst, P.G. *Alternatives to hierarchies.* Leiden: Martinus Nijhoff Social Sciences Division, 1976.

Herzberg, F., Mausner, & Bloch, B.S. *The motivation to work.* New York: Wiley, 1959.

Hinrichs, J.R. *Practical management for productivity.* New York: Van Nostrand Reinhold Company, 1978.

Homans, G. C. What do we mean by social "structure"? In P.M. Blau (Ed.), *Approaches to the study of social structure.* New York: The Free Press, 1975, 53-65.

Horner, B. A union perspective on quality of worklife. *Perspectives on quality of working life.* Ontario: Quality of Working Life Advisory Committee, 1980, 22-36.

Hunnius, G., Garson, G.D., & Case, J. (Eds.). *Workers' control: A reader on labor and social change.* New York: Vintage Books, 1973.

Ingalls, J.D. *Human energy: The critical factor for individuals and organizations.* Reading, MA: Addison-Wesley Publishing Co., 1976.

Jahns, I. Training in organizations. In Grabowski, J. and Associates, *Preparing educators of adults.* San Francisco: Jossey-Bass Publishers, 1981, 94-114.

Jenkins, D. *Quality of working life — Current trends and directions.* Ontario: Ontrand Directions, 1981.

Kanter, R.M. *Men and women of the corporation.* New York: Basic Books, Inc., 1977.

Kanter, R.M., & Stein, B. *Life in organizations.* New York: Basic Books, Inc., 1979.

Katzell, R. A., Bienstock, P., & Faerstein, P. *A guide to worker productivity experiments in the United States, 1971-75.* New York: New York University Press, 1977.

Katzell, R., & Yankelovich, D. *Work, productivity and job satisfaction: An evaluation of policy-related research.* New York: Harcourt Brace Jovanovich, Inc., 1975.

Kerr, C., & Rosow, J. *Work in America: The decade ahead.* New York: Van Nostrand Reinhold Company, 1979.

Keohane, R.O., & Nye, J.S. *Power and interdependence.* Boston: Little Brown and Co., 1977.

Kluckholn, F.R., & Stodbeck, F.L. *Variations in value orientations.* Evanston, IL: Row Peterson and Co., 1961.

Kraus, W. *Collaboration in organizations: Alternatives to hierarchies.* New York: Human Sciences Press, 1980.

Leepson, M. The big business of worker education. Northampton, MA: *Daily Hampshire Gazette,* January 17, 1981, 7.

Lewin, K. *Field theory in social science.* New York: Harper, 1951.

Loughran, E. *Collaboration in work settings.* Unpublished doctoral dissertation, University of Massachusetts, 1981.

Maslow, A.H. *Toward a psychology of being* (2nd ed.). New York: D. Van Nostrand Company, 1968.

McGregor, D. *The human side of enterprise.* New York: McGraw-Hill, 1960.

McNeil, I. AT&T: Psychologists in the American Psychological Association. *APA Monitor,* November 1981.

McQuigg, B. The role of education in industry. *Phi Delta Kappan,* 1980, 61, 324-5.

O'Toole, J. (Ed.). *Work and the quality of life: Resource papers for Work in America.* Cambridge: The M.I.T. Press, 1974.

Ouchi, W. *Theory Z: How American business can meet the Japanese challenge.* Reading, MA: Addison-Wesley Publishing Co., 1981.

Parnes, S. *Productivity and the quality of worklife.* Scarsdale, NY: Work in America Institute, 1978.

Pascale, R.T., & Athos, A.G. *The art of Japanese management.* New York: Warner Books, Inc., 1981.

Pateman, C. *Participation and democratic theory.* Cambridge: The University Press, 1970.

Rosow, J. Quality of worklife issues for the 1980's. In Kerr, C. & Rosow, J. (Eds.), *Work in America: The decade ahead.* New York: Van Nostrand Reinhold, 1979, 157-87.

Seaman, D., & Dutton, D. The future of human resources development. In Grabowski and Associates (Eds.), *Preparing educators of adults.* San Francisco: Jossey-Bass Publishers, 1981, 123-132.

Taylor, F.W. *The principles of scientific management.* New York: W.W. Norton and Co., Inc., 1911.

Thayer, F.C. *An end to hierarchy: An end to competition: Organizing the politics and economics of survival.* New York: New Viewpoints, 1973.

Thorsrud, E. Democracy at work: Norwegian experience with non-bureaucratic forms of organization. *Journal of Applied Behavioral Sciences,* 1977, *13,* 410-21.

Thorsrud, E., Sorensen, B.A., & Gustavsen, B. Sociotechnical approach to industrial democracy in Norway. In R. Dubin (Ed.), *Handbook of work organization and society.* Chicago: Rand McNally College Publishing Co., 1976, 421-64.

Toffler, A. *Future shock.* New York: Bantam Books, 1970.

Toffler, A. *The third wave.* New York: Bantam Books, 1980.

Trist, E. Collaboration in work settings: A personal perspective. *Journal of Applied Behavioral Sciences,* 1977, *13,* 268-78.

Varney, G. Productivity in the 80's: Are you ready? *Training and Development Journal.* March, 1981, *35,* 13-17.

Walton, R.E. Criteria for quality of working life. In L.E. Davis & A.B. Cherns and Associates (Eds.), *The quality of working life: Problems, prospects and the state of the art.* New York: The Free Press, 1975, 91-104.

Yager, E. Examining the quality control circle: A participatory technique that benefits trainers, managers and employers alike. *Personnel Journal,* 1979, *58,* 682-4.

Yankelovich, D. New rules for American life: Searching for self-fulfillment in a world turned upside down. *Psychology Today,* April 1981, *15,* 35-91.

Zwerdling, D. *Workplace democracy: A guide to workplace ownership, participation and self-management experiments in the United States and Europe.* New York: Harper & Row, 1980.

Journals

Journal of Applied Behavioral Science
Journal of European Training
Organizational Dynamics
Training
Training and Development Journal
Training World
Workplace Democracy

Resource Centers

Association for Workplace Democracy
1747 Conn. Ave. N.W.
Washington, D.C. 20009

Association for Training and Development
600 Maryland Avenue, Suite 305
Washington, D.C. 20024

National Center for Employee Ownership
1611 S. Walter Reed Drive
Room 109
Arlington, VA 22204

National Training Laboratory Institute
P.O. Box 9155
Rosslyn Station
Arlington, VA 22209

Ontario Quality of Working Life Center
Toronto, Ontario

The Tavistock Institute of Human Relations
London, England

Work in America Institute
Scarsdale, New York

8
HUMAN SERVICES
AS EDUCATOR

Jeanne Martin

Good physical and mental health is an essential element for a productive and satisfying life. Yet, like so many essential life functions, health is only a peripheral concern of the formal school curriculum. For the most part, the health habits that are learned beyond the influence of family and peer group are learned from various components of the human services profession. For this reason, the human services are an extremely important part of a total educational system.

This essay examines the various human service models as educators. There are numerous different approaches to delivering health care, each of which operates quite differently in its function of providing education. It is the thesis of this paper, however, that the oft neglected role of education is critical to the attainment of physical and emotional health. The purpose here is to heighten the awareness of both caregivers and consumers as to the potential impact of various health care strategies as encouragers of good health.

Definitions

What do we mean by human services? Human services, as a field, encompasses many areas aimed at improving the quality of life of people and communities. Ranging from institutional to community-based operations, serving a population from the very sick to well, human service programs deliver a wide variety of services. For the purposes of this essay, human services includes the entire range of programs developed to serve the health and mental health needs of communities. Institutions, such as hospitals, and programs located within institutions, such as counseling and advocacy programs in the criminal justice systems and in schools, are included along with health care facilities involving in-patient and out-patient services, advocacy services, residential treatment centers, hotline and drop-in centers, and self-help groups.

Levels of Prevention

These functions take on many dimensions, but tend to fall into three distinct categories. Approaches which aim at primary prevention call for efforts to reduce the numbers of new cases of disease or problems by affecting the population before the problems occur. Secondary prevention approaches involve early identification and treatment of a problem in order to reduce its severity. Tertiary prevention strategies attempt to reduce and/or prevent relapses of problems and so prevent chronic, ongoing problems through rehabilitation and integration into the community (Mann, 1978).

Target Populations

What populations do human services serve? Programs cut across the entire range of community populations from infancy (childcare, well-baby clinics) to old age (elderly advocacy services, hot lunch programs). Most programs are funded for tertiary prevention services and so are targeted for those people already identified as needing help: the physically and mentally unwell, the addicted, the abused, those in trouble with the law, the homeless, the destitute, and generally down and out. Human services programs involved in primary and secondary prevention are much fewer in number and tend to target specific populations such as college students or welfare mothers. Goals of these programs may be more specialized, such as the reduction of the incidence of alcoholism or infant mortality within a given population.

Closely associated with the human services are those community caregivers who are not classified as human services workers, but interact often and share clients with human services staff. Examples of these community caregivers are teachers, clergy, and police. These people are often called upon to perform counseling and other health-related tasks, and their training is a concern to the human services field (Caplan, 1970).

Educational Approach in the Human Services

Human services programs engage in education in two major ways — formal and nonformal. Formal education is characterized by an emphasis on cognitive learning, such as classifying information, the use of symbol systems, and the building of systematic problem solving. Formal education may be a component of patient education in a hospital and may involve the didactic teaching of health education. Formal education too is widely utilized in the training and development of human service staff, especially professional workers. Nonformal education focuses on more experiential, participatory learning which actively involves the learners in a more fluid dialogue with their teachers. Advocacy groups and neighborhood community organizations are more likely to utilize this form of education.

The use of consultation as a frequent educational approach exemplifies the blending of formal and nonformal educational components. Caplan (1970) defines consultation as a process of interaction between two professional persons: the consultant, who is a specialist, and the consultee, who invokes the consultant's help. This help may be in regard to a current work problem which the consultee has decided is within the other's area of specialized competence (p. 19).

Much consultation and education work is undertaken by psychiatric social workers with a strong background in consultation and education and by community psychologists. Both of these professional groups work with a variety of community caregivers and community groups with the goal of increasing their psychological awareness and skills for handling difficult situations. For example, staff from a local mental health center may regularly work with school teachers to help them recognize and deal with a variety of problems confronting students. Consultation can focus on a specific problem with a client, a problem that the consultee is having in working with a client group, or may be focused on program development or administrative improvement. In recent years, the use of consultation has expanded from use by such traditional groups as police, clergy, and schools, to work with alternative youth programs, half-way houses and other residential facilities, and programs serving the mentally retarded (Rogowski, 1979).

Consultation as an educational approach is formal in its reliance on experts and yet more nonformal in its emphasis on problem solving among colleagues. Both the consultant and consultee are professionals, though from differing fields, and both have a valuable perspective on the problem.

As an educational approach, however, consultation emphasizes the education of the expert or caregiver. The fact that the most frequent learner in the human services is the expert rather than the consumer is of critical importance in understanding how this approach functions educationally. In turn, the emphasis on the expert in the human services is a result of a long history.

Historical Roots

Removing the Sick

Several key elements of the human services system in the United States were imported from England early in the nation's history. The first was the practice of institutionalizing people with severe or chronic health or mental health needs. Large hospitals were formed to care for the physically ill, and insane asylums, institutions for the retarded, and jails were created for a wide variety of people who did not fit into the rest of society. While most of these institutions had some altruistic motive, they also were based on the belief that illness was a menace to the rest of the population, and healthy, normal people needed to be protected from contamination (Wolfensberger, 1969). It is also true that the poor formed the vast majority of the people institutionalized for a chronic disability.

Treating the Individual

Another key element of the modern human service system is the casework model of delivery which was adapted from Britain's Charity Organization Society in the late 19th century. These societies provided an organized system of investigation of people requesting relief. "Friendly visitors" assessed those in need and recommended help for those who qualified. This individualized approach later evolved into the casework method of social work, where individuals, usually called clients, are seen individually. The goals of casework range from helping the client manage difficult situations to more complex resolution of personality conflicts. Implicit in the casework approach is that the individual is the locus of change. It is the individual that is sick and must be cured.

The Community Approach

A third element of the modern human service system, the idea of small, community-based health care services, developed in this country through the efforts of Jane Addams in Chicago. In 1889, Jane Addams and Ellen Gates Starr established the Hull House in the slums of Chicago. The Hull House was modeled after Roynbee Hall, a settlement house established to provide education and recreation for the poor of London. Jane Addams worked for better housing and the advancement of progressive education in Chicago. Addams' work and the settlement house movement shifted the focus of social services and "charity" work from institutionalization to neighborhood activity services. An essential component of this type of program was education of neighborhood people to ameliorate their life situations. Implicit in this approach is that it is not just the individual that is sick or at fault, but that a great number of social conditions contribute to illness.

Thus, at the beginning of the 20th century, there were three major approaches to health care: (a) To remove the sick person to an institution; (b) To treat the individual client through individualistic techniques; or (c) To develop community services which addressed social as well as individual ills.

During the first half of the 20th century, the first two approaches became much more prevalent than the last. The century saw great advances in modern medicine which brought with it enormous optimism for a potential cure for all sicknesses. Even mental illnesses seemed much reduced through the development of psychotropic medication. At the same time, the influence of Freudian and neo-Freudian psychologies greatly increased the effect of individual dynamic therapy. In most cases, the belief was that it was just certain individuals who became sick, and that these individuals could be cured by well-trained experts with access to the wonders of modern science. For those chronic illnesses that science had as yet not affected, there existed institutions for long-term care.

Social Causes

The settlement houses persisted, however, and during the Great Depression the approach was reinforced by the belief that many types of ill health (particularly those types that ended in the person's inability to find employment or the commitment of a crime) were caused by circumstances beyond the individual's control. The solution to this problem was twofold: (a) the government would offer the client work on some form of public works project; or (b) the government would take care of the clients. It is interesting that it is the second of the two approaches that has persisted to modern times, giving rise to the enormous variety of welfare programs still in existence. While there is an acknowledgement of the social causes of illness, the cure still centers on the individual, carefully singling out the person and designing a basic level of subsistence appropriate for his/her condition.

The 1960's brought an even greater increase in emphasis on the social causes of poor health and on community-based treatment modes. While the vast majority of services today are still individually based, there has been important growth in small, community-centered approaches.

The passing of the Community Mental Health Centers Act of 1963 was an early and important shift in this direction. This federal legislation mandated the establishment of community mental health centers nationwide serving catchment areas of 200,000 people. Five service components were mandated for each center: in-patient services, partial hospitalization, out-patient services, emergency services, and consultation and education services. For the first time, the provision of consultation and education services was made mandatory in a publicly supported mental health program. Consultation and education services as defined by the Community Mental Health Centers Act provided for health care professionals to work with community caregivers in a consultative, collaborative and teaching capacity in order to enhance those caregivers' skills in working with community people. Although the establishment of these community mental health centers has been slow (Mann, 1978) and has been criticized at times as not accountable to consumers (Cher and Trotter, 1974), this legislation did acknowledge and support the pivotal role of education as a part of community mental health, and additionally signaled a movement away from large centralized institutions.

De-institutionalization

The de-institutionalization movement, another facet of this same community-based movement, has been supported by the philosophy of normalization brought to this country from Scandinavia by Wolfensberger (1972). According to this theory, institutions cause as much illness as they cure. Institutions house people in back wards, leaving them ignored and supported in dependency behaviors. The majority of people (the exceptions being people dangerous to themselves or others) can be supported at similar or perhaps lower cost and in much more humane, normal ways in small community-based apartments and group homes. While handicapped people will, in many cases, need varying levels of lifetime supports, they nonetheless can develop quite extraordinary levels of independence given the proper environment.

However, the success of de-institutionalization has been uneven. Frequently, handicapped people have been relocated without necessary community supports. In addition, the development of small community-based programs has been vulnerable to fiscal cutbacks such as those that occurred during the early 1980's.

The same problem has plagued the development of many other community-based health care facilities. The 1960's, with a heightened awareness of the degree to which society regularly discriminated against large groups of people, brought with it an enormous growth in small community-based clinics: drop-in centers, centers for abused wives, hotlines, low cost health care centers in minority neighborhoods, planned parenthood clinics, etc. Despite their different focal points, most of these clinics shared a commitment to serving a relatively defined neighborhood where people suffered from illnesses that were to some degree socially, as well as individually, caused.

Theoretical Models

The development of human services over the past several hundred years has left us with three basic models of human service delivery which will be explored in depth below. By far, the most prevalent is the Disease Model which assumes that the individual is the cause of the illness or problem and that the solution is either an individually based cure or institutionalization. The second most prevalent is the Welfare Model which assumes that many problems are socially caused and that society ought to support people until they can enter the mainstream. The third, much less frequent model is the Social Change Model which assumes that much ill health is caused by society, and therefore, society ought to be cured as well as the individual.

The Disease Model

The Disease Model is the prevailing modus operandi of most health and mental health services in the United States. Basic to the Disease Model is the notion that change is rooted within the individual. In order to get better, feel better, do better, the individual must change. How this change takes place varies widely depending on which theory of personality development the human services practitioner uses; ego psychology, behaviorism, and Rogerian theory are a few popular examples. Delivery services may take many forms but always focus on the individual (not society and other people) as a locus of change. Delivery services vary from the "expert" treating the "sick" person, who is the passive recipient of care, to self-help groups which call for each individual to take responsibility for his/her improvement. The Disease Model, however, is by no means a singular or simplistic treatment approach. When one begins to examine in detail how the basic assumption that "the individual is sick" gets translated into educational approaches, there are in fact a number of quite distinct approaches that can be investigated.

The most common is the medical model where the expert doctor or psychiatrist treats the patient. For the most part, it is a tertiary prevention program where the disease is already identified. However, other tertiary prevention programs such as Alcoholics Anonymous or group therapy, while developing from the same set of assumptions, nonetheless function very differently as educational approaches. Still different are such secondary approaches as information and referral systems and Employee Assistance Programs. Both seek to identify problems early, before they become major. Information and referral services such as crisis centers or drug hotlines provide immediate access to help, while Employee Assistance Programs within the workplace train supervisors to identify and refer troubled employees to adequate help before they experience a severe loss to the company and themselves.

Two of these approaches will be explored here in order to provide the reader with some understanding of the variety of teaching situations that might be found within the Disease Model. The medical model has been chosen because it is still the most dominant approach in the field. The second choice is information and referral services which have become quite common since the 1960's. Elsewhere in this book is a description of self-help groups which the reader might also wish to read in conjunction with this discussion.

The Medical Model. The medical pattern is the most common human service approach today. It is the basis for treatment in both medical and psychiatric hospitals, for the doctor-patient relationships and for most psychologist, social worker-client relationships. The individual patient is assumed to be ill, and the cure for the illness is treatment by an expert.

It is interesting to examine the underlying assumptions behind this approach that fits so easily into the prevailing cultural context of the Western world. As a social change model, it is preeminently a top-down pattern, with its roots deeply embedded in a faith in scientific progress. The expert has the answers and will treat for the illness. There is great optimism about the potential for improved mental and physical health as long as a national effort continues in basic medical research. Clearly, it is also an evolutionary approach, assuming slow improvements in the overall health of the population without the necessity of changing any fundamental social structures.

The learning theory implicit in the doctor-patient relationship reflects this medical pattern. Certainly the assumption is that the basic authority is external to the learner. The learner is largely passive and needs only to follow directions exactly in order to get well. It is also a segmented and incremental approach to learning. Generally, the disease is considered as distinct from the patient; it is the illness that is treated, not the whole person.

The underlying assumptions behind the medical model are certainly those most basic to Western culture: a belief in individualism, a faith in scientific progress, a preference for slow, incremental change, a belief in the power of the expert. It is no wonder that, of all the human service approaches, this one is the most common.

On the other hand, if one begins to describe the medical approach as an educational approach, one begins to see some of the tensions that exist within it. These tensions are perhaps reasons why the medical pattern, despite its frequent success in treating disease, has been less effective when its purpose has been to educate clients about health-related issues.

The medical model uses both formal and nonformal educational variables. Clearly most objectives of the medical pattern are nonformal; they are immediate, psychological and physical, and of critical importance to the individual. The patient or learner also fits the criteria usual for less formal approaches in that all ages are involved, and there are no pre-requisites for learning. On the other hand, the approach is quite formal in its reliance on a professional staff and a bureaucratic organization along with highly technical and expensive equipment, buildings and resources.

Not surprisingly, the teaching-learning approaches employed are mixed. Practitioners or experts operating under this model may utilize formal education by encouraging their patients or clients to learn didactic information, such as signs and symptoms of disease. Yet this education has less formal aspects too. Usually the information conveyed has immediate and useful applicability for the learner and is conveyed not in a classroom but in an office setting. The more formal qualities of the education tend to center on the teacher-learner encounter, in which the teacher is expert and the learner the passive recipient of knowledge.

Less formal learning, also taking place in these encounters, may be more powerful and subtle. This information teaching may be intentional or unintentional, verbal or nonverbal. It may more likely involve learning about the relationships of practitioners and clients, and affect clients' attitudes about themselves and their situations. Such informal learning may serve to keep clients rooted in beliefs about themselves and their relation-ships to the human services program. This informal education teaches the consumers of human services the behaviors that will most readily help them get their needs met by becoming "good" and compliant patients or clients. This transmission of information reinforces "good" and discourages "bad" behavior through a host of human interactions and can be used in a variety of arenas, from gestalt groups to traditional psychotherapy.

Viewed as an educational approach then, the medical model presents a number of contradictions. The use of a highly professional staff, technical and expensive resources, and bureaucratic delivery system often does clash with the more immediate, concrete, and problem-oriented needs of consumers. Additionally, the emphasis on the role of expert can have the effect of lessening the learner's active involvement in the process.

Information and referral services pattern. The second type of less traditional human services incorporating the Disease Model approach is information and referral. These services, however innovative, are based on the assumption that individuals need information, support, and possible referral to a wide variety of community services. The individual is still considered sick.

These programs grew out of the early drug scares and countercultural movements of the late 1960's. Although not treatment programs themselves, these services provide information about and referral to community agencies and conduct crisis telephone counseling. Originally developed as drug crisis hotlines, many of these programs and their progeny have been incorporated into larger human service agencies or community mental health centers. Some have become specialized, serving special needs like suicide prevention, and special populations like abusive parents. Many services have expanded their repertoire to include drop-in crisis counseling. These information and referral services make seeking help easy, accessible, and relatively nonthreatening and provide an important entry into the human services system.

If a telephone call or drop-in is handled sensitively by program staff, she/he may be encouraged to seek further help, if needed. These programs also provide important linkages to other community agencies like police, hospitals, and advocacy programs. Staff are trained to act quickly in an emergency situation and to cut through the bureaucracy of larger institutions.

These information and referral services are generally low budget operations and employ a work force of volunteers. The training and education of these volunteers is often an ongoing proposition, as high turnover is a fact of life in these programs. The training of volunteers emphasizes readily acquired and useable crisis counseling skills and referral techniques such as empathetic listening, concrete questions about the client's address and immediate intentions, and quick, common sense use of police and emergency assistance. Volunteers may view this training as a way to learn skills that can translate into paying jobs elsewhere. In order to operate effectively, program trainers must be cognizant of the ramifications of this less formal training and prepare themselves for continual training and recruitment of personnel.

Unlike the medical model, the educational components of information and referral are basically less formal in nature. The objectives are immediate and applied to specific persons and situations. By definition, the objectives are noncredentialed. Learners are general—anyone can call for information. The teachers or conveyers of information act as facilitators. They may define themselves as links or bridges to information and services. They encourage learners to take an active role by taking cues from the learners in terms of what to do. Perhaps the only real formal educational variable is the very directive action taken in serious crisis situations. For example, the teacher may take predictable drastic and direct action like sending out the police to save a suicide victim. These crisis responses, however, do not generally alter the tone of the less formal climate of acceptance and learner-oriented service.

Information and referral programs are highly dependent on effective uses of education, both through the dissemination of information and education to consumers and the training of staff. Such programs also contribute to community networking because they compile and keep updated lists of community referrals. In this way, these programs can encourage ongoing communication about services with a cross section of community agencies.

This brief account of two approaches emanating from the disease model makes it clear that, though many approaches share the basic assumptions that the individual is ill and needs treatment, they vary widely in the ways they function as educational approaches. Practitioners who function as educators within these patterns may wish to become acquainted with some of the techniques used in other approaches.

The Welfare Model

Human services programs based on the Welfare Model are those primarily concerned with the administration and delivery of public assistance and child welfare programs. Included in this category are programs like Aid to Families with Dependent Children (AFDC), old-age assistance, aid to the blind, aid to the permanently and totally disabled, and general assistance and child welfare programs. Such public assistance is administered by federal, state and community agencies. These programs generally employ large numbers of staff and service many public assistance recipients. The task of the staff in these human services agencies is to investigate applicants and to provide them with money, services, and goods. Workers in public assistance often have too much to do with too few resources, and consequently are burdened by too many people to serve. Clients in the system often feel overwhelmed by the stringent financial requirements and impersonal treatment they encounter.

The Welfare Model parallels the Disease Model in that both serve individuals rather than wider social and community systems. However, the Welfare Model sees the cause of the individual's problem differently. The individual is not ill or diseased, but rather the victim of some force beyond his or her control: unemployment, poverty, old age, youth, handicap, discrimination, etc. The philosophy behind public assistance and other similar programs is that all persons deserve respect, and that the meeting of basic needs is a right, not a privilege. This is both the strength and limitation of the Welfare Model. Done with sensitivity and respect, these programs encourage human growth and movement toward autonomy. Done poorly, they can damage and further limit human energy and spirit. The philosophy of "we will take care of you" can be helpful or harmful.

There is an additional paradox in that the Welfare Model identifies social causes of the problem, but does not have as its purpose changing society. Rather, it reinforces basic social norms by relying on the government to provide minimum support to individuals who have been identified as needy. The inequities caused by the economic and social structures of society are not challenged as such; rather assistance is available to those who have the bad fortune to have been born "on the wrong side of the tracks."

The Welfare Model is also somewhat suspect as an educational model. In fact, the educational means, more often than not, have the effect of teaching the precise opposite of the behaviors desired. If one were to ask a welfare caseworker what he or she would like a client to learn, the answer would be some version of "greater independence." However, the welfare system, through its reliance on an excessively bureaucratized set of procedures and a highly professionalized staff, tends to reinforce dependence. First steps towards getting a job are penalized by losing benefits. The skills actually learned by a person on welfare tend to be how to stay on welfare rather than how to become independent.

The Welfare Model functions quite similarly to the Disease Model, despite the different view concerning the causation of the problem. Both view the individual as having the problem and seeing the solution as being some application of external means (modern science or government subsidy). The role of the patient or recipient is largely a passive one, thus teaching a set of dependent behaviors. While success rates can be high when the problem is short-term or amenable to a surgical or chemical cure, the success rate is much lower if a long-term change in behavior is needed for improvement.

The Social Change Model

The last theoretical model of intervention is the Social Change Model. It is based on a community organization approach to change. Growing out of the community organizing component of both social work and health education, human services programs based on this model work to organize groups of people to change society. Enhanced quality of life is seen not as solely the responsibility of the individual, but rather as a function and responsibility of society. The Social Change Model may differ from the Disease Model in etiology of illness as well as method of alleviating social problems. For example, a Disease Model practitioner may believe alcoholism to be caused by individual disease, possibly genetic in origin, while a social change agent would view alcoholism as a result of social and enviromental factors.

Human services personnel operating in a Social Change Model organize groups of people concerned about community issues. For example, a community organizer might work with neighborhood groups to pressure local government for better waste disposal or to work toward the creation of an after school program. Usually, the human services worker acts as a facilitator—a change agent helping community people create better living conditions for themselves and their neighborhoods.

Many of the programs working from a social change perspective are primary and secondary prevention efforts. The disease causing effort is located in society, and the main thrust of the program is to prevent its effects from harming individuals. Drug education and nutrition, day care and after school programs for children are examples of the many activities operating from this model.

There are, however, also tertiary prevention programs which are based on this model. The small group homes for mentally ill or retarded people assume that part of the problem of these individuals is the way they have been devalued and institutionalized by society. Treatment consists as much in changing normal people's behavior towards the handicapped person as in teaching the handicapped person community survival skills.

For this reason, education is an essential component of the Social Change Model. At times, community education may be both the means and the end of the project. Education plays a critical role in the process of community organizing, as community people inform and educate themselves about their adopted issues and the methods of community change. As a group, they may investigate and gather information about an issue, prepare a plan of action, and then embark on a process of educating other people. Examples of such a project may be educating community people about how to prevent lead paint poisoning, learning hygiene methods to reduce rodent infestation, or learning to accept a handicapped person as a next door neighbor.

Human service workers may utilize classic nonformal education techniques such as role playing and simulation exercises to prepare community people for social action endeavors. Or nonformal education concepts may be used more tangentially through the encouragement of group-centered, participatory learning. In the community organizing or Social Change Model, the human service facilitator is often seen not as an expert but as a teacher and co-worker, who acts to enhance the skills of community people.

Another effort within the human service movement within the past twenty years which belongs, in general, to the Social Change Model is the trend towards far greater community participation and control of human service delivery systems. In 1963, the Community Mental Health Centers Act called for community input into decision making about policies of mental health centers. These federal regulations have encouraged the establishment of local boards representing their regional catchment areas to assist in the governing of the health centers and to advise on problems confronting the agency. These community board members must, therefore, be familiar with relevant health issues and the workings of the health center. They must have the skills necessary to participate in viable decision making with agency personnel (Beigel and Levenson, 1972).

The effort has not been a complete success, however. Ralph Nader in *The Madness Establishment* (in Cher and Trotter, 1974) has charged that community mental health centers have not been accountable to consumers and community citizens, but rather have become the domain of psychiatrists. The establishment and workable functioning of community boards has brought some successes and several problems. Consumers cannot assume participation in decision making without acquiring the means to do so, and community boards cannot be effective unless the members are able to deal realistically with issues confronting these health centers. In many ways, the uneven success of these boards represents the clash between the Disease Model that informs the thinking of most mental health professionals and the Social Change, community involvement model of lay board members.

Conclusion

The three models described—Disease, Welfare, and Social Change Models—involve different approaches to education. The most prevalent approach, the Disease Model, is for the most part the weakest of the three. Its emphasis on tertiary prevention dictates a largely passive role for the patient. However, as the Disease Model moves from tertiary to primary prevention modes, it seems to incorporate more educational strategies, techniques and philosophies, utilizing the idea that people can learn skills to help themselves for the prevention of illness and social problems. The integral use of education facilitates empowerment; the absence of education tends to make these programs stagnant and stale.

While programs operating from a Welfare Model framework have more overt educational elements, they nonetheless reflect the ambivalence with which society views the "needy" or destitute. On the one hand education is important, and on the other hand much of the outer structures of these programs reinforce the dependent behavior that the educational programs are supposed to change.

Social change programs, in contrast, very frequently have education as a major goal of the program. The learners in this case are not only the sick but society at large. However, programs operating from this model are still rare in Western society and are only a peripheral influence on the overall quality of health care offered.

One must conclude that human service providers, taken as a collective, offer inconsistent and contradictory health education to citizens. It is no accident that the most well-articulated educational approach, consultation, for the most part is offered to professionals in the field. The greatest educational effort is on staff development, ongoing consultation and further education for the experts. In contrast, the programs that aim at enabling lay people to take charge of their own physical and mental health in a coherent, ongoing way are much less frequent and tend to reach only small groups on the margins of society. There remains an enormous need for human service programs to develop educational programs that are equal in quality to treatment programs.

Suggested Resources
Human Services as Educator

Bibliography

Acuna, H.R. Community participation in health. *World Health,* September, 1977.

Beiger, A., and Levinson, A. (Eds.). *The community mental health center: Strategies and programs.* New York: Basic Books, Inc., 1972.

Caplan, G. *The theory and practice of mental health consultation.* New York: Basic Books, Inc., 1970.

Cher, F.D., and Trotter, S. *The madness establishment: Ralph Nader's study group report on the National Institute of Mental Health.* New York: Grossman Publications, 1974.

Clinebell, H.J. *Community mental health: The role of church and temple.* Nashville: Abington Press, 1970.

Gartner, A., and Riessman, F. *Self-help in the human services.* San Francisco, CA: Jossey-Bass Publishers, 1977.

Green, L.W., Krenter, M.W., Deeks, S.G., and Partridge, K.B. *Health education planning: A diagnostic approach.* Palo Alto, CA: Mayfield Publishing Company, 1980.

Grover, P.L., and Miller, J. Guidelines for making health education work. *Public Health Reports,* 1976, *91,* 249-53.

Iseve, I., Bloom, B., and Spielberger, C.D. (Eds.). *Community psychiatry in transition: Proceedings of the National Conference on Training in Community Psychiatry.* New York: John Wiley and Sons, 1977.

Karno, M., and Schwartz, D.A. *Community mental health: Reflections and explorations.* Flushing, NY: Spectrum Publications, Inc., 1974.

Lauffer, A. *The practice of continuing education in the human services.* New York: McGraw-Hill Book Company, 1977.

Macht, L., Scherl, D., and Sharfstein, S. (Eds.). *Neighborhood psychiatry.* Lexington, MA: Lexington Books, 1977.

Magoon, T.M., Golann, S.E., and Freeman, R.W. *Mental health counselors at work.* New York: Pergamon Press, 1969.

Mann, P.A.,. *Community psychology: Concepts and applications.* New York: The Free Press, 1978.

Mehr, J. *Human services: Concepts and intervention strategies.* Boston: Allyn and Bacon, Inc., 1980.

Munk, R.J., and Lovett, M. *Hospitalwide education and training.* Chicago: Hospital Research and Education Trust, 1977.

Munoz, R.F., Snowden, L.R., Kelly, J.G., and Associates. *Social and psychological research in community settings.* San Francisco, CA: Jossey-Bass Publishers, 1979.

National Commission on Allied Health Education. *The future of allied health education.* San Francisco, CA: Jossey-Bass Publishers, 1980.

New Schools for Old: Interview with M. Dowling, J.J. Gilbert, and F.M. Katz. *World Health,* April, 1977, 12-15.

Riddick, C.C., Cordes, S.M., and Crawford, C.O. Educational needs as perceived by community health decision makers. *Public Health Reports,* 1978, *93,* 474-8.

Rogawski, A. *Mental health consultations in community settings.* San Francisco, CA: Jossey-Bass Publishers, 1979.

Salber, E.J., Beery, W.L., and Jackson, E. The role of the health facilitator in community health education. *Journal of Community Health,* 1976, *1,* 5-20.

Sarason, S., Carroll, C., Maton, K., Cohen, S., and Lorentz, E. *Human services resource networks.* San Francisco, CA: Jossey-Bass Publishers, 1977.

Sinacore, J.S. Priorities in health education. *The Journal of School Health,* April, 1978, *48,* 213-17.

Skillern, P.G. A planned system of patient education. *The Journal of the American Medical Association.* August 22, 1977, *238,* 878-9.

Truelove, J., and Linton, C. *Hospital-based education.* New York: Arco Publishing, Inc., 1980.

United Way of America. *A taxonomy of social goals and human service programs.* Alexandria, VA: United Way of America, 1976.

Wolfensberger, W.A. The origin and nature of our institutional models. In R. Kugel and W. Wolfensberger (Eds.). *Changing patterns in residential services for the mentally retarded.* Washington, D.C.: President's Committee on Mental Retardation, 1969, 59-171.

Wolfensberger, W.A. *The principles of normalization in human services.* Toronto: National Institute of Mental Retardation, 1972.

Journals

American Journal of Community Psychology
Journal of Community Health
Public Health Reports
Social Work

Resource Centers

National Association of Social Workers
1425 H. Street, N.W.
Suite 600
Washington, D.C. 20005

Project Share: National Clearinghouse for
    Improving Management of Human Services
P.O. Box 2309
Rockville, MD 20852

The Society for Public Health Education
703 Market
San Francisco, CA
(415) 546-7601

9
COMMUNITY
LEGAL EDUCATION

Ismael Ramirez-Soto

One of the major vehicles all modern societies use to ensure the smooth functioning of society is the law and its necessary partner, the judicial system. Complicated societies need clear rules, and they need clearly specified mechanisms to decide conflicts both about the rules themselves and the way they are applied in particular cases.

Just as obvious as the need for laws and courts is the need for education to use the legal system. Traditionally in the United States and in most industrialized countries legal education has been reserved for a very select group of people. Until recently by far the majority of law school students were white males from the middle or upper social classes. Law schools had very select admission requirements and consisted of a very rigorous, formal curriculum. In addition potential lawyers needed to pass a very difficult set of examinations in order to be licensed to practice. In summary, legal education was almost exclusively seen as preparation for a very elite career and was reserved for a select few. It was assumed that this small group, once educated, would ensure that the rest of the population had adequate legal services.

Though there have been some important reforms within law schools, notably an increasing effort to recruit qualified minority and women students, nonetheless, most legal education in this country remains very selective and formal. Not surprisingly, this educational approach has not created a legal system noted for its attention to the poor. Even attempts to

increase minimum access of low income groups to low cost legal consultation and representation have proved to be more of a band-aid than
substantive answer to the issue. Though considerable resources are
involved, it is estimated that only 20% of the legal needs of the poor are
addressed (Tapp and Levine, 1974).

Community Legal Education developed as an alternative educational
strategy. It is an alternative not just to traditional law schools but also to the
idea that the legal needs of the poor can be taken care of by providing them
with more low cost lawyers.

Definitions

Community Legal Education is a movement that seeks the eradication of
legal illiteracy among the people in the United States, at least in those areas
of the law that directly affect them as individuals or as a group. It is expected
that learners will become aware of their rights and obligations; they will
learn to whom to turn for assistance in using the legal system (Carlin,
Howard & Messinger, 1967; Levine & Preston, 1970; Tapp & Levine, 1974).

In practice, Community Legal Education, hereinafter referred to as CLE,
may involve many educational activities directed towards the following
areas:

1. Broad dissemination of legal information concerning
    — general legal knowledge of a substantive nature (e.g., land-
      lord/tenant) and/or procedural area (Small Claims Court,
      Pro se Divorces);
    — legal and social services available in the community.
2. Advocacy training for
    — individuals about ways in which they can assert their rights by
      themselves or with very little assistance from an attorney or
      paralegal;
    — groups and community programs that provide services or are
      organized around particular interests or needs.

Activities vary according to the size and characteristics of the intended
audience(s), the geographical dispersion (urban or rural), financial resources
available, and the staff's background and interests in CLE. Some emphasize
media (radio, television, newspapers) and audio-visuals (filmstrips, videos,
slides, posters). Almost without exception, CLE projects engage in direct
contact with the people in the community by providing classroom
instruction, community workshops, lay and pro se (on one's own behalf)
advocacy clinics and teach-ins.

CLE has taken place in schools, community centers, community colleges,
churches, courtrooms, community street festivals, and people's living
rooms. It has also taken place in migrant workers' camps, mental institutions,
prisons, shelters and nursing homes. It has been a movement that has
approached community education by an aggressive outreach to the
community it serves. Institutional support has primarily come from state
and federal programs in education, aging, community development and
juvenile deliquency prevention. There has also been significant involve-

ment from bar associations, community organizations, private schools and police departments.

There is a wide variety of people that get involved and exposed to legal education activities. In many respects, CLE has benefitted from the experience of many groups and people involved in teaching about the law: judges, teachers, attorneys, paralegals, community leaders, social services staff, policemen, probation officers, retired people.

CLE covers a wide selection of the spectrum of formal and nonformal settings, reaching segments of the population where access to justice is most critical and most neglected (e.g., people in mental institutions, prisons, migrant farms, nursing homes). Practitioners have contributed to the teaching of law through the development of teaching innovations like the advocacy clinics, self-instructional modules, use of audio-visuals, simulations, and adaptation of the case study method for teaching children. These innovations stem from the need to develop activities that center on the learner rather than on the subject matter. Law is not taught as if to prepare lawyers but rather to gain an understanding of how the law relates to the individual, and how the legal system operates. Law is not abstract and complicated; people can understand it, if properly taught. That has been the experience with teaching law in community-based settings and schools.

Some CLE projects teach law in a very traditional form, relying on lectures and question/answer formats while others teach through role plays, games and simulations, and peer teaching. Again, the activities and their successes depend on many factors, among them those relative to the background and interests of the teaching staff. CLE has been conceived as one of several means to reduce the caseloads in legal services, as well as a means to reduce delinquent behavior and foster a positive attitude towards law and the American legal system. It may be carried out either through the initiative of one staff person or by the entire staff of a program or community organization. Some of the educational services may be provided on an ad hoc basis while others may be part of the regular services the project has to offer.

This chapter describes a community-based approach to legal education. First its historical antecedents are traced; like many out-of-school educational approaches, much of the fortunes of CLE are tied to larger social and economic trends. Next basic themes common to the movement are examined as well as the underlying assumptions supporting them. Last the various delivery mechanisms are described in detail and several evaluative surveys reviewed.

Historical Antecedents

CLE is far from being an established educational movement in this country. It is still fighting for legitimacy and slowly consolidating networks to avoid duplication of efforts. CLE is a by-product of several experiments with alternative delivery systems for legal services for the poor that were created in the early 1960's.

Legal Aid Societies

Although the concepts of preventive law and *pro se* advocacy date from the 19th century, it was not until the growth of the legal aid movement in the first half of this century that they became associated with the provision of free legal representation and minimum access to justice for the poor. The legal aid movement was small, poorly financed and relied almost entirely on the donations of time and resources of private citizens and community chests. To provide some perspective on the problem, Johnson (1977) estimates that in 1962 the combined budgets of all the legal aid societies in the country represented less than two-tenths of one percent of the nation's annual expenditures for lawyers. The task of these societies, in contrast, was to represent the interests of 25% of the nation's population.

NAACP and ACLU

During the same period of time, however, two major public interest law organizations were formed and eventually developed quite successful litigation strategies. The NAACP Legal Defense and Education Fund, Inc. was created in 1939. It worked with its parent organization to develop a comprehensive legal approach to the problem of racial discrimination. The victory of *Brown vs. Board of Education* of Topeka, Kansas, 1954, leading to a major restructuring of public education, was the work of this organization. Likewise, the American Civil Liberties Union, founded in 1920, became well known as the instigator of many important civil liberties cases.

Both of these organizations were voluntary organizations and relied on the vehicle of the test case to secure rights and benefits for the disenfranchised. While the work of these organizations was extremely important, they did not address either the issue of procuring adequate legal representation for the poor nor the problem of educating disenfranchised groups about their legal rights.

Public Financing

In the 1960's a number of social and economic forces converged, creating favorable conditions for what became a tremendous expansion of the role of public financing of legal services for the disenfranchised, as well as the first major attempt to provide legal education outside of schools. The nation's consciousness of the effects of discrimination and poverty was heightened, resulting in the Civil Rights Movement and the War on Poverty. In 1964 the Neighborhood Legal Services Program became part of the Office of Economic Opportunity and began its dual purpose of providing direct legal services to the poor and engaging in law reform. In 1974 this program was replaced by the Legal Services Corporation, a public organization whose directors are appointed by the president. It is this organization which funds both direct legal services to individuals and community education services.

Now there are approximately 75 CLE projects which are funded by the

Legal Services Corporation. While this effort is still very small, it must be seen as a part of a greatly increased interest in legal education by a number of public and private organizations.

Advocacy Groups

Many district attorney's offices, the League of Women Voters, bar associations, agricultural extension programs, and others have developed curriculum materials, courses and lectures on legal issues relevant to their needs and interests. Programs like VISTA and church parishes have also gotten involved either by providing resources to other groups for legal education programs or by organizing activities to educate their constituency about certain legal issues. National institutes and centers have organized as advocacy centers for particular issues or as public interest law firms. The American Civil Liberties Union, The Center for Law and Education, Sierra Club Legal Defense Fund, and Mexican-American Legal Defense and Education Fund have been involved in delivering educational services and logistical support to others, although such involvement has been somewhat erratic and modest and usually related to impact litigation.

In short, the educational efforts within many communities is considerable when the interplay of all these groups is taken into account. Clearly a wide variety of organizations such as those listed above have varying conceptualizations of the purposes of community legal education. Some people in legal services programs view CLE as a strategy to promote in their clients a sense of self-esteem and competency to deal with many legal problems and develop alternative methods of conflict resolution (Houseman, 1978; Tapp & Levine, 1974; Youells, 1980). On the other hand, in many public schools the teaching of law is seen more as a means of helping students understand, appreciate and develop a positive attitude towards the way justice is administered in this country and to learn to prevent legal problems.

Despite the difference in focus, all CLE efforts are designed with the ideas of raising people's consciousness, empowering them by learning how to use the legal system effectively, and preventing legal problems from taking place if they can be avoided. It is a strategy for promoting the development of a more ethical legality and participatory democracy (Tapp & Levine, 1974). Its effects are designed to last even if the programs cease to exist and if access to lawyers becomes more remote in the future. In other words, CLE is predicated on the push for more self-help, socio-economic reform, and consumer protection.

Legal Education Surveys

Despite widespread interest in legal education in many organizations, coordination and evaluation of many separated local projects has become sparse and funding very precarious, especially in times of fiscal austerity. Only two nationwide surveys on the topic have been conducted; their results are reviewed later in this chapter. In addition, only two national conferences have been held. Their history provides insight into problems currently facing the movement.

In 1978 a conference sponsored by the Legal Services Corporation was held on CLE, and 48 programs were selected to participate. This conference was instrumental in setting up, for the first time, an opportunity for CLE practitioners to exchange views and ideas on CLE and set a national agenda. The emphasis was on developing curriculum materials, manuals for setting up instructional activities and a network of resources. The main distribution center of these materials was to be the National Clearinghouse for Legal Services in Chicago, Illinois. Regional conferences were (and still are) given around the country mostly on a one-shot basis, but no unified support system emerged from this effort. In that same year the Legal Services Corporation funded eight programs to conduct effectiveness studies on instructional methods and strategies of CLE with the goal of judging the impact of CLE efforts in their client community (Legal Services Corporation, 1980, 1981).

In September, 1980, another national conference was organized, but it aborted while in progress. Frustration and pessimism among many CLE "veterans" and newcomers was widespread on all levels. The election of Ronald Reagan signaled a decrease in funding nationwide. CLE was to rest on local initiative, resources and creativity. No significant logistical support could be expected from the national offices of the Legal Services Corporation.

As of today, still no systematic institutional support exists for CLE. Much of what existed before is currently being dismantled or entering into a period of retrenchment. CLE is still not perceived as one of the core services to be provided by a legal services office in its community. At the local level, in some programs, CLE staff has been terminated or charged with new or added roles, making it much more stressful and harder to maintain current work output.

In Summary

The development of community legal education has been very much affected by major socio-economic trends in the United States. Out-of-school education projects were virtually nonexistent before the 1960's, grew sizably during the late 1960's and early 1970's, and have experienced a considerable decline in the 1980's due to the combination of recession and a noticeable growth of conservative ideology in the country. Nonetheless, the idea of empowering the disenfranchised via education about their legal rights has gained acceptance by a wide variety of public and private agencies. Although the fate of the publicly funded Legal Services projects is in doubt, the larger concept of legal education as an important corollary to both public service law and legal services to the poor has a much greater chance of survival. It is an important facet of the out-of-school educational system.

Pervasive Themes

A number of themes recur throughout the literature on legal education.

The two purposes most frequently mentioned are providing equal access to justice and a more equitable distribution of wealth. These purposes are major themes of the movement. Similarly some of the strategies of the legal education movement are so pervasive as to be major themes. The need to empower or increase participation of clients, the idea of advocacy as a strategy, and the importance of systemic reform of the legal system are common concerns of a wide number of commentators.

Equal Access to Justice and Equal Distribution of Wealth

The primary purpose of providing legal services for the poor has been that of equalizing justice and eradicating those conditions that perpetuate poverty. The majority of the legal problems of the poor are believed to arise out of their poverty. Poverty is seen as a problem of nonequitable distribution of goods and services. The law is viewed as a mechanism to facilitate that distribution of resources. The role of the lawyer is to put the mechanism in action for the clients. The intent, therefore, is to marshal the resources of the private and public institutions to provide a better standard of living and greater opportunities for the poor. This organizing of resources focuses on:

- Securing and/or advancing the emergence and institutionalization of socio-economic and political rights that will benefit the poor in state and federal legislatures, administrative agencies and the judiciary.
- Reforming the current judicial system and increasing dispute resolution forums in communities to ensure adequate access and nondiscriminatory treatment.
- Developing and utilizing legal strategies and remedies to effectively address and resolve the social and legal problems of the poor within the justice system.
- Changing the internal structure of the legal services movement, whether private (*pro bono,* judicare, legal clinics) or public (The Legal Services Corporation, Public Defender Programs) to assure that clients also have access to the legal services programs and to develop focused advocacy on local, state and national problems effectively.

Given these concerns with equalizing access to justice and to a reasonable level of affluence, it is no accident that most CLE efforts are aimed at the poor and at racial and ethnic minorities. The purpose of these projects is to educate disenfranchised groups to use the legal system for their own benefit. The assumption is that poverty is largely a structural problem rather than an individual problem which has been caused in part through misuse of the judicial system. With education, however, poor people can learn to use the law to ensure fair access to such things as employment, medical care, welfare, and education.

Empowerment and Participation

Traditionally the legal system has operated under the assumption that clients' needs are well served if they can hire good lawyers. The client's major activity is choosing the lawyer; after that initial action the client for the most part is a passive bystander.

CLE operates under the assumption that this system has failed to serve poor and minority groups. Themes that occur over and over in the literature are the need to empower clients and to raise their capacity to participate as knowledgeable consumers of legal services. Groups need information about what their legal rights are and how they can use the system for their own purposes. They need to know where they can go for free or low cost legal services. Education in this sense is empowering to the learner, providing the learner with the information necessary to access the legal system.

In experimenting with alternative delivery systems, legal services has paid increasing attention to strategies that involve the clients in the pursuit of their interests. Some of these strategies are:

- Increasing the poor's general knowlede about their rights and obligations as citizens and workers and the benefits to which they may be entitled in the various social service programs funded by the state or federal government.
- Enhancing the poor 's legal competency so that they can recognize, avert, and, in some cases, advocate by themselves disputes which do not require a lawyer for their resolution.
- Enhancing and disseminating political and legal consciousness among the poor with respect to their status within the American legal culture and helping them in the process to organize as effective advocacy groups.
- Maintaining a continuous outreach activity to inform the client about the program, what kind of legal assistance can be obtained and how such services can or cannot be used.
- Providing legal help to poor people for whom the program has been unable to provide individual case aid (institutionalized, language minorities, isolated rural residents, handicapped, migrants, etc.).
- Providing incentives for more client participation in the policy making process of the legal services program to prevent program priorities and services from becoming monopolized by the staff's perceptions and those who already know and have used the program's services.

In short, CLE enhances the ability of the poor to seek a more equitable distribution of the goods and services. Its effects are meant to last even when there may not be any legal services for the poor (Barrett & Youells, 1981; Houseman, 1978).

Advocacy

While the legal system as a whole is basically an advocacy system (lawyers advocate on behalf of clients), CLE education often uses the concept of advocacy in a somewhat different sense. The assumption is that many populations, because of ignorance, handicaps or poverty, are not in a position to use normal legal channels. What they need are fewer individual advocates and more class or group advocacy. Thus, CLE projects are often connected to advocacy programs where lay people or paralegals work on behalf of a certain group of people.

One example of this kind of approach is the advocacy programs for retarded or mentally ill people living in institutions or in community settings. Lay or paralegal advocates work on behalf of the handicapped person and at the same time provide education to both the client and the community about basic legal rights. Sometimes these advocacy programs work in conjunction with public interest law firms which use the vehicle of the class action suit to secure the right of handicapped people to live in less restrictive and more humane settings than are provided by the usual state institutions.

Reform of the Legal System

A recurrent theme of the community legal education movement is the need for fundamental reform of the legal system. A number of realities force a reevaluation of the traditional methods of legal advocacy, namely litigation and legal advice. One of these realities is that people in this country are basically ignorant of their rights and the benefits to which they are entitled; for many of them legal services is their first formal contact with the legal system. Ignorance and the cost of using the legal institutions to address grievances are conditions that deter the poor from relying on the law to improve their socio-economic conditions.

Participation in the law, therefore, is unfairly concentrated among those groups who have adequate access to a lawyer and can bear the costs of providing enough funds to supply each potential client with access to a lawyer for advice and representation. In addition to the enormous cost (at present there are over 5,000 attorneys and 300 million dollars which handle approximately 20% of the estimated legal needs of the poor), this solution focuses on a case litigation approach which is

> not conducive to the realization of prevention and systemic reform. Individual, situation-specific legal services do not enhance a teaching-learning exchange relationship between the lawyer and client. It reinforces a view of this separateness of the legal system from other problem solving approaches, and it reduces the possibility for shared activity basic to the quest for justice.

This type of legal service is a bandaid and lollipop endeavor because access to the institution of law remains in the exclusive control of the lawyer. It sustains the profession's monopolistic, gatekeeper role toward law. Individuals function only at the periphery of shaping and mobilizing the legal institutions. In essence, isolated legal experiences tend to be system maintenance oriented and do not encourage people, including lawyers, to utilize their skills to establish reciprocal rights, build a sense of self-esteem and competency, foster internal judgement and control, and develop alternative methods of dispute settlement. (Tapp & Levine, 1974, 52-3.)

Community legal education, in other words, is a social change movement. It seeks a major shift in power in this society through using means which have traditionally been used to maintain the middle- and upper-classes in power.

In Summary

The themes that emerge from a study of CLE sources are similar to those that have pervaded many of the social change movements of recent years. There is the assumption that the current system is inequitable in the way it allocates both power and resources. Legal education projects see as their purpose to increase poor and minority groups' access to resources and to the judicial systems. Methods seek to empower clients. Advocacy is on behalf of the collective, not just the interests of one individual. Systemic reform is seen as essential if basic purposes are to be attained. These themes, in turn, are based on some fundamental values and assumptions.

Underlying Assumptions

It is not hard to uncover the value structure implied in the typical CLE project. The notion of equality of justice for all receives more than lip service. The barrier to that basic right is assumed to be the current system, not any individual defect or problem. There is a belief in the potential of all kinds of people, including the handicapped, the poor, and minority groups, to be productive members of society. These values, in turn, dictate the need for major change in the social system. While advocates of CLE support the legal rights listed in the Bill of Rights and the economic rights of the New Deal reforms, they feel that many groups of people do not have these rights guaranteed in actual practice. It is the day-to-day procedures of the legal system that discriminate unfairly.

A major reason for the inequity is the individualistic bias of the legal system. While it is true that some poor, handicapped, and minority people have access to quality legal services and enjoy the same rights as more privileged groups, nonetheless the collective needs of these groups are not met by the system. The system works very well to advocate for rights that individuals are willing to pay for. It does not work as efficiently for groups unwilling or unable to pay; nor does it advocate as efficiently for community-wide issues. Traditionally the legal system has not addressed such collective issues as the right to clean air and water or safe products (Weisbrod, Handler and Komesar, 1978).

The CLE movement is a part of a larger group of legal reform groups which are developing legal procedures that work on behalf of the collective good. While the concept of *pro bono* (for the public good) law is old, nonetheless the effort was, for the most part, voluntary and quite small until the 1960's. Since that time there has been a marked growth in the number of collective approaches: public interest law firms, advocacy projects, legal aid, citizen lobbying groups are examples. All are interested in the legal rights of the entire community rather than concentrating exclusively on the rights of individuals within it.

What differentiates CLE programs from many of these groups, however, is its assumption that basic change must occur simultaneously at the local level as well as at the national level. Most of the other approaches assume that key changes such as the successful test case, class action suit, or legislative reform will make the difference. Legal educators believe that an educated community is also essential. It is not enough that certain laws and regulations are changed; people must also be empowered to use them.

The concept of empowerment, in turn, is essential to the learning theory implied in most community legal education projects. The techniques seek to activate the learner, to enable learners to advocate on their own behalf. The assumption is that the learner has the inner resources necessary in order to use the system effectively. The task of the educator is to remove barriers that have prevented the learner from acting effectively. Thus in general, methods are highly participatory. Methods also assume that the lessons to be learned are not unduly difficult, but can be learned quickly and efficiently. Learning, when conceived as the removal of barriers to understanding can be seen as a "light dawns" type of process rather than the laborious, step-by-step process typical of schooling.

In Summary

Assumptions and values underlying this educational approach take seriously the right of each person to be considered equal and to have an equal opportunity to develop his/her potential. CLE assumes social change to be essential if the goals of the movement are to be attained. This change will procure the collective rights of society as well as individual rights and must simultaneously take place at the bottom as well as top layers of society. Education therefore seeks to remove barriers that have prevented people from learning and allow them to attain fundamental knowledge about how to use the system very efficiently and quickly.

Delivery Systems

CLE activities vary according to the client population characteristics (literacy levels, age, language and ethnicity distributions), geographical dispersion (urban or rural), financial resources available (within the legal services program's budget or special funds) and the staff's background and interests in CLE. Many emphasize mass media as one delivery vehicle for their educational services (radio, television, newspapers), while others emphasize direct contact with the clients (advocacy clinics, teach-ins, classroom instruction, community workshops).

The settings where these activities can take place vary according to the needs of the population, logistical convenience for the instructors, and the types of activity that are required to meet those needs. Thus, CLE practitioners have been involved in curriculum development and instruction in public high schools, adult education programs, radio education, commercial and cable television, community centers, church basements as well as clients' living rooms, migrant workers' camps, and community festivals.

Most of the instructional materials utilized are made by people in the program. They will produce information leaflets, posters, newsletters, filmstrips, videotapes, self-help kits, and tapes (Tel Law) which can be used in a variety of ways. Very little commercial material is used, perhaps because of its unavailability, cost, and lack of orientation to the poor.

In many respects, CLE has benefitted from the experiences of other nonschool educational movements, but may have also tried to reinvent the wheel in the process. Very little is known among CLE practitioners about the community education and nonformal education movements in this country. The literature does not mention these at all. But in the process of maturing as an educational movement, CLE has also been original and creative. It has contributed to the teaching of law through the development of teaching innovations such as the lay and *pro se* advocacy clinics, the people's law schools, and self-instructional modules. These innovations stem from the need to develop activities that center on the needs of the clients rather than on the constraints that law as a subject matter may appear to impose on teaching.

In CLE, law is not treated as an academic discipline as it is in law schools . The emphasis is on the clients' empowerment. This issue has been well recognized in several law schools where certain clinical programs have actually sent students to prisons, public schools, and community settings to teach about the law (Association of American Law Schools, 1980; Harrington, 1969; Macey, Singleton & Thompson, 1977; McAuliffe, 1967). These law schools have found that teaching law to a law student is subject-oriented rather than person-oriented. Thus, new methods and materials need to be developed to successfully teach lay people about the law. The significant contributions in this particular area of curriculum development are to be found in the literature, not in CLE, but in the areas of legal socialization (Grossman & Sarat, 1981; Levine & Preston, 1970; Sarat, 1977; Tapp & Levine, 1974) and Law-Related Education (American Bar Association, 1975, 1976; Gerlach & Lemprecht, 1975).

The organizations engaged in CLE activities are varied in their structure and process. The major public provider, the Legal Services Corporation, is a government bureaucracy. Projects need to contend with a hierarchical system where many crucial decisions such as the amount of funding available are made far away from the projects. However, many of the voluntary organizations providing CLE have less bureaucratic processes and often make decisions in a more democratic fashion.

CLE as an educational approach is characterized by its flexibility and variety. For the most part, such key variables as content, methods, settings, and staff are very nonformal in their orientation, particularly when the project is located in a community rather than school setting. The key exception is that the major publicly financed programs are run by a highly formal organization—the United States government.

Evaluations of CLE Activities

In recent years there have been two major evaluations of the CLE projects financed by the Legal Services Corporation. While these evaluations only concern government financed projects, they do provide the major coordinated data available about the characteristics and major issues facing CLE programs. In 1977, the Office of Program Support of the Legal Services Corporation launched a survey of all its funded programs to determine what educational efforts were underway and what the corporation might do to support these local efforts. Forty-eight projects were identified as the result of this study. It represented a "first step towards establishing some much-needed communication by and about community education efforts" (LSC, 1977). A directory of CLE programs was compiled and distributed through the Clearinghouse Service of the Legal Services Corporation. It was to be updated regularly every year. This plan failed, and it was not until January of 1982 that it was finally updated, although its publication is not contemplated.

The 1977 survey uncovered, for the first time, data that could assist policy makers at LSC in building a monitoring and support system to address the program's needs. These survey findings were corroborated and furthered one year later by the U.S. Comptroller General's report to Congress on the LSC operations. Their final report recommended that the LSC should:

- Expand training sessions on CLE and require grantees to submit plans for addressing CLE with their budget submissions.
- Provide individual projects with needed technical assistance in developing CLE programs suitable for their clients' needs. (U.S. General Accounting Office, 1978.)

From the 1977 study, a follow-up report was prepared with the following four suggestions:

1. That technical assistance was needed in at least two areas,
   a. training of local staff and client board members, and
   b. funding of direct training services and materials development and strategies to seek outside funding.
2. That collection and distribution of curriculum materials reported in the survey needed to be done.
3. That the directory needed to be updated regularly.
4. That experimental grants for development and evaluation of preventive law techniques were also needed since the LSC knew "very little about how to do genuinely preventive legal education, and even less about how to evaluate it." (LSC, 1977.)

These two major surveys indicate the tentative nature of the publicly funded projects. Given the greater difficulties that private projects have with funding, it is likely that they experience similar concerns.

Conclusion

CLE may become an essential form of advocacy work for the legal services movement in the next years, in view of such recent developments as:
- restricted funding;
- further congressional restrictions concerning the type, cases and litigation forums that the Legal Services Corporation can become involved in;
- the increasing role of the private sector in the provision of legal services for the poor; and,
- the self-help movement among client groups as a strategy of empowerment and pressuring government for more public accountability.

At present these developments are instrumental in redefining the client/attorney and client/legal services office relationships. In this transitional process, close contact with clients is essential, and the need to develop legal competence among the poor is an imperative reality that has to be addressed as soon as possible.

Failure to invest time and resources in improving the quality of CLE programs and extending their successes to other communities may mean relegating CLE to a soon-to-be-forgotten fad. The energy and creativity already invested by many individuals could be wasted. The community legal education movement is still fighting to be recognized and institutionalized within the Legal Services Corporation. It is an educational movement well worth rescuing.

Suggested Resources
Community Legal Education

Bibliography

American Bar Association. *An annotated catalogue of law-related audio-visual materials.* Chicago: American Bar Association, 1975.

American Bar Association. *Bibliography of law-related curriculum materials.* (2nd. ed.). Chicago: American Bar Association, 1976.

Association of American Law Schools. *Directory on teaching law outside law schools.* Washington, D.C.: Association of American Law Schools, 1980.

Barrett, J.C., and Youells, R. The statewide poor people's platform congress: Building coalitions for social justice. *Clearinghouse Review,* 1981, *14,* 1168.

Beryl, M. Community legal education for senior citizens. *Clearinghouse Review,* 1980, *14,* 784.

Carlin, J., Howard, J., and Messinger, S.L. *Civil justice and the poor: Issues for sociological research.* New York: Russell Sage Foundation, 1967.

Duncan, G.A. Public access to law in the 80's: Current trends in broadening public access. *Saskatchewan Law Review,* 1979-1980, *44,* 123.

Erlanger, H. Lawyers and neighborhood legal services: Social background and impetus for reform. *Law and Society Review,* 1978, *12,* 253.

Ferry, Michael. Legal services can use local media for community education. *Clearinghouse Review,* 1980, *14,* 731.

General Accounting Office. *Review of Legal Services Corporation's activities concerning program evaluation and expansion.* Washington, D.C.: U.S. Government Printing Office, 1980.

General Accounting Office. *Free legal services for the poor: Increased coordination, community legal education and outreach needed* (U.S. Superintendent of Documents, HRD-80-103). Washington, D.C.: U.S. Government Printing Office, 1978.

Gerlach, R., and Lamprecht, L. *Teaching about the law: A guide to secondary and elementary school instruction.* Cincinnati: Anderson Publishing Company, 1975.

Grossman, J.B., and Sarat, A. Access to justice and the limits of the law. *Law and Policy Quarterly,*1981, *3,* 125.

Harrington, E.M. Preventive law for low income groups: The Texas Southern experience. *Journal of Legal Education,* 1969, *21,* 339.

Houseman, A. Legal services and equal justice for the poor: Some thoughts for the future. *National Legal Aid and Defenders Association Briefcase,* 1978, *35,* 44-9.

Houseman, A. The Houseman memorandum. *The Congressional Record,* February 6, 1981, 1209.

Johnson, E. *Justice and Reform.* New York: Russell Sage Foundation, 1977.

Kalmowitz, G. Legal services: Marching to a different drummer. *National Legal Aid and Defenders Association Briefcase,* March 1978, *35,* 66-71.

Katz, J. Lawyers for the poor in transition: Involvement, reform and the turnover problem in the legal services program. *Law and Society Review,* 1978, *12,* 275.

Kocher, E.G. The legal check-up: An approach to the problem of access to legal services. *Clearinghouse Review,* 1980, *13,* 728.

Legal Services Corporation. *Quality improvement project: Community legal education and client involvement demonstration projects: Final evaluation reports,* 1981.

Legal Services Corporation. *Quality improvement project: Status reports, Demonstration projects,* 1980.

Legal Services Corporation. *Preventive law community education survey results.* Clearinghouse Document #22,460, 1977.

Legal Services Corporation. *Directory of community education projects.* Clearinghouse Document #22,497, 1977.

Legal Services Corporation. *Community legal education directory: Appendix with working papers and proposals.* Clearinghouse Document #22, 498, 1977.

Levine, F., and Preston, E. Community resource orientation among low-income groups. *Wisconsin Law Review,* 1970, *80.*

Macey, N.L., Singleton, S.M., and Thompson, A.C. The prison project: A proposed model for clinical course. *Journal of Legal Education,* 1977, *28,* 573.

McAuliffe, J.W. The urban law program of the University of Detroit. *Journal of Legal Education,* 1967, *20,* 83.

McDonald, R.A. Law schools and public legal education: The community programme at Windsor. *The Dalhousie Law Journal,* 1979, *5,* 779.

Moore, P. People as lawyers—Lay advocacy and self-help in the legal system. *British Journal of Law and Society,* 1978, *5,* 121.

Nagel, S.S. *Improving the legal process.* Lexington: Lexington Books, 1975.

Pearcey, P. Public legal education: How, what and why. *Saskatchewan Law Review,* 1979-80, *44,* 131.

Press, A., et al. Counsel to the poor. *Newsweek*, January 14, 1980, *95*, 89-90.

Sarat, A. Studying American legal culture: An assessment of survey evidence. *Law and Society Review*, 1977, *11*, 427.

Stumpf, H.P. *Community politics and legal services: The other side of the law.* Beverly Hills: Sage Publications, 1975.

Tapp, J., and Levine, F. Legal socialization: Strategies for an ethical legality. *Stanford Law Review*, 1974, *27*, 1.

Weisbrod, B.A., Handler, J.F., and Komesar. *Public interest law: An economic and institutional analysis.* Berkeley: University of California Press, 1978.

Youells, R. Designing a low-cost community legal education. *Clearinghouse Review*, 1980.

Journals

Clearinghouse Review

National Legal Aid and Defenders Association Briefcase

Journal of Legal Education

Resource Centers

National Street Law Institute
605 G Street, N.W.
Washington, D.C.

Center for Law and Education
Gutman Library, Graduate School of Education
Harvard University
Cambridge, MA

Massachusetts Law Reform Institute
2 Park Square
Boston, MA 02116

Native American Materials Development Center
407 Rio Grande, N.W.
Albuquerque, New Mexico 87104

New Orleans Video Access Center
2010 Magazine
New Orleans, LA 70130

10

SELF-HELP GROUPS AS EDUCATION

Robert G. Ross

Self-help groups have become an increasingly common phenomenon over the past two decades. The phenomenon crosses all ages, races, social and economic levels, and a multitude of conditions. These groups have become a major educational approach, facilitating learning about very central and important issues facing members.

Though diverse in their intent, membership, characteristics, processes, and philosophies, all self-help groups are educational. They build skills, provide new information, and perhaps most importantly, provide a setting for changing attitudes on immediate, pressing issues facing group members. The approach is practical and functionally oriented, and as such has been frequently demonstrated to be successful in areas where more professional approaches have failed.

The self-help group is one aspect of a groundswell of lay support programs, services, organizations, and clubs which have emerged and developed outside of the traditional professional helping structure. As a consequence of their relative newness, rapid growth, anti-professional stance, and extreme diversity, the research on self-help groups is limited. Only recently have they received the in-depth attention by several small groups of active researchers. An indication of its newness as an area of research is that no computerized literature search currently recognizes the terms "support group," "self-help," or "mutual aid" as descriptors. Thus, this work has been manual and owes a debt of gratitude to the groundbreaking works of Caplan and Killilea (1976), Gartner and Riessman (1977), and Lieberman and Borman (1979) for providing the foundation.

It is the intent of this chapter to provide an overview of the self-help group as an educational approach. The chapter is divided into three sections. First, the various types of self-help groups will be explored with examples of each. Second, the various components of the approach will be analyzed; how do the objectives, methods, staffing and so forth of self-help groups distinguish this educational approach from other approaches? Last, the assumptions underlying this approach will be explored in more depth. Various themes characteristic of the approach will be examined for their significance; the cultural conditions that foster or inhibit self-help will be noted; theoretical assumptions concerning the nature of personal and group change will be investigated; and the potential negative uses of self-help discussed.

The purpose of this chapter, in other words, is to explore in-depth a significant, out-of-school learning approach which has proved effective and helpful to people facing a wide range of problems. The fact that the approach is inexpensive, adaptable, and appropriate for a wide variety of issues heightens its importance as a major educational technique.

Definitions and Examples

Self-Help Groups in the Wider Context of Support Systems

The literature to which self-help groups belong is the general milieu of support systems, a complex and varied set of phenomonon. Support systems perform a range of enabling functions in a wide variety of formats to individuals with varying degrees of need. The word support easily could be construed as suggesting weakness or inadequacy on the part of the individual. However, the majority of self-help group members would argue to the contrary. Support in this context implies "augmenting of a person's strengths to facilitate his mastery of his environment" (Caplan, 1974, p. 7). Support systems have several functions in common: they aid individuals in activating and mobilizing their psychological resources; they share in the individual's task accomplishment; they provide individuals with additional needed resources in a multitude of forms (Caplan, 1974).

In considering the support system, one is struck by its multiplicity, diversity, and extent. So basic is the need for and provision of support that it pervades virtually every corner of human activity and interaction. As a consequence, much of the effort by researchers has been in ordering and categorizing groups and data to make the topic more manageable. In this essay, three broadly defined divisions of support systems (natural, nonprofessional and professional) have been employed to look at the self-help group in context. Although much of what occurs within the realm of the nonprofessional and professional is in fact very natural, the distinction is helpful in isolating characteristics, differences, and similarities.

Natural support systems are those structures which occur spontaneously within society. These systems are natural and occur in all cultures throughout history. Within the natural support system one locates the nuclear family, extended family, friendships, informal groups, neighbors, as well as religious denominations. The major distinction here is that of "kith and kin," kith being friends, neighbors, and acquaintances and kin being members of the nuclear and extended family (Caplan, 1974). The basic training ground for all support systems is in the natural support system, specifically the family. It is in the nuclear family that children first experience support, learn its methods, its rules, its costs, and its rewards. For many, it is an effective, reliable system which continues to function throughout life. For others, subject to a multitude of perils, it is only partially effective.

The second division to be considered is the professional support system. Included are the individual and group services provided by psychiatrists, psychologists, counselors, and social workers; the settings are private offices, community mental health centers, schools, and hospitals. Many of those support functions identified with the natural systems are exhibited by professional supports; however, the method of delivery and nature of relationships are considerably different. The style of communication and support are unidirectional rather than mutual; the professional is usually part of a hierarchical bureaucratic institution; access to support is limited; the type and quality of professional support is often predetermined by proximity to agencies and ability to pay; perceived and actual commonality of the individual seeking support and the professional is lacking. Professional support services tend to focus around the theoretical base of the professional helper rather than the specific needs of the client (Dewar, 1978).

The third division and the main focus of this study is the nonprofessional or self-help support system. Within this division are intentional communities, self-help groups, and peer counseling. Levy (1979, p. 239) describes this segment of support as

> a vast array of alternative social arrangements by which people today are seeking to improve the quality of their lives without recourse to professional care givers, ranging from communes to peer counseling to community crisis hotlines, and including proprietary organizations such as Smoke-Enders and Weight Watchers.

A brief discussion of two types of nonprofessional support systems can begin to provide a context for understanding the self-help group approach. Intentional communities are one example which have a long and varied history.

> An intentional community is a group of persons associated together (voluntarily) for the purpose of establishing a whole way of life. As such, it shall display to some degree each of the following characteristics: common geographical location; economic interdependence; social, cultural, educational, and spiritual interexchange of uplift and development. (Zablocki, 1971, p. 19.)

Whether motivated by religious interests, economic, political, social interests, or health interests, these characteristics are common to all successful communities. Whether one is investigating the religious and socio-political communities of the 19th century, or the alternative lifestyle and therapeutic communities of the mid-20th century, one finds the same banding together of individuals without outside or professional help to attain goals of utmost importance to members (Kanter, 1972; Wilson, 1978).

Another nonprofessional type of support system is peer counseling. Within this category are a host of varied programs and services provided by indigenous peer helpers. Individual counseling, co-counseling, peer-led group counseling, hot lines, rap room, and drop-in centers in myriad settings and formats compose this rapidly growing area of support. The proliferation of peer counseling services has been encouraged by evidence that indigenous helpers are more effective in working with the poor, drug abusers, alcoholics, college students, minorities, and subcultures than professionals. Brown (1972), in extensive work with college peer counselors, found that the counsel offered by fellow students achieved greater acceptance due to the commonality of language, experience, and problems. Peer programs have been effective in working with minorities, with gays, in a variety of formats with college students, with older students returning to education, with junior and senior high school students, and with members of the clergy. The popularity of programs of peer counseling is a result of this success, as well as its cost-effectiveness, its ability to expand service, and its freeing-up of professional helpers to perform more intensive work. It can also be postulated that the popularity and consequence of institutional and professional support are the results of the integration of a nonprofessional support system with the professional, and the degree of control and influence maintained by the professional through training, supervision, and accountability through varied reporting systems to funding agencies.

Most notable throughout the peer counseling literature is the impact of training and the activity of helping upon the peer counselors themselves. Through both subjective observation and empirical research, it is clear that the counselors experience remarkable personal growth, improved self-concept, improved self-acceptance, and decreases in personal problem areas.

The Self-Help Group: A Definition

The self-help group is one more example of a nonprofessional support group. Katz and Bender provide the following definition:

> Self-help groups are voluntary, small group structures for mutual aid and the accomplishment of a special purpose. They are usually formed by peers who have come together for mutual assistance in satisfying a common need, overcoming a common handicap or life-disrupting problem and bringing about desired social and/or personal change. The initiators and members of such groups perceive that their needs are not or cannot be met by or through existing social institutions. Self-help groups emphasize face-to-

face social interactions and the assumption of personal responsibility by members. They often provide material assistance as well as emotional support; they are frequently "cause-oriented," and promulgate an ideology or values through which members may attain an enhanced sense of personal identity. (1976b, p. 9.)

While the goals and processes of self-help groups are quite diverse, there are some rough categories that have wide support throughout the research. The most common of these is the distinction between "inner"-focused or "outer"-focused groups (Katz and Bender, 1976a; Sagarin, 1969; Steinman and Traunstein, 1976). The inner-focused group concentrates on personal growth and direct service to members while the outer-focused groups are involved in altering social norms.

These categories are not, however, mutually exclusive. It has also been found that self-help groups over time may change their focus from inner to outer or outer to inner. Tracy and Gussow (1976) found this change in the function and overlapping of focus in health related groups. Bond and Reibstein (1979) found several changes in the focus of women's consciousness raising groups. In the early period, they found the groups to be quite political and activistic. Then, during the early 1970's, the groups functioned as personal support groups. More recently, they have again become political, activistic, and more highly structured. This changing focus may be the simple organic development of a fledgling movement: taking action, attracting new members, building support on a wider base, and resuming action.

Common Characteristics of Self-Help Groups

The literature identifies a consistent cluster of characteristics which are common throughout self-help groups. Finding both their origin and sanction for existence from within their memberships, they are voluntary associations. Members within each self-help group have a common life experience or problem which is not dealt with, or not dealt with effectively, by professional helpers. The groups always involve a face-to-face interaction with the primary purpose of providing members with mutual aid and support.

Self-help is characterized by the collective assumption of personal responsibility for the members' destinies. Within this collectivity, each member is provided with a new role as helper. In so doing, members find the group fulfilling needs for reference, reinforcement, identification with others, and a base for action. They are empowered and experience an increased sense of personal value, self-respect, and capability. An additional characteristic involves the role of the professional. A majority of self-help groups are independent of professionals; those which involve professionals have done so in an ancillary manner.

In contrast with professional support systems, the self-help group orientation "is more activistic, consumer-centered, informal, open, and inexpensive." The experience of self-help groups is one which stresses "the concrete, the subjective, the experiential and the intuitive" while the experience of the professional stresses "distance, perspective, reflection, systematic knowledge and understanding" (Gartner and Riessman, 1977, p. 14).

The overriding difference is the empowerment of the individual and the group through the self-help experience. Autonomy, self-reliance, group solidarity, and active helping of others all contribute to an increased sense of personal power and its actuality. In addition to empowering members, self-help groups validate the need for the strength of basic human qualities in caregiving systems, such as feelings for one another, common sense, shared experience and person to person availability.

Examples of Self-Help Groups

There are numerous types of self-help groups which illustrate the characteristics described above. Gartner (1976) and Gartner and Riessman (1977) provide a compact set of categories which are inclusive, easily remembered, and identify groups by core elements of both purpose and methods. *Anonymous groups* are identified by a set of organizational commonalities; these are, anonymity, individual responsibility for the problem, belief in a rigid system such as the Twelve Steps and the Twelve Traditions of Alcoholics Anonymous. These groups are further identified by member commonalities: members have hit bottom; are self-degraded; see no other alternatives; and believe that only within the group are they able to control their behavior. Included in the Anonymous groups are Alcoholics Anonymous, Gamblers Anonymous, Narcotics Anonymous, Neurotics Anonymous, and Parents Anonymous.

Synanon type groups share many of the same commonalities. They are, in addition, residential communities and share more vigorous and rigid belief systems and processes. Synanon type groups rely heavily on the influence of ideology and/or a charismatic leader. Included in the Synanon type groups are Synanon, Daytop Village, and Delancey Street.

Ex-patient groups are an emerging form of self-help which focus on an individual's coping with and adjusting to the acute phase of a long-term disease. Visitation, information sharing, support and encouragement are key elements in programs such as Mended Hearts, Stroke Club, Reach for Recovery, International Laryngectomy Association, Paralyzed Veterans, National Foundation for Ileitis and Colitis. They also perform an outpatient maintenance function for patients with psychological disorders. Groups such as Recovery Inc. and Integrity provide ongoing support and systematic maintenance of ex-patients.

"Living with" groups are characterized by their membership. They are composed of the family members and relatives of persons suffering from some form of affliction. Al-anon, Gam-anon, Alateen, Parents of Gays, Prison Families Anonymous, parents of retarded persons, and parents of children with a multitude of medical conditions all provide information, support, referral, and encouragement to members.

Transitional groups is the final category presented by Gartner and Riessman (1977). Earlier Gartner (1976) had divided this group into People Alone and Transitional Groups. Within this expanded category, one finds a host of groups supporting individuals experiencing a transitional phase of life which in some way separates the individual from former or usual peer groups. Included here are Parents Without Partners, North American Conference of Separated and Divorced Catholics, La Leche League (issues of mothering), Senior Companions, Foster Grandparents, and a host of other age-related groups for children, adolescents, and adults. In this study, the support group is added to the Transitional category. Whether considering consciousness raising groups for women, men, lesbians, or gays, or support structures for high-risk students, older students returning to education, or individuals in adult development crises, the support group aids in the transitional experience of changing one's lifestyle, social milieu, peers, and goals and attitudes about oneself. The term "support group" is beginning to be used in the literature with some frequency. It is a nonthreatening term appropriate to a variety of self-help groups.

In summary, the self-help group is a nonprofessional support group through which members provide mutual assistance in meeting a commonly identified need. Self-help groups are organized around a wide variety of issues, but share the characteristics of being informal, open, and empowering to helper and helpee alike.

Educational Aspects of Self-Help Groups

The self-help group is, in the broadest sense, educational and, like other educational approaches, can be analyzed into its component parts. It has goals and objectives which are embodied in content and can be compared and contrasted to the objectives and contents of other educational approaches. Learners and staff differ in characteristics from those in other approaches, as does the methodology, the type of resources used, and the organizational structure. Analyzing the self-help group using this framework provides the reader with the tools to compare this approach to other out-of-school settings highlighting the specific usefulness of various techniques.

Self-help as an educational approach can be, broadly speaking, characterized as nonformal; it is, in fact, one of the most consistently nonformal approaches that is widely practiced both in North America and worldwide. As a nonformal approach, one finds that its concerns are immediate and practical; it is lay-oriented, flexible, learner controlled, and holistic in its worldview. Several of these characteristics are described in more detail below. The major emphasis in this section, however, is a detailed description of the methodologies used in self-help groups which are unique in educational practice.

Objectives and Content

The catalogue of the issues of self-help groups presented above provides an indication of the objectives of the self-help approach. Alcoholism, gambling, divorce, illness, handicap, impending death, drug use, major life transitions, sexual preference, poverty, unemployment, discrimination all are powerful, immediate, central concerns to the lives of the people who experience them. There is little that is abstract or purely rational about these issues. Rather, the issues involve pressing problems that need immediate solution if the quality of members' lives is to be improved substantially.

These objectives are translated into a content that is quite distinct from a formal school curriculum. There are no prerequisites or carefully sequenced steps in helping a group member survive a divorce or conquer a drinking problem. Rather, the approach is experiential and pragmatic. Members seek to help each other find what works concretely and specifically in that individual's life.

Learners

Within the self-help group movement a wide variety of individuals participate as learners. The common characteristic of members is the perceived existence of some form of internalized problem (personal, physical or social) for which relief is sought. According to Katz and Bender, the potential member acts on the basis of two assumptions: "(1) The group will help solve his problems more effectively than he can himself. (2) The goals of a particular group — its ideology and socialization, its program and procedures — are compatible with his view of his own needs and outlook" (1976b, p. 33).

In that the types of problems addressed by the varied self-help groups are myriad, the membership is likewise, crossing age, race, sex, educational, and income levels. There is, however, some inconclusive data pointing toward more involvement among the poor and the various minorities within the self-help group movement.

Staff

For the most part, staffing within self-help groups is informal and nonhierarchical. Members of long standing often serve as leaders and models for newer members. In some groups, a charismatic leader emerges as a formal leader. The typical charismatic leader is an individual who is perceived as knowing "the way," having pulled him/herself "up by the bootstraps."

Generally, professional staffing does not exist within the self-help movement. Groups typically evolve in response to member needs not being effectively met by professional caregivers. Even in those self-help groups which include professionals, their role is peripheral. Gartner and Riessman have identified several potential roles for professionals in the self-help movement. "They may initiate such a group; they can refer persons to such a group; they may develop a group; they can consult with the group; they can staff the group, and finally, they can help the group become independent" (1977, p. 133). Stephens (1972), the originator of Compassionate Friends, recommends that the professional remain in the background as a support, to refer members and serve as public representative. Mowrer, the founder of Integrity Groups, states that:

The most useful thing that the professional can do at this point, especially in the community mental health movement, is to give support to these indigenous groups and to refer to them and to learn how to become facilitators or expeditors for the development of these indigenous groups. (1975, p.49.)

Methods

Self-help groups most frequently are involved in promoting personal change, and for that reason the methodology or change mechanism is critical for understanding the approach. Because the end result is essentially that of individual growth or change, a major resource for understanding the methods used is the literature on individual and group therapy and change. One such description, that of Yalom (1975), is used here to explore the relevance of these well-tested methods for self-help groups.

Yalom identifies eleven curative factors involved in group therapy. Included are the following:

(a) Instillation of hope; (b) Universality; (c) Imparting information; (d) Altruism; (e) The corrective recapitulation of the primary family group; (f) Development of socializing techniques; (g) Imitative behavior; (h) Interpersonal learning; (i) Group cohesiveness; (j) Catharsis; and (k) Existential factors.

Of Yalom's eleven factors, ten are intensively involved in self-help groups. The single exception, the corrective recapitulation of the primary family group, has clearly and rightfully remained the province of the professional therapist. Some groups use some of these change mechanisms more than others, but all are found in the self-help movement.

In exploring each of these factors in relation to the self-help group literature, it is appropriate to begin with the area of hope. The instilation and maintenance of hope are especially important curative factors in self-help groups. Those individuals who seek out self-help groups tend to perceive themselves, their condition, or life situation as hopeless, beyond the ability of the professional caregiver, beyond their own ability, or if professional care might work, it is beyond their reach. In self-help groups, as in therapy groups, hope is instilled by the faith of the leader (if there is one), by the process, and by past and current members' successes. The faith and hope of the new member is often inspired by the use of the testimonial in group meetings. In this process, the new member and older members are constantly reminded that this group and this belief system has worked and is working for someone else who shares their problem. People believe they can take charge of their own lives when given the processes available in self-help groups. That belief is very powerful.

The second factor, universality, is intimately connected to the instillation of hope. To believe in the group, its belief system, and processes, individuals must see themselves as similar to the other members, to the testimonial givers. The value of commonality of experience among group members is that each member's identity is validated while providing support in not being alone. Though many terms are used to express this need for universality (the common experience, affinity, etc.), the basic need is to remove the sense of being alone, of being the only one. The stigmatized person experiences the stigma lifted as he/she joins with others of similar condition.

The imparting and acquisition of information is another important mechanism for change in groups. Sometimes it is not the information itself that is important as much as the sense of interest and caring transmitted with the information. At other times, however, the offer of a cognitive framework is very helpful, particularly to individuals in transitional self-help groups who experience themselves as confused and unprepared for the transition. By understanding their experience, the members gain mastery and control over the experience. In any case, it is important that information is shared in a way that takes into account the affective as well as cognitive needs of group members.

Another aspect of self-help methodology, altruism, is intrinsic to all forms of helping, but finds a special role in the self-help group. There is a therapeutic strength in groups as members share in helping each other. The helper finds that it is possible to give to another, and the helpee receives support and information. Riessman (1965) coined the term, *helper therapy principle*. The principle simply states that those who help are helped most. Cressey (1965), in working with incarcerated men, noted the same phenomenon which he called "retroflexive reformation." It requires the helpee to perform helper roles and gain experience in the desired role. The helper in this altruistic process receives substantial gains. The helper feels and is less dependent. The helper moves from a helpless state to a helpful one. The process permits the helper to get distance from the problem. By focusing on the same problem in someone else, the helper is able to be more objective and dispassionate. The process of helping gives the helper a sense of purpose and a feeling of usefulness. The helper's sense of self is reinforced as being okay. Through aiding another, the helper is directed from focusing internally on the helper's own problem. As the helper persuades others, the message is internally persuasive.

Face-to-face interactions characterize the self-help methodology. The face-to-face interactions of self-help groups, peer counseling, and support systems are social situations, and opportunity exists within them for the members to develop socializing techniques. For the alcoholic or the drug addict, it involves learning how to interact when not under the influence; for the person recovering from acute illness, or radical surgery, or transition, it is learning how to relate to others now that "everything" is different. Groups and counseling interaction provide the opportunity and safety to try out new behavior; they provide the norms and mechanisms to "be" in a new way. It is this mechanism of change which most enables the individual to hold on to gained ground outside the support relationship. Yalom notes the social skill gains of members of group therapy, "They are attuned to process, they have learned how to be helpfully responsive to others, they have acquired methods of conflict resolution, they are less prone to judgmentalism and more capable of experiencing and expressing accurate empathy" (1975, p. 16).

Imitation is another mechanism of change. Just as children learn first by imitating, the person undergoing change is, at first, much like a child. Imitative behavior and modeling are active aspects of the change process in therapy and in self-help groups. The role of the old-timers in self-help groups is a venerable one. They are the models of "methods for coping with stress and changing behavior" (Levy, 1979, p. 249). The dynamics which function to encourage and reinforce change in the helper therapy principle are also at work here. The individual who imitates is trying on the demeanor and attitudes of another. In consort with other elements of change, the person begins to feel natural in the new model.

An emphasis on interpersonal learning is another key component of self-help methodology. The member, having first sought to reduce some form of pain, turns attention to improving relatedness, the learning of communication, warmth, and love. Within many self-help groups, membership tends to be ongoing and intense. In this climate, there is opportunity to learn about oneself and others. There are considerable mechanisms for feedback and movement toward greater intimacy.

Group cohesion is among the most important elements of change in groups. Yalom defines cohesiveness as "the resultant of all the forces acting on all members to remain in the group" (1975, p. 46). Tuckman (1965) notes the development of group cohesion as one of the four essential stages of development occurring in social/emotional groups. Among communal groups such as the Bruderhof, unity is considered the highest value of life. It serves to intensify collective behavior, provides a base for consensus, and maintains group procedures and norms. Therapeutic communities encourage both group solidarity and high levels of member autonomy.

Lieberman (1979) discusses the self-help group's ability to develop a sense of belonging and group cohesion among members. This is accomplished through a shared sense of similar suffering, and a shared sense of deviance. The groups develop aspects of primary groups, becoming family-like and developing their own norms, rules, and traditions. Yalom considers group cohesiveness a "necessary precondition for effective therapy" (1975, p. 47). Yalom notes Roger's assessment of the importance of group cohesiveness, "member-member acceptance and understanding may carry with it a greater power and meaning than acceptance by a therapist" (1975, p. 55). This is certainly the case in leaderless groups and self-help groups in which the leader plays a minimal background role.

A vital curative process in counseling, group therapy, and self-help groups is catharsis. The emotional release of the very painful and the very private is an essential part of personal and emotional growth. The cathartic experience is most often connected with a confession-like experience. Antze concludes that "self-help groups achieve their results through a relatively simple cluster of social-psychological processes, most notably confession, catharsis, mutual identification and the removal of stigmatized feelings" (1976). Lieberman includes catharsis as a primary element of the self-help groups' processes. "It appears as if what unifies all types of helping groups results from the simple procedure of individuals joining a group of fellow sufferers in high states of personal need, with a requirement that some aspects of their painful affliction be shared in public" (1979, p. 232).

Wrestling with existential issues is a common curative factor in groups and counseling. In the self-help groups they are especially pronounced. "Joining a mutual support group involves varying degrees of public affirmation of an aspect of oneself which is generally stigmatized or at best ignored" (Spiegel, 1976, p. 151). The nature of stigma raises a multitude of varied existential issues which the person must address: the meaning of life, the individual's fate, the status of being alone. The singular step of becoming involved in the change process is one of existential recognition and taking action. Spiegel notes, "By asserting that he has a particular stigmatized or unacceptable attribute, the group member is saying, 'Okay, I am such and such, but see me as a whole person who has rights'.... The act...becomes an act of self-assertion and self-respect" (1976, p. 139).

Lifton articulates one of the major factors affecting the success of support groups of veterans, calling it "self-generation, the need on the part of those seeking help, change, or insight of any kind, to initiate their own process and conduct it largely on their own terms so that, even when calling in others with expert knowlege, they retain major responsibility for the shape and direction of the enterprise" (1973, p. 77). Gartner and Riessman (1977) discuss this aspect of self-help groups calling it "consumer intensivity." Consumer intensivity occurs when the consumer is both deliverer and receiver of a service.

Each of these factors is powerful in contributing to the growth of the individual. They function, however, in consort with each other geometrically increasing the overall impact upon the group member. Together they form a methodology that is unique as an educational approach.

Resources and Organizational Structure

The methods described above clearly are quite distinct from those found in other educational approaches. Just as distinct are the kind of resources needed and the organizational framework employed.

Resources used within self-help groups are largely nonmaterial. Help comes from within the individual or from other members. Material help usually manifests itself in the form of helping members utilize the generic resources within the community, or at best, providing emergency, neighborly concern.

Similarly, the organization is the antithesis of the bureaucracy common to many educational approaches. The group is small, face-to-face, quite personal, and for the most part, organized horizontally rather than vertically. Leaders tend to be chosen because of demonstrated competence (e.g., conquering alcoholism) and tend to create a structure that leads to empowerment rather than control.

Summary

The self-help group is as pure a nonformal education approach as one can find widely practiced in many settings. As such, it provides a great deal of potentially valuable information to practitioners in other out-of-school settings. A number of variables have been discussed here; one variable, methodology, has been examined in great depth. It is in the intuitive use of the therapeutic and personal change strategies by individual and group counselors that self-help approaches are most unique.

Persistent Themes

Clearly, an educational approach, as distinct from schooling as it is usually practiced, has behind it some very different assumptions about the nature of learners, about how people learn, and about how groups and societies change. Clues to these assumptions can be found by investigating the persistent themes or concerns that are evident in discussions about self-help. Further illumination comes from taking some of the major characteristics described above, for instance, methodology or objectives, and exploring the underlying beliefs behind these practices. This exploration is a final step in describing the self-help phenomenon and in allowing the reader to understand, in depth, how it is similar and different from other out-of-school approaches.

Community vs. Alienation

When reviewing the literature of self-help, one is struck by the constant emphasis on building a sense of community as a central goal of the groups or as a resultant side effect. Nisbet defines community in terms which simultaneously define the nonprofessional support system. Community is "the product of people working together on problems, of autonomous and collective fulfillment of internal objectives, and of the experience of living under codes of authority which have been set in large degree by persons involved" (1971, p. xvi).

In opposition to this definition is what one generally recognizes in modern communities. The qualities of community to a great extent are gone.

> Family, local community, church, and the whole network of informal interpersonal relationships have ceased to play a determining role in our institutional systems of mutual aid, welfare, education, recreation, and economic production and distribution. Yet...we continue to expect them to perform adequately the implicit psychological or symbolic functions in the life of the individual. (Nisbet, 1971, p. 49.)

The family is the primary base of community. Yet, the family has extremely little natural interdependence in today's technologically advanced, "future shocked," and alienated world. When mankind looks beyond its families for community, it is struck by huge impersonal megalopolises, multinational corporations, and by urban and suburban sprawl. People are confronted with a seeming contradiction: increased closeness to the world through vastly improved transportation and communications systems and isolation from it. It is its vastness, its mechanization which overwhelms and isolates the individual.

The present dissolution and lack of community is the result of several hundred years of progress in industrialization, urbanization, and belief in individualism. In an effort to both improve the quality of life and to guarantee individual freedom, Western society has successfully eroded the personal sense of community. This pessimistic view of modern man's alienated situation and tendency toward irrational and damaging mass movements and nationalistic responses is evident on the front pages of today's newspapers. It is a possible response to the desire for personal belonging and empowerment. It is, however, not the only response; an alternative can be seen in the recent development of the nonprofessional support system. Emerging from several long-standing traditions, these new support systems offer substantial hope for avoiding nationalistic frenzy and war.

Individualism and Group Cohesion

One tradition of powerful influence is the ethic of individualism. Although it has had its cost in separating individuals from community, it has also fostered a practice of individuals helping other individuals to help themselves. In considering the historic antecendents of self-help groups, Hurvitz states that "Helping others and helping oneself is the American way" (1976). The tradition in this country of barn raisings, common grazing, and community volunteer fire departments is a strong one even if never experienced firsthand. The coming together of groups is so important in this culture that the Founding Fathers guaranteed it as a right in the First Amendment. De Tocqueville noted that "Americans of all ages, all conditions, and all dispositions constantly form associations." This tradition is of great importance in mitigating the sense of alienation and loss of community. It is a tradition clearly alive and expressing itself in the self-help movement.

Schmalenbach's (1965) consideration of the categories of communion provides an explanation of the seeming contradiction between the continued belief in individualism and the search for belonging and community. He distinguishes between community and communion. He states that community pre-exists, and out of its existence arise the emotions associated with it. Communion, on the other hand, exists as a result of the emotions of coming together. Schmalenbach explains that:

> Those social relations within a community that suggest communion are the ones preferred by people who are not, in fact, members of a community. Much of the present-day yearning for communal coherence assumes this character. Such yearning is usually less directed toward a specific community than toward coherence as such. (1965, p. 338.)

Thus, it is possible to reconcile both individualism (leaving one's home and family, going off on one's own, rejecting the limits of small town or church) and the desire for connectedness.

Empowerment

A final theme that is persistently encountered in the self-help literature is the theme of empowerment. Self-help by definition is personal empowerment; the focus on groups implies a power that transcends individual members. The self-help group, in its rejection of professional forms of helping, provides both the ideal setting and an effective methodology for empowering participants. As long as professional staffing is present in an educational approach, there is some dilution of the possiblity of full equality of learners and staff. The expert will most usually have more power than the apprentice and very rarely is full empowerment possible. In self-help groups, the power is quite literally in the group, and full empowerment of each member is the aim of the group.

Theoretical Assumptions

The Nature of Human Nature

The notion of self-help and the importance of community as well as the possibility of individual and group empowerment imply a very deep belief in human potential and human cooperation. It is no accident that both past and present theoreticians of the movement are strong exponents of this belief structure.

For instance, one of the earliest investigations of mutual aid (or self-help) was Petyr Kropotkin (1955). Kropotkin, a Russian anarchist, presented an opposing view of the nature of man to the prevailing Social Darwinist, "Law of the jungle" perspective of the survival of the fittest. Through an examination of animal behavior, anthropological data, and historical records, Kropotkin built a powerful case. He proposed that a trait of mutual aid and cooperation within species was as equally strong an evolutionary force as competition and aggression. The debate continues today. Leakey and Lewin (1979) argue that aggression and territoriality exist, but are biologically necessitated or environmentally triggered. Instead of believing that mankind was made up of violent aggressors, they propose that early mankind "would have been just the opposite, with a network of acknowledged kinship easing the contact between separate groups" (pp. 216-217). The extensive history of the hunter-gatherer society, they believe, required "extreme selective pressure in favor of our ability to cooperate as a group" (p. 223).

Another powerful tradition which has encouraged the development of self-help programs is found in the Judeo-Christian tradition. The belief in the power of caring for one another is powerfully ingrained. Central to most self-help groups is a tradition of public confession of one sort or another. The roots of this tradition can be traced to the practice of exomologesis in the primitive Judeo-Christian tradition.

The practice denoted by this term involved complete openness

> about one's life past and present to be followed by important personal changes with the support and encouragement of other members of the congregation, which was a little group. (Mowrer, 1975, p. 35.)

Out of this practice came a sense of fellowship and mutuality known as Koinonia. The experience and sense of community was very powerful, enabling the early Christian church to endure through more than 300 years of persecution. When the early church became formalized and accepted as the Church of Rome under Constantine, the confession gradually became closed and private — the experience of the confessional. The experience of group confession re-emerged in the Anabaptist movement which was condemned by the Roman Catholic Church. Its survivors today are known as the Amish, Hutterites, Mennonites, and Brethern and Moravians, all of which are successful intentional communities continuing this practice. Group confession and mutuality were central to Luther and other reform churches. Most directly connected to the self-help movement was Frank Buchman, a Lutheran minister, who founded the Oxford Group Movement. The Movement advocated group confession, an absolute value system and redressing of past sins. Two members of the Oxford Movement founded the organization Alcoholics Anonymous in 1939 (Hurvitz, 1974; Katz and Bender, 1976a, 1976b; Mowrer, 1975).

A more modern theoretician often referred to in the self-help movement is the psychologist Carl Rogers. Rogers believes that the drive toward fulfilling one's potential is innate in all humans.

> Biologists, neurophysiologists, and other scientists, including psychologists, have evidence that adds up to one conclusion. There is in every organism, at whatever level, an underlying flow of movement toward constructive fulfillment of its inherent possibilities. There is a natural tendency toward complete development in man. (1977, p. 7.)

It is also known that a multitude of environments, situations, and significant others work in opposition to this development. Rogers poses the question, "What psychological climate makes possible the release of the individual's capacity for understanding and managing his life?" The climatic conditions he presents are very familiar; they include "genuineness, realness—congruence. . .acceptance, or caring or prizing—unconditional positive regard. . .empathetic understanding" (1977, pp. 9-11). These conditions, in addition to their centrality in client-centered therapy, are usually present in self-help groups as well.

Thus, self-help as a concept is firmly anchored to that branch of philosophy that is accepting of human nature, that implies a more cooperative rather than aggressive nature and that puts a drive towards becoming or self-actualizing at the center of human nature. There is the potential in each person, no matter what their current condition, of reform, revitalization, and growth.

Assumptions about Learning

Clearly, the most important assumption that self-help groups make is that all members can learn. There are, however, some additional beliefs about how people learn implicit in self-help practice. These beliefs take quite consistent positions on whether people learn largely from external sources (Locke's *Tabula Rasa* Theory) or through an internal unfolding process, and whether people learn through organized, logical, segmented methods or through more holistic, body, mind, spirit approaches.

Clearly, a brief review of the methods described above demonstrate that the emphasis is on an internal developmental process. External events provide a rich and helpful environment, but key learning—the acquisition of hope, the carthartic experience, the struggle with existential meaning—are all essentially internal to the learner. Even those methods that are group focused (attaining group cohesion, interpersonal learning, participating in universal experiences) are conceived of as the collective unfolding of all individuals in the group, not the learning of the "truth" of one member from another.

The gestalt or holistic nature of that learning is equally apparent from a review of those methods. While cognitive learning is important (sharing information, understanding the issue), so too are powerful affective, and to some extent, physical experience (cartharsis, becoming one with a group, confronting one's existential aloneness; working together). The learning that occurs is hard to dissect into component parts; it is all of one piece, a heightened awareness, a sudden understanding and capacity to move on.

Assumptions about Social Change

In order to understand and more fully develop an understanding of self-help groups as vehicles for social change, one has to go back to the distinction made earlier in this essay between inner- and outer-focused groups. The majority of the examples used in this essay are inner-focused groups; their aim is to enable individual members to grow (to stop drinking, become employed, survive the death of a loved one, etc.). These groups are largely evolutionary in their approach to change as they do not challenge any of the basic norms of society. This emphasis is no doubt both an indication of the power of this approach when focused individually and a reflection of the more personalized concerns of the 1970's and 80's. In any case, social change is only a peripheral result.

There are, however, increasing indications that the self-help group can be used as a very powerful catalyst for social change. In this sense, they can be quite revolutionary in their effect on society. The women's movement is perhaps the best example of a social change movement built on small consciousness raising and support group foundations. Another example, the cooperative movement, is an older movement that is experiencing a renaissance of popularity. Other human rights groups (handicapped, retarded, senior citizens, gay rights) have used the social potential of a network of self-help groups concerned with similar issues.

Though self-help as a social change mechanism is less practiced than as a personal growth phenomenon, nonetheless it has demonstrated some effectiveness and is interesting in its radical departure from other social change mechanisms, particularly in North America. It is, for instance, entirely a bottom-up mechanism, change comes not from the federal government, big business, national foundations, large universities, but from many small, nonprofessional groups interested in improving their own lives. Women in innumerable settings explore and help each other to change their status as women in their societies, and over time social roles and norms change in very profound ways.

The approach is also significant in the degree to which it molds individualistic and collective change strategies. Normally, these two approaches are seen as mutually exclusive. Capitalist strategies stress individual choice and growth as do most formal school educational approaches; socialist approaches stress the growth and change of the collective. What is unique in the self-help approach is its blend of intense emphasis on both individual progress and group cohesiveness and solidarity. Change is seen as a complex intertwining of both facets, neither more desirable than the other; no one really possible without the other.

Summary of Themes and Theory Bases

The themes that occur so frequently in the self-help context—community versus alienation, personal and collective growth and empowerment—provide very direct indications of the assumptions underlying this educational approach. There is a strong belief in human potential and an equally strong belief that individual human potential is not in basic conflict with the collective good. Learning, which is a universal phenomenon, consists of a holistic, individual and collective unfolding in the context of a rich and demanding environment. Frequently, the learning, or personal growth, is an end in itself. Other times it has the potential of causing radical changes in society through the collective effect of intense individual growth. As such, it is a pervasive change, emanating from a wide base of support, and very difficult to reverse.

Self-Help: A Warning and a Potential

Amidst the acclaim given to the nonprofessional helping system are valid concerns over the processes involved in programs and in the professional and community response. Perhaps the greatest danger is the focus on ideology and/or a charisma among many self-help organizations. The worst scenario has already become reality in the People's Temple mass suicide under the deranged leadership of charismatic Jim Jones. There is clearly a potential danger involved in the leadership of such organizations and in the member's surrender to the group and its ideological base. The professional community and society need to be watchful of such groups, but need also to remember the power of ideology as a healing force and successes and responsible nature of many groups.

One is struck by the similarity between some self-help group processes and our conceptualization of mind control or brainwashing. In his book *Thought Control and the Psychology of Totalism* (1961), Lifton researched the processes and impact of this control among people who had experienced it in China. He enumerates the criteria of thought reform as follows:

- Individual communication, both external and internal, is controlled through a milieu group.
- There is a mystical manipulation of the individual by the milieu.
- There is a demand for absolute purity which creates a guilty or shaming milieu.
- There is a focus on personal confession.
- There is commitment to the ideological way.
- Language is controlled through reductionist thinking and use of "thought terminating cliche." The most far-reaching and complex human problems are compressed into brief, highly reductive definitive-sound phrases easily memorized and easily expressed.
- The ideology takes precedence over the individual and his experience.
- The group milieu and leaders have the power of dispensing or not dispensing with the continued existence of the member.

This cluster of criteria, as a whole, is applicable to a very few intentional communities or self-help groups. Elements of thought control are involved in all forms of personal change. The distinctions of totalism, of control over life and death, should be our major concern. One disaster is enough. It is important to be able to distinguish between the benefits of the processes of personal change and the dangers when those processes are misused. This caution points to the importance of opening communication between professionals and self-help groups.

Lifton contrasts open personal change to thought reform. Although there is a degree of similarity, the differences are obvious. He sees it as a three-step process of confrontation, reordering, and renewal. Confrontation is the combination of both inner impulse and outer challenge to change. Reordering includes an emptying process of some type of confession and exploration of existential issues and an absorption process of new ideas and emotions. Renewal he defines as "the new sense of fit between personal emotions and personally held ideas about the world. . . a new interplay between identity and ideology in which both have been changed" (1961, p. 464).

Another danger of the emergence of self-help is the possibility that needy individuals will seek ineffective self-help instead of available and effective professional care (Gartner and Riessman, 1977). Social service decision making concerning the types of services to be made available may be based on cost rather than effectiveness (Gartner and Riessman, 1977). The existence of self-help programs may be used as rationale for not providing professional community services (Gartner and Riessman, 1977; Henry, 1976; Sidel and Sidel, 1976). Because the groups are informal, they may participate in exclusionary practices which would be unchallenged (Henry, 1978).

A final caution is that the self-help programs may lead to greater inequality in the delivery of services with the poor receiving self-help care, while the rich receive professional care, regardless of which modality is more appropriate (Gartner and Riessman, 1977; Sidel and Sidel, 1976).

The cautions and dangers, however, must be contrasted with the demonstrated protential of self-help as an educational approach worldwide. It has the possibility of becoming a paradigm for change in educational thinking, particularly when one considers the needs of the out-of-school, disadvantaged learner or of the developing world. The fact that professional staffing and a high degree of capital outlay are not necessary factors for success is a major advantage. So too is the emphasis on the solution of immediate and pressing problems, and the potential for simultaneous individual and collective development. While self-help is in no way a substitute for formal schooling (it will never produce physicists, mathematicians, and engineers), it is a self-, and increasingly collective, approach to many of the out-of-school learning needs of a wide range of learners.

Suggested Resources
Self-Help Groups

Bibliography

Antze, P., The role of ideologies in peer psychotherapy organizations: Some theoretical considerations and three case studies. *Journal of Applied Behavioral Sciences.* 1976, 323-346.

Bond, G.R., and Reibstein, J., Changing goals in women's consciousness raising. T.M. Lieberman and L. Borman (Eds.), *Self-help groups for coping with crisis.* San Francisco, CA: Jossey-Bass Publishers, 1979.

Brown, W., *Student-to-school counseling.* Austin: University of Texas Press, 1972.

Caplan, G., *Support systems and commuity mental health: Lectures on concept development.* New York: Behavioral Publications, 1974.

Caplan, G., and Killilea, M., *Support systems and mutual help: Multidisciplinary approaches.* New York: Grune and Stratton, 1976.

Cressey, D.R., Social psychological foundations for using criminals in the rehabilitation of criminals. *Journal of Research on Crime and Delinquency,* 1965, 49-59.

Dewar, T.R., The professionalization of the client. *Social Policy,* 1978, 8, 4-9.

Gartner, A., Self-help and mental health. *Social Policy,* September 1976, 7, 28-33.

Gartner, A., and Riessman, F., *Self-help in the human services.* San Francisco, CA: Jossey-Bass Publishers, 1977.

Henry, S., Dangers of self-help groups. *New Society,* 1976, 44, 654-656.

Hurvitz, N., The origin of the peer self-help psychotherapy group movement. *Journal of Applied Behavioral Sciences,* 1976, 12, 283-94.

Kanter, R.M., *Commitment and community.* Cambridge: Harvard University Press, 1972.

Katz, A.H., and Bender, E.T., Self-help groups in Western society: History and prospects.*Journal of Applied Behavioral Sciences,* 1976, 12, 256-82.

Katz, A.H., and Bender, E.T., *The strength in us: Self-help groups in the modern world.* New York: New Viewpoints, 1976.

Kinshenbaum, H., and Glaser, B., *Developing support groups.* La Jolla, CA: University Associates, 1978.

Kropotkin, P., *Mutual Aid.* Boston: Extending Horizons Books, 1955. (Originally published, 1914.)

Leakey, R.E., and Lewin, R., *Origins.* New York: E.P. Dutton, 1979.

Levy, L.H., Processes and activities in groups. In M.A. Lieberman and L.D. Borman (Eds.). *Self-help groups for coping with crisis.* San Francisco, CA: Jossey-Bass Publishers, 1979.

Lieberman, M.A., Analyzing change mechanisms in groups. In M.A. Lieberman and L.D. Borman (Eds.). *Self-help groups for coping with crisis.* San Francisco: Jossey-Bass Publishers, 1979.

Lieberman, M.A., and Bond, G.R., Self-help groups—problems of measuring outcomes. *Small group behavior,* 1978, *9,* 221-241.

Lieberman, M.A., and Borman, L.D., *Self-help groups for coping with crisis.* San Francisco, CA: Jossey-Bass Publishers, 1979.

Lifton, R.J. *Thought reform and the psychology of totalism.* New York: Norton, 1961.

Mowrer, O.H., Small groups movement in historical perspective. In L.D. Borman (Ed.). *Explorations in self-help and mutual aid.* Evanston, IL: Center for Urban Affairs at Northwestern University, 1975.

National Training Laboratory Institute. Self-help. *Journal of Applied Behavioral Sciences,* 1976, *12.*

Nisbet, R.A., *Quest for community.* London: Oxford University Press, 1971. (Originally published, 1953).

Riessman, F., The helper-therapy principle. *Social Work,* 1965, *10,* 27-32.

Riessman, F., How does self-help work? *Social Policy,* 1976, *7,* 41-45.

Rogers, C., *On personal power.* New York: Delacorte Press, 1977.

Sagarin, E., *Odd man in.* New York: Quadrangle Books, 1969.

Sarason, S.B., *The pscyhological sense of community: Prospects for a community pscychology.* San Francisco, CA: Jossey-Bass Publishers, 1977.

Schmalenbach, H., The sociological category of communion. In T. Parsons (Ed.). *Theories of society.* New York: Free Press, 1965.

Sidel, V.W., and Sidel, R., Beyond coping. *Social Policy,* 1976, *2,* 67-9.

Smith, D.H. and Macauley, J., *Participation in social and political activities.* San Francisco, CA: Jossey-Bass Publishers, 1980.

Spiegel, D., Going public and self-help. In G. Caplan and M. Killilea (Eds.). *Support systems and mutual help: Multidisciplinary approaches.* New York: Greene and Stratton, 1976.

Steinman, R., and Traunstein, D.M., Redefining deviance: The self-help challenge to the human services. *Journal of Applied Behavioral Sciences,* 1976, *12,* 347-361.

Stephens, S., *Death comes home.* New York: Moorehouse-Bailow, 1972.

Tracy, S., and Gussow, Z., Self-help health groups: A grassroots response to a need for service. *Journal of Applied Behavioral Sciences,* 1976, *12,* 381-396.

Tuckman, B., Developmental sequence in small groups. *Psychological Bulletin,* 1965, *63,* 384-399.

Wilson, S., *Informal groups: An introduction.* Englewood Cliffs, NJ: Prentice-Hall Inc., 1978.

Yalom, I.D., *The theory and practice of group psychotherapy* (2nd ed.). New York: Basic Books, 1975.

Zablocki, B., *The joyful community*. Baltimore: Penguin Books, Inc., 1971.

Journals

Community Mental Health Journal
Journal of Applied Behavioral Sciences
Personnel and Guidance Journal
Social Policy
Social Work

Resource Centers

National Self-Help Clearinghouse
184 5th Avenue
New York, New York 10010
See Directory of self-help groups. In A. Gartner and F. Riessman, *Self-help in the human services*. San Francisco, CA: Jossey-Bass Publishers, 1977, for an extensive listing of self-help groups and national office addresses.

11
MUSEUM
EDUCATION

Judithe D. Speidel and
Sue E. Sturtevant

As museums search for ways to ensure a "usable future" and appeal to new audiences, they are placing increasing emphasis on their educational role. While realizing that the most effective long-term method of interesting the public is probably through the schools, museum educators are also actively seeking relationships with their local communities and developing programs for special populations such as the physically handicapped, the economically disadvantaged, and the elderly. Consequently, the traditional image of museums as self-perpetuating, elitist institutions designed to preserve treasures donated by the affluent and to serve the requirements of scholars is undergoing a transformation.

Opinions differ as to how, where, and in what proportion a museum's efforts should be directed to education, but programs in a variety of museums reflect a new sensitivity to the responses of visitors. In many instances, museums have augmented their usual lectures and guided tours with participatory and sensory experiences and have shifted from a stress on communicating factual information to providing more personal encounters with objects in their collections. Evaluations of these new efforts indicate that a corresponding change is taking place in the attitude of visitors, who are beginning to view museums as less intimidating and more enjoyable.

Definition of Museum Education

In the broadest sense all museums are educational. Just the existence of a collection of artifacts itself will encourage learning. However, as is true with other approaches, museum education can be found to be formal, informal, or nonformal in its delivery. Many museums offer school-like programs for children. On the other hand, some museums concentrate on displaying collections with almost no interpretations available. Such education as occurs is almost completely up to the viewer. In addition there are many nonformal programs where the museum intentionally interprets the collection to the viewer using a wide variety of nonformal educational techniques. While all three approaches can be defined as museum education, it is the latter that is more the focus of this essay.

What constitutes museum education varies in kind and quality with the type and location of the museum, financial resources available, size of collection, attitudes of trustees, director, and curators. Thus, any generalizations about characteristics and trends must be offered with reservations.

Insofar as a relationship with formal schooling is concerned, some museums take a passive stance. These museums offer free admission for groups of students when accompanied by their teachers, and the services of a docent to direct attention to exhibits that have been preselected for the occasion, but little more than these encouragements are offered. At the other end of the scale is cooperative involvement with the schools. Museums in this category make vigorous efforts not only to send staff members and even sample artifacts into classrooms to interest students in what the museum contains, but they also provide courses and workshops to inform teachers about the collections and ways to use them in their classes. These museums produce curriculum kits, permit their slides to be borrowed, generate background information on items in the regular collection, and circulate announcements of special exhibitions.

Other types of schooling that take place within large museums include professional training in studio art, painting workshops for adults and children, nature study classes, and internships in museum work for college students. Also, many universities and colleges maintain their own small museums and galleries which are used for instruction in art history and in the natural sciences.

As for educational efforts directed toward the nonschool population, in the broad sense, museums, by their very nature, function educationally whether or not they have formal programs. In the past, the assumption was that museum visitors could educate themselves by browsing through the objects on display (usually arranged chronologically in crowded glass-covered cases), making their own choices of which yellowing explanatory labels to read for information. But today we are increasingly aware of how sophisticated the techniques are for supplementing the act of viewing a painting or an object, how skillfully the visitor's attention and response are manipulated. Devices like slide lectures, tours by tape recorder, sale of reproductions and gift items, isolating objects in dramatically lighted display cases, the block-buster exhibition, all these modern developments have permitted expansion of the educational activities of museums. A current subject of debate is whether or not they have served to enhance or overwhelm the actual exhibits themselves.

A Brief History

Ever since their inception, museums have acquired, cared for, and displayed objects judged to be of lasting interest or value. However, their educational rewards were generally reserved for the scholar or connoisseur. In the seventeenth and eighteenth centuries, European museums and galleries were privately owned, their collections gathered from royal palaces, military plunder, or bequests from wealthy donors. Often run by autocrats who asked for no one's advice, they admitted visitors as a privilege not a right.

In America, on the other hand, the idea of a public museum established for the benefit of a whole community came before the formation of the great private collections. The first museum in this country, for example, was begun in 1773 by group efforts of the Charleston Library Society, which solicited the cooperation of local gentlemen farmers in putting together a natural history collection (Hudson, 1975). Charles Willson Peale's museum in Philadelphia, which opened in 1782, was an individual effort, but was planned expressly "to please and entertain the public." Visitors could buy a season ticket for a nominal fee. Originally intended to display the portraits of Revolutionary War heroes painted by Peale, the collection was soon expanded into a heterogeneous repository for "Natural Curiosities" and "Wonderful Works of Nature," including a number of oddities such as a mastodon's bones and a four-legged chicken. Although animal specimens were arranged according to species and an attempt was made to simulate habitats through the use of painted backgrounds, artificial grottos, and re-flecting mirrors to suggest water, the primary attraction for the public was probably the satisfaction of curiosity rather than the desire to be educated. Nonetheless, both the Charleston and Peale museums were culturally sig-nificant as reflections of the growing consciousness of America as a unique country, with distinctive animal and plant species, and as a national identity with its own important history.

In the nineteenth century, American museums developed in two directions—one in the popular tradition of Peale's museum, the other in the elitist tradition. The Old Boston Museum and Gallery of Fine Arts, which opened in 1841 and flourished for fifty years, was typical of the popular style. Primarily housing a collection of paintings as well as curiosities, it also offered "platform entertainments" that evolved into vaudeville shows. This trend toward entertainment and showmanship in museums reached a peak under the entrepreneurship of Phineas T. Barnum (once favored for the directorship of a proposed national museum), but has had a resurgence in the late twentieth century.

Parallel to the growth of museums devoted to pleasure was the establishment of European style institutions designed to preserve collections of the fine and decorative arts, ethnographic material, and natural history specimens. In addition to the factors that motivated financeers like Henry Clay Frick, J.P. Morgan, and Andrew Mellon (the "proud possessors") to compete with each other in cultivated acquisitiveness, the impetus for establishing our major museums came from a series of industrial exhibitions and world fairs. These occasions made clear that not only could museums be assets to a community, but that there were potential benefits from linking museums to industry. Just how effective this sort of linkage turned out to be was amply demonstrated in the next century when an industrial participation plan was instigated at the Chicago Science Museum (Danilov, 1979). This plan, which has become a model for many other science museums (it also inspired the founder of Disneyland), provided continual sponsorship for new exhibits and placed the museum in a position to promote technological advancement through its educational endeavors.

By the beginning of the twentieth century, increased state and federal support for museums reinforced endowments from private benefactors. As a result, museums acquired considerable social power. Although they saw themselves as providing opportunities for the public to achieve self-improvement and aesthetic refinement, their sense of educational mission was most often subordinated to their functions as preservers of our cultural heritage.

For affluent citizens, museums tended to be sites more often visited for social reasons than for uplift. Motivated individuals of whatever socio-economic group always found their own enrichment in museums, of course, but for a large segment of the ordinary population museums had no connection with everyday life. To these people, regardless of pronouncements about serving the needs of the public, museums were awesome, or even foreboding temple-like edifices, guarded by marble columns and daunting flights of granite stairs.

The monolithic institutions have retained their power during the twentieth century, although recent years have seen the emergence of smaller, more specialized museums. The whole notion of what constitutes a museum has been expanded to include new developments like restored villages, environmental centers, and recreated seaports. A movement to redefine the role of museums in terms of social mission, desired type of audience, and the nature of service to be rendered emerged during the Depression. It was the social upheaval of the late sixties, however, that brought the strongest challenge to the idea of museums as custodians of high culture. The ensuing crisis (as it has been called) in the museum world provoked heated debates. Conservatives argue that the increasing attempts to allure the widest possible public are debasing works of art, setting up barriers between the visitor and firsthand encounters with paintings and objects, and are drastically transforming museums into places hostile to scholarship. Against this criticism is the argument that the increase in attendance is a sign that museums now have a responsibility to a new kind of audience, one much more diversified than in the past. And since museums have obligations to the present as well as the past, they should respond to current social movements by directing their attention to meeting the needs and interests of special populations such as minorities, the handicapped, and the elderly within their local communities.

Perhaps the answer lies in a compromise between the requirements of scholarship and the pressure to serve the public at large. As Germain Bazin has predicted in *The Museum Age* (1967), the future will probably see a proliferation of small-scale museums that are a pleasure not an ordeal to visit. On the other hand, the large institutions with their vast holdings will function like research libraries do today—available for scholars who wish access to whole collections but not for the casual browser.

Sources for Change

Given their generally acknowledged role as preservers of culture, it is hardly surprising that museums have not been in the forefront of social change. But neither have they remained static and unresponsive to pressures for change. As the numbers and types of visitors have increased, museums have taken steps to formalize their educational mission and to improve the status of their education departments in relation to the curatorial side. Changes are not always initiated within the museum itself, though, because many boards of trustees are still chosen in the traditional way (i.e., on the basis of patronage), and their directors come from the academic or business establishments. An instance of how people from outside the museum world can bring pressure to bear occurred when a group of directors of New York State museums met in 1969 to discuss the development of neighborhood museums as branches of large national ones. To the organizers' surprise, this seminar grew into a gathering of several hundred participants from nineteen states, most of whom came because they were concerned about racism as it relates to the function of museums. At issue was the relevance of museums for neighborhoods burdened with poverty, unemployment, poor housing, and a widening gap between social classes. Whether or not the communities needed or even wanted museums was one of the questions debated at this meeting, along with contentions about community control and the relevance of Western European art to the interests of Blacks and Hispanics of African and Caribbean origins (Harvery and Friedberg, 1971).

Repercussions from this meeting have been evident in later attempts to create connections between museums and their communities, such as the establishment of cultural centers that house collections of African art and the work of local Black artists, as well as demonstration projects like the Culture Voucher Program in New York City. This program which was funded for three years was intended to raise public awareness of the benefits to be gained from services offered by museums, and at the same time, reward institutions for devising programs that were especially responsive to community needs (Culture Voucher Program, 1977). Some other museums have virtually turned themselves into community centers by sponsoring a series of festivals or science fairs.

The creation of facilities to accommodate special needs is a further indication that museums have kept in step with social changes. The National Air and Space Museum, for example, is just one of the hundreds of museums that have remodeled their buildings to permit easier access by handicapped persons and have refashioned their means of conveying information. In his preface to a manual containing guidelines for museums to follow, Michael Collins, Director of the Space Museum, reflects a new attitude toward the kind of visitor who has seldom been able to go to a museum. He writes: "We have met the handicapped and he is us. When we begin to acknowledge this truth—that it is only a matter of degree—we will surely improve the quality of life for all of us" (1977).

In some cases, educational programs that were initially planned for the handicapped visitor such as the tactile gallery for the blind at the Wadsworth Atheneum, Hartford, have proved to be successful with all types of museum goers (Calhoun, 1974). They offer aesthetic experiences and direct contact with objects in a manner not usually possible in a museum setting.

These successes with exhibits that are independent of verbal explanations and offer opportunities for active participation have indicated to museums some additional ways in which they can be involved in social change on a worldwide basis. UNESCO and the International Council of Museums have supported innovative approaches to adult education in developing countries through the use of nonverbal displays of cultural artifacts (Zetterberg, 1969).

Learning Theory

What is the difference between the kind of learning that takes place in a museum and that which occurs in a classroom? Aside from the innovative approaches referred to above—permitting objects to be handled, exhibits that instruct without relying on verbal explanations—most museum techniques of instruction are similar to those employed in schools. Yet museum directors and their staffs agree that museums should not compete as educational institutions with schools, colleges, and libraries. They must recognize their special function as havens of the varied and differentiated where both the intellect and the emotions work together to produce an influential experience that is possible in no other setting.

In the case of art museums, critics have maintained that they are still serving primarily as places where art is embalmed, a subject of worship removed from its purpose of reflecting and responding to life, whereas it should be presented as an activity to be engaged in. The so-called aesthetic experience, consequently, is not engagement with artists' works so much as with their reputations. Still other commentators have observed that the problem may be that art itself has evolved to the point where effective display of it is no longer physically or conceptually possible. Thus, educational outcomes have become increasingly tied to reproductions or translations rather than the real thing (O'Doherty, 1972; Van der Haag, 1971).

Despite these negative views of the kind of learning museums provide, the majority opinion appears to support the trend toward the hands-on, "please touch" type of museum display as the most effective learning device. Participatory museums, especially those for children, and industrial and scientific collections are the fastest growing types of museum. Because of the fragility and value of their objects, many museums, naturally, cannot allow visitors to handle or even get close to the displays. In these museums, educators are turning to various kinds of participatory games to encourage involvement with what is exhibited. That museum educators, like their counterparts in the schools, have become aware of developmental and learning theories is evident in professional publications like the American Association of Museum's *Museum News* and the American Association for State and Local History's *History News*. These publications are full of recommendations for how to adjust techniques of instruction to the characteristics of learners and how to organize presentations for maximum assimilation and retention.

With the growing interest in teaching history through material culture, historic houses have assumed new importance for their educational potential. These houses, together with reconstructed villages and factory complexes, can give visitors a sense of continuity with the past that is more intensely felt than impressions gained from reading historical texts. The danger is, as Thomas Schlereth has pointed out, that historical museums interpret our past only through the eyes of a certain segment of the population. Also, reconstructions at best can be only interpretations, subject to distortions according to current tastes (Schlereth, 1978).

Apparent to most museum educators and the teachers who collaborate with them is the continuing need for research into what effects museums have on visitors. So far we have no substantial evidence as to just how museums educate. Displays are seldom tested for effectiveness, objectives are rarely defined, nor are visitors systematically consulted for their reactions. In recent years, museums have been trying to determine the character of their audience so that exhibits and programs will have the desired impact (for instance, give an ethnic group a sense of pride in their cultural heritage or stimulate a disadvantaged child to try painting). During the course of these efforts, they have looked to sociological survey methods as a means of identifying visitor expectations. Results have indicated that visitors of all ages and backgrounds want to be presented with something of personal interest in a way in which they can participate in and relate to their previous experiences.

Hays' (1967) investigation into methods for improving the use that schools make of museums prompted an HEW-sponsored study; since then, various models, including ones based on the computer, have been proposed for evaluating exhibits, teaching techniques, and visitor responses. Concurring in the dissatisfaction with controlled experimental models for research studies that many educators and social scientists have been expressing lately, museums are turning to naturalistic evaluation methods— observations of behavior, interviews, and nonobtrusive measurements like worn spots on carpets (Wolf and Tymitz, 1978). Through these interpretive means, they hope to find answers to questions about what changes in attitudes occur after a museum visit, whether a visit improves receptivity to learning an academic subject matter, and whether what visitors experience carries over into other learning situations.

The Museum and Community Education:
The Example of the Maine Maritime Museum

The subject of the following case study has been selected because it typifies (insofar as anything complex and diversified can be represented by a single example) museum education in both its traditional and innovative aspects.

The Maine Maritime Mueum reflects 375 years of shipbuilding along the banks of the Kennebec River in Bath, Maine. There are five waterfront, city-wide sites connected, in season, by a roundtrip passage aboard the *M/V Sasanoa*. Free second-day admission is provided through a validated ticket for 30,000 annual visitors. Most tours begin at the Sewall House, an 1844 mansion now housing fine art and folk art forms. Many of the museum's 15,000 artifacts are displayed interpretively by way of dioramas, labels with provocative questions, instructions to try-your-hand at marine crafts, or stories about the lives of sea captains and their families. Signs in the Children's Room ask that small visitors please touch the ship wheel, bell, tackle and pulley; other unique features include a gangplank entrance, very low ceiling, and eyepieces through which to view the interior of a modern destroyer.

The second stop along the museum route is at the Winter Street Center. Once a well-attended church, it is now used as a working site for the museum staff to prepare new exhibits and programs. Half the space is reserved for displaying ship models, historical photographs and regional maritime artifacts. The building belongs to the Maritime Museum, but is also used extensively by other community groups.

The three remaining sites are concerned with actual boatbuilding. Percy and Small Shipyard is the only surviving shipyard in America to have built large wooden sailing ships. Here space is leased to various individuals who work on special restoration projects: *Seguin*, the oldest U.S. registered wooden steam tug, has her restoration and heavy-hull trainee program open for public inspection.

Nationally recognized educational opportunities in small craft skills are available at the Apprenticeshop where men and women build and repair boats to sell. The emphasis is on learning the old handcraft and teaching it to others. Three miles away, at the Restorationshop, students replicate traditional designs of workboats as they prepare to be both woodworkers and museum trainees. Along with a large, open workspace, there is a whole floor for displaying old boats of classic design. These boats are left in the condition in which they were found with planks missing and sprung, hollow thwarts and peeling paint. Alongside the original craft is a contemporary example built in the shop.

The Maine Maritime Museum has grown with its success in the ten years since it was founded. Each site has been an expansion in response to a special need in the community. Besides an audience of transient summer tourists, the museum had to take into account the concerns of the people in

Bath. As a result, it now offers three night boatbuilding sessions a year, half-model lessons for elementary and high school students, a sail training program which stresses the importance of power by sail, and various seminars in local maritime history. The high school program believes that the right age to apprentice is fourteen through sixteen; some eighty students have taken classes in drafting, modeling, fishing, sailing and building small craft to use in the waters of the Kennebec River. An outgrowth of the museum's formal role as educator has been an annual three-day symposium where maritime scholars meet to deliver papers on museological problems of artifact restoration and storage, preservation, and maintenance.

This institution is not without the problems that most museums have to face today. There is an ongoing search for new members and new sources of funding, as well as for ways to entice first-time visitors. At present, no studies have been done on the types of visitors, their motivation for coming, and their evaluation of the visit. The winter months are very slow for the Sewall House when attendance drops severely; on the other hand, it is the most productive season for the boatbuilders. Other areas which need strengthening are staff to deal with the elementary school tours and handicapped visitors.

The additions and changes that have been made in the museum's functions have developed naturally from a combination of creative leadership and the willingness to take chances with new ideas. Masterbuilders at the Apprenticeshop and Restorationshop learn from novices as well as the other way around. Each site affiliated with the Maritime Museum is complementary to the others. The director of the Sewall House and the directors of the boatbuilding yards collaborate on themes, goals, and cooperative projects. Because the museum has such distinct programs, its educational theories emphasize several modes of learning and social change.

The three living museum programs see each intern, apprentice, or volunteer as the important component of change. The personal growth of each individual takes precedence over the growth of knowledge concerning objects. However, as each person's life is shaped by hands-on learning, so too is the entire group of workers molded and formed by the experience. And out of that communal effort, comes change for the future of the entire museum organization. The individual's learning experience is powerful enough to influence the structure of the institution.

The two more traditional centers of the museum emphasize learning from viewing objects rather than by the process of making them. However, they must accommodate thousands of learners instead of the sixteen participants in the other in-depth programs. Even so, they are initiating more dramatic ways to affect the casual learner. The riverboat rides, for instance, set a nautical tone which makes many visitors more receptive to learning maritime history.

The general learning theory which the entire Maine Maritime Museum espouses combines conventional academic devices—classes, lectures, guided tours, and written resources—with the kind of longer-term education which comes from thinking with one's hands. The staff believe museums do a good job of preserving artifacts of past generations, but there is also the need to preserve the skills that went into making and using those artifacts.

Lance Lee, director and founder of the Apprenticeshop, wants people to serve and support a group effort while achieving something of excellence. He strongly believes that preservation should apply not to vessels or paintings, but to the skills, practices, and attitudes of the past.

Sixteen apprentices have hands-on training for eighteen months to two years in a number of endangered skills. Using hand tools to build beautiful wooden boats seems to lead to patience, resourcefulness, and competence that is rare in today's marketplace. The apprentices also learn to live cooperatively in an intentional community on a spit of land north of the city. Taking turns, each day someone stays at home to clean and prepare meals for the others. During the summer, they rotate as interpreters for the visitors who have questions and comments.

Boats built at the Apprenticeshop are either sold or used in the Sail Training Program. One boat carries sardines to Nantucket, another cord wood to Monhegan. Many of the sloops have won races; all have proven to be handsome and seaworthy.

Lee is proud of the way the Restorationshop was built by volunteers, who gathered salvaged parts of old barns and recycled materials. Old boats are used as references for learning all that is possible from the original models, both the good and the bad. New lines are taken, drafted for posterity, and placed in a technology bank being built up by the Research Department. Publications of sets of plans and templates have been issued and tapes of interviews of Maine boatbuilders and boat users are available so that their knowledge and experience will not disappear. As a contemporary maritime museum, the example in Bath covers three major aspects: preservation of old examples, perpetuation of the skills and techniques involved, and documentation of construction details for the future. Thus, continuity between the past and present ensures a vital, realistic setting for this form of community education.

Future Directions

Indications are that in the foreseeable future, museums will not abandon their traditional role as preservers of our cultural heritage nor depart from standards of scholarship in their activities of acquisition and exhibition. They will probably further broaden the scope of their undertakings as they extend their efforts to attract a varied clientele. Although they may still have the aura of social and economic prestige because of their history, museums will no doubt continue to be responsive to changes in society. Since attempts to tailor programs to the requirements of individuals with special needs and to communities with distinctive cultural backgrounds have been endorsed by groups within the museum profession, they are likely to be continued.

The policies of the Council of Museums and Education in the Visual Arts, although formulated for art museums, are an indication of how the profession sees its future direction. By highlighting aspects of educational programs that need improvement, the Council's recommendations point to where the energies of museum educators ought to go during the next several years. Among these recommendations is the injunction that museums should be candid about their motives and limitations when they plan programs for communities with different sets of priorities from those of the museum staff and that they should accommodate to and learn from these communities. Also, educational programs of all types should be given repeated tryouts, evaluations, and revisions in different social contexts before being judged effective. Increased attention must be given to the search for evidence as to how and in what ways museums can educate. But, the Council warns, "the pressure to expose ever greater numbers of people to museums must be resisted so that a way can be found to provide access to more in-depth learning" (Newson and Silver, 1978).

Needless to say, the implementation of any of these recommendations, as well as the very existence of organized educational programs within the museums, depends on long-range commitments from both museum management and from private and public funding sources. Without this support, there can only be entrenchment. The hope is, however, that in reaching out to their communities, museums are insuring their future vitality.

Suggested Resources
Museum Education

Bibliography

Alexander, E.P. *Museums in motion: An introduction to the history and functions of museums.* Nashville: American Association for State and Local History, 1979.

Bazin, G. *The museum age.* New York: Universe Books, 1967.

Berrin, K. Activating the art museum's experience. *Museum News,* March/April 1978, 42-45.

Blocker, M.D., and Gurian, B.S. *Outreach program in the arts for the low-income elderly,* 1979. ERIC Document No. Ed185467.

Borun, M. *Measuring the unmeasurable: A pilot study of museum effectiveness.* Washington, D.C.: Association of Science-Technology Centers, 1977.

Breun, R., and Sebolt, A. (Eds.). *Museum-school cooperation: A summary of school projects.* Washington, D.C.: American Association of Museums, 1976.

Calhoun, S.N. On the edge of vision. *Museum News,* April 1974, 36-41.

Ethnic Discovery. Boston: Children's Museum, 1975.

Cohen, L. How to teach family history by using an historic house. *Social Education,* November/December 1975, 466-469.

Danilov, V.J. Chicago's trail-blazing museum. *American Education,* March 1979, 19-25.

DuTerroil, A. *Museum Education: Recent trends in learning environments.* San Antonio: Texas University, 1975.

Feild, B. *Hands-on museums: Partners in learning.* New York: Educational Facilities

Laboratories, 1975.

Gatto, J.A. The sustained visitation program. *School Arts Magazine*, April 1979, 22-25.

An Evaluation of the 1972-73 Guggenheim Museum Children's Program: "Learning to read through the arts." New York: Board of Education, 1973.

Harvey, E.D., and Friedberg, B. (Eds.). *A museum for the people.* New York: Arno Press, 1971.

Hayes, B.H., Jr. *A study of the relation of museum art exhibits to education.* Washington, D.C.: HEW, 1967.

Houlihan, P.T. Museums and American Indian education. *Journal of American Indian Education*, October 1973, 20-21.

Hudson, K. *A social history of museums: What the visitors thought.* London: Macmillan, 1975.

Johnson, J.R. The college student, art history, and the museum. *Art Journal*, 1971, 260-264.

Kenney, A.P. Women, history and the museum. *The History Teacher*, August 1974, 511-523.

Kohn, S.D. It's ok to touch at the new-style hands-on exhibits. *Smithsonian*, September 1978, *78*, 81-83.

Krawiec, W.E. Van-Ripper House: A case study of the local historical museums of Wayne Township, NJ, as resource for community continuing education. (Doctoral dissertation: Walden University, 1976).

Larrabee, E. (Ed.). *Museums and education.* Washington, D.C.: Smithsonian Institution, 1967.

Linn, M.C., and Laetsch, M. *Informed decision making: Evaluation you can use.* Berkeley: University of California, 1976.

Mead, M. Museums in a media-saturated world. *Museum News*, September 1970, 23-25.

Moore, D.T. *Urban resources as educators.* New York: Columbia University, 1978.

Culture Voucher Program. New York: Museums Collaborative, Inc., 1977.

Museums and handicapped studies: Guidelines for educators. Washington, D.C.: National Air and Space Museum, 1977.

Newsom, B. The art museum and the school. *American Education*, December 1977, 12-16.

Newsom, B., and Silver, A.L. (Eds.). *The art museum as educator.* Berkeley: University of California, 1978.

O'Doherty, B. (Ed.). *Museums in crisis.* New York: Braziller, 1972.

Rebetez, P. *How to visit a museum.* Strasbourg: Council for Cultural Cooperation of the Council of Europe, 1970.

Rothman, E.K. The Worcester sourcebook. *Museum News*, March/April 1978, 31-37.

Schlereth, T.J. It wasn't that simple. *Museum News*, January/February 1978, 36-44.

Stevens, E. Black arts centers. *Museum News*, March 1975, 19-24.

Taylor, J. To catch the eye and hold the mind: The museum as educator. *Art Education*, October 1971, 18-24.

Museum techniques in fundamental education. New York: UNESCO Publications Center, 1956.

Unterberg, A.P. Art, the natural sciences and a museum. *School Arts Magazine*, April 1979, 34-35.

Van der Haag. Art and the mass audience. *Art in America*, July 1971, 52-57.

Wittlin, A.S. *Museums: In search of a usable future.* Cambridge: MIT Press, 1970.

Wolf, R.I., and Tymitz, B.L. *A preliminary guide for conducting naturalistic evaluation in studying museum environments.* Washington, D.C.: Smithsonian Institution, 1978.

Zetterberg, H. *Museums and adult education.* New York: Augustus M. Kelley, 1969.

Journals

History News

Museum News

Resource Centers

Association of Science-Technology Centers
1016 16th Street, N.W.
Washington, D.C.

Center for Museum Education
George Washington University
2121 I Street, N.W.
Washington, D.C.

Museums Collaborative, Inc.
15 Grammercy Park S.
New York, NY

Smithsonian Institution
1000 Jefferson Drive, S.W.
Washington, D.C.

12
COMMUNITY EDUCATION IN CONTEXT

Elizabeth L. Loughran

If one asked the ordinary citizen "What is the center of learning in this community?" the most usual answer would be, the school. In fact, as many other chapters in this volume point out, education takes place in many institutions besides the school. Nonetheless, the school is a very important educational resource. Clearly, it has the potential of being a major force for community learning.

The purpose of this essay is to describe a form of schooling variously titled the community school movement or community education. The aim of this movement has been to forge much closer ties between the school and its community than has been common practice with most schools in North America. The usual school takes a small portion of the community's inhabitants (those ages 5-18) and tutors them in several abstract symbol systems (reading, writing, and arithmetic) using materials and methods that have only minimal derivation from the community. The community school resembles in many ways this usual school, but it adds several important components. Its educational activities involve participants of all ages from preschool children to senior citizens. The curriculum and materials make much greater use of community resources. Lay people are involved in volunteer and advisory roles in the school and as instructors in a variety of afternoon, evening, and vacation activities. After school activities provide a wide range of avocational, practical, and community-oriented problem solving learning experiences in addition to the usual formal school activities. The school makes a much greater effort to collaborate with other community agencies.

The intent of this essay will be to describe the history of this movement, to abstract and analyze some of the themes and theoretical bases underlying everyday practice, and to use the lifelong learning variables to analyze a typical community school so that this approach can be compared with others presented in this volume. The purpose is to look critically at the educational movement which has been the most explicit advocate for close ties between education and the community. How close are these ties in reality? How effective is a community school as a center for community learning? What is the future? The answers to these questions can inform not only school practice, but also can provide guidance to those who practice community education in other institutions.

The History of the Community Education Movement in the United States

Current community education programs in the United States have their immediate beginnings in Progressivist philosophy and in its implementation during the Depression. John Dewey provided the beginnings of community education theory (Dewey, 1900, 1916). He sensed that only a small portion of educational aims were pursued by formal schools. Because learning took place in many settings through the exercise of a wide variety of life functions, it made little sense to wall off the portions that were the traditional concerns of schools. Schools needed to be more permeable, to allow their curriculum and methods to reflect the immediate concerns of the wider community. In doing so, they would also more nearly meet the intrinsic needs of the students attending them, thus bringing daily processes more closely in tune with general aims.

A number of other Progressivists have been important in furthering community education theory. Perhaps the most frequently cited is Joseph Hart whose concern with creating an institution that fostered democracy reflected the idealism prevalent in this country after World War I:

> The democratic problem in education is not primarily a problem of training children; it is a problem of *making a community* within which children cannot help growing up to be democratic, intelligent, disciplined to freedom, reverent of the goods of life, and eager to share in the tasks of the age. A school cannot produce this result; nothing but a community can do so. (Hart, 1924, pp. 382-383.)

The combination of this philosophy and the more collectivist, egalitarian economic and political attitudes stemming from the Depression led to the founding of a number of community schools during the 1930's. Several fascinating accounts of these schools (Clapp, 1939; Everett, 1938; Seay and Meece, 1944) emphasize their concern with the immediate and pressing problems of the community. Food needed to be grown and preserved so people could survive the winter, and workers needed to be retrained for the few jobs available.

Given the depth and severity of the Depression, it is not surprising that some of these schools became critical of some of the major elements of the social order. Myles Horton's Highland Folk School (Clark, 1978; Everett, 1938; Oliver, 1976) represents one of the more radical of these schools, but nonetheless illustrates the directions these schools were exploring. A number of Horton's comments still sound radical today:

> The facts selected for teaching do not include those that would give children a just pride in the workers' struggle to better society through their own organizations. Instead, it is the individuals who have gained power through ownership and the generals of the armies who are pictured as citizens worthy of emulation. (Everett, 1938, pp. 265-266.)

However, the Depression ended, and World War II initiated a renewed support and admiration for American values such as productivity of American corporations, opportunities for individual advancement in schools and industry through merit, efficiency and productivity through bureaucratic and professional management. The community schools that expanded through the 1940's and 1950's, including those which were to become very important in Flint, Michigan, emphasized more conserving values. Instead of radical reform of basic institutions, commentators praised such organizations as the PTA and the use of volunteers in the classroom (Olsen, 1945). While the emphasis on such community development activities as improvement of nutrition or agricultural practice persisted in the rural South, even these programs no longer involved major social reforms. Black women were prepared for domestic service, white women for housework and child care, and the males of both races for farm or factory labor.

The Flint Program

The Flint Program fits into the latter phase of the community schools movement. The differences and the sources of its continued importance are two-fold. First, the Flint Program developed in a severely depressed and decaying urban area and, consequently, it is a model that has relevance to more modern schools than the programs typical of Appalachia during the same era. Second, the program attracted the support of a major foundation, the C.S. Mott Foundation. Foundation support in itself is not unique. Other foundations, notably the Sloan and Kellogg Foundations, have offered significant support to the movement. What has made the difference is the continuous and expanding nature of that support. Mott funding is still a major factor to community education and has come to be counted on during periods when governmental sources are strained.

The Flint Program began as an after school recreation program aimed at curbing delinquency rates. Later, summer programs were added. With Mott's help, the program expanded through the late 1930's and 1940's into many other social service areas: nutrition, health education, vocational training. Flint was the home of the General Motors Corporation which was headed by Mr. Mott. Throughout his lifetime, Mr. Mott supported the community school as a major vehicle for improving the quality of life for his workers and their families.

During the late 1940's, the idea spread to other Michigan communities through the Kellogg-funded Michigan Community School Service Program. In the 1950's the Flint Program itself became more established, employing community school directors and constructing buildings designed with considerable input from the community. The increasing degree of local support for the idea was made evident through the greater support of bond issues and local funding efforts. In addition, programs added numerous, very creative community-school interconnections such as advisory councils, volunteer and apprenticeship programs, and community needs assessments.

The basic philosophy behind the program involved the importance of increasing the self-reliant strength of individuals in deprived areas through the more efficient use of established institutions (Decker, 1972, p. 62). That philosophy is common to the progressive reforms in many other areas of American life. The intent is to marshall the resources of the established institutions (the corporation, all levels of government, schools, health care facilities) to provide a better standard of living and greater opportunities for the poor. The poor, during the early years of these programs, were immigrants; in later years they have more usually been racial and ethnic minorities. The poor are often described as being deprived. One author described them as being "virtually helpless when they walked into the classroom" (Campbell, 1969, p. 27). The philosophy embodies an evolutionary theory of social change and does not see anything fundamentally wrong with American social structures.

The Community Education Movement

The basic philosophical stance has not changed within the community education movement as it is largely practiced today. What has changed has been the content and methodology advocated. By the 1960's, many community school practitioners began to realize that individual growth programs (typically adult basic education, vocational training, and recreation) were not reaching many people in large urban areas. Those kinds of programs had been very important to earlier immigrant groups who wished to join middle class society; they were not and are not attractive to groups who either do not wish to join, or for racial reasons have been prevented from joining, the dominant society.

The movement's response to these problems led to rapid growth in the 1960's (funded in key ways by the Mott Foundation), to a change in methodology, and to a change in name. By the mid-1960's, the movement was being termed *community education* and was distinguishing itself from community schools by emphasizing several process variables more heavily. Theoreticians of the movement began to stress such concepts as lay participation, interagency cooperation, and responsiveness to community needs rather than the programmatic emphasis of community schools (LeTarte & Minsey, 1972; Seay, 1974). In addition, the Flint Program now became more clearly a national movement with some 400 school districts participating by 1974 (Crinshaw, 1974), a professional organization (The National Community Education Association), and a journal (*The Community Education Journal*). The federal government acknowleded this national significance by offering modest incentive funding through the National Community Schools Acts of 1974 and 1978. In the 1980's diminished federal funding continued through block grants.

Community education, the process, is the dominant theoretical perspective and definition of the movement today (Deaver, 1980). However, two factors limit its importance. The first is that there is widespread disagreement between experts and practitioners on the nature of process (Cwik, et. al., 1975). Second, the community school's definition (individual growth programs offered at local schools for all ages, community participation through advisory councils, volunteer programs, social services available through the school) dominates actual practice (Deaver, 1980).

Many observers see the movement at a crucial point — choosing which of these views will predominate. The federal government with its modest incentive funding, most university theoreticians, and a significant number of National Community Education Association and Mott Foundation personnel support the broader community education concept, but the weight of the past and the present social and institutional forces in American society support the community schools.

Another movement which has also employed the term *community school* is interesting both as an alternative conceptualization of the relationship between school and community and for the perspective it provides on the Flint Program. The community control movement developed explicitly in relationship to one of the major social forces of the 1960's, the Civil Rights Movement.

The community control movement was largely a growth of the Oceanhill-Brownsville controversy in New York, though other more moderate versions occurred elsewhere, notably in Detroit. The controversy stemmed from the numerical impossibility of desegregating New York public schools given the heavy in-migration of minorities and out-migration of whites during the 1960's. Community members, with the later very important support of the Ford Foundation, wished to explore the feasibility of improving segregated schools by transferring significant control over such issues as hiring, firing, content choice, and graduation standards to the community, in this case the Black and Hispanic community. Though these groups got significant support from political leaders, they failed to gain control over personnel matters which were controlled by the union (overwhelmingly white). Despite a series of strikes and boycotts, New York's schools are not significantly different in their degree of lay control and parent participation today than they were before the controversy began (Scribner, 1980).

Summary

This brief historical account should provide a context for understanding today's community school. The community school which developed from the Flint Model is still a formal school; it offers a K-12 curriculum and is staffed by professionals with control vested in an elected school board and its chosen superintendent. What distinguishes it from other public schools is more extensive use of facilities for nonschool populations, greater use of community participation through devices like advisory councils, and use of community resources. Community education retains all of the formal school control apparatus while increasing interaction with the community through a number of processes, the effect being to increase lay participation and to increase the emphasis on community development.

However, neither the community school nor community education retain the focus on community development and reform of oppressive institutions that characterized the movement during the Depression. Nor is the emphasis on actual control of key matters (such as the choice of personnel and of the curriculum) that characterized the community control movement of the 1960's supported by practitioners or theoreticians. Community schools are clearly mainstream institutions which extend educational resources to the community, but in no way do they challenge the major values underlying the American social order.

Pervasive Themes

Importance of Community

The most pervasive theme of the community education movement is the importance of community. The community is a significant source of support, of the curriculum, and of teaching and learning resources. Additionally, there is an obligation to better serve people in the community.

However, a comparison of the differences in the ways in which community members are used, in the ways education is seen to relate to the community, and in the very conceptualization of community itself between the community education movement and the community control movement of the 1960's is interesting. Most of the early Depression community schools, including the Flint schools, saw the community ideally as a unified, coherent phenomenon. That concept is based on the experience, or perhaps the memory, of communities as rural or medium-sized towns. Though the typical definitions of community acknowledge diversity as an element, they nonetheless emphasize what is held in common. The direction of the community schools and the community education movement is towards establishing a unity of purpose:

> Men live in a *community* in virtue of the things which they have in common; and *communication* is the way in which they come to possess things in *common*. What they must have in order to form a

community or society are aims, beliefs, aspirations, knowledge — a
common understanding — like-mindedness as the sociologists say.
(LeTarte & Minzey, 1972, p. 44.)

In contrast, community control schools were initiated more in reaction to a
sense of diversity within communities. Their answer to differences of race,
culture, abilities, and aspirations was to attempt to institutionalize these differences through pluralistic patterns of governance and/or educational
approach.

This difference in conceptualization has been reflected in differences in
the type of lay participation and in the leadership patterns of each movement. The community schools and community education movement, with
their emphasis on the commonalities within the community, have not
sought to encourage participation and leadership of one segment of the
community more than any other. Perhaps, as a result, the movement has
tended to resemble most other American educational groups with relation
to these characteristics. Specifically leadership, at least through the early
1970's, was predominantly white and male, and citizen participation tended to involve more middle- and upper middle-class groups than lower socio-
economic groups (Manser, 1976). In contrast, the community control
schools place a positive value on serving one specific community. Consequently, they have made greater efforts to appoint or involve professional
and lay leaders from the particular racial, ethnic, and cultural groups that
the schools serve (Grant, 1979).

None of these movements, however, has developed either a rationale or
a set of programs that is as explicit as were some of the early Progressivist
community schools (i.e., the purpose of education is to enhance the quality
of life in communities). One characteristic that most community schools
and community control schools share with more formal schools is that they
all place a priority primarily on the individual progress of the young people
who attend them. The progress of the community as a collective entity is a
secondary concern. Thus, these schools will use the community via intern-
ship programs, work-study, or guest speakers. Community affairs may also
become the topic of the curriculum as in the core or project curricula. However, the purpose in most cases is first to serve the needs of individual
students; rarely are community needs considered as primary.

It is no accident that, of the key process variables introduced above (e.g.,
participation, interagency collaboration), community development is one
of the least implemented in this country. Implementation would question
some of the major assumptions behind the individualistic philosophy that
permeates all facets of American life. Aside from the few Depression-era
community schools, one has to look to other countries (Yugoslavia, Tan-
zania, The People's Republic of China, Sri Lanka, and other Third World
countries) to find large scale examples of educational projects aimed specifically at community improvement (Barnard, 1979).

Participation

All community schools put a heavy emphasis on the theme of participation: participation by citizens, by parents, by learners. However, the different emphasis on community as a unitary concept, contrasted with community as a pluralistic phenomenon, is reflected in somewhat different implementations of the idea of community participation. Community education potentially has a more inclusive vision of community involvement. The inclusion of all ages as active learners, as well as concerned participants, permits a much more natural role in the community's educational system. Other programs aimed at school-aged children only theoretically permit participation in a much narrower realm.

In practice, however, community education's support of the traditional management systems restricts participation particularly in large urban areas where school boards have frequently not reflected community concerns. Because major decisions are made by professional administrators, subject to school board ratification, citizen participation is restricted to giving advice, to being consumers, and to being lay volunteers. In small districts, those roles, coupled with a more community-based school board, can be very meaningful. In urban areas, and particularly in urban areas where professionals belong to racial or cultural groups different from those of the community, those roles have been less attractive.

The community control movement clearly advocated a more intensive form of participation. Parents and community members were to make the major decisions facing the schools. However, that approach has not proved successful over long periods of time. Community decisions to fire certain teachers in the Oceanhill-Brownsville district sparked a major confrontation with the teacher's union which led to the end of that experiment.

Thus, in the 1980's, participation is still a theme that is the subject of a great deal of rhetoric, but seems to elude widespread implementation. At least in urban areas, participation in advisory or voluntary forms seems unable to attract large groups of people over a sustained period of time; participation in the form of exercising real power runs the risk of major conflict with established groups. Only in relatively small communities is there widespread involvement in the schools, and that seems more a function of social setting than educational philosophy (Peshkin, 1978). Yet, a community school without community involvement is clearly an abuse of the term. Increasing citizen participation in urban community schools remains one of the key problems facing the movement (C.S. Mott Foundation, 1979).

A Broader Definition of Education: The Learning Society

Another theme common to all community schools, a reflection of their common debt to Progressivist theory, is a broadened definition of education. Education is considered a much wider concept than schooling; it is an organized effort to influence people and is carried on daily by a host of community agencies including unions, businesses, the media, welfare offices, scouts, and churches. All community schools recognize the vitality of nonschool education and try to integrate that energy into their programs in many different ways, some of which are work-study, internships, community volunteers, field trips, school camping.

In addition, the community education movement has significantly extended this concept by combining it with a commitment to lifelong learning. A number of Depression-initiated community schools included a commitment to adult learning, but of the modern inheritors only the Flint Model retained that emphasis. The community control schools were schools for youths only.

Community school programs based on the Flint Model and community education, the process, include significant emphasis on preschool and adult learning experiences. In the community school model, the emphasis has been on providing opportunities for individual development. Programs of after school recreation for adults and youth, career training, adult education classes, and enrichment activities are offered at community schools in the late afternoon and evening hours, and during weekends and summer vacations. Community education theorists (very seldom practitioners) extend that emphasis with concern for community development activities: citizens working to beautify a neighborhood, lobbying for a drop-in center, building a cooperative housing project. The school is occasionally a meeting place for these activities, but more commonly is only one of several agencies involved.

Efficient Use of Educational Resources

One of the reasons that community education weathered the more conservative attitudes of the 1970's is that a major rationale for the concept emphasizes conservation of resources. Operating a major public facility for only eight hours a day is clearly wasteful. A school can provide many learning opportunities in the early morning hours and after children leave in the afternoon for populations not normally served by public education. The majority of these programs can be offered at only minimal public expense financed by user fees or run by community volunteers. The beauty of the idea, of course, is that it is a very liberal educational concept: lifelong community-centered learning, financed conservatively. It is in part this combination that has enabled community schools and community education to expand equally during periods of social conservatism such as the 1950's and 1970s as well as during more liberal decades.

Interagency Collaboration

The community education movement has moved one step further than the community schools, believing that not only should building resources be used more extensively, but that education as a whole can be provided more efficiently. If education is more than schooling, then hospitals, local government, scouts, neighborhood renewal agencies, welfare agencies, etc., can also be educators. Often they can provide better educational services more efficiently than the formal schools. The staff of a drop-in center might have an excellent drug abuse program; a lawyer or judge, a program on juvenile justice; a local business, a career training program. Again, the attraction of the idea is the union of a philosophically meaningful process and a conserving economic base. Not only should collaboration among community agencies lead to greater citizen participation in community affairs, but it is also a vehicle for expanding educational opportunities at little additional public expense.

As with many other aspects of the community education process, interagency collaboration is more a theory than a fact. Most actual programs depend heavily on the school (Ringers, 1976). In addition, many successful collaborative programs use new and quite expensive facilities which house social service programs and recreational facilities in a K-12 school facility (Educational Facilities Laboratory, 1973). While such facilities do further collaboration as an important element in the philosophy of community-centered learning, they do not necessarily save money (Baillie, et. al., 1972). Programs not dependent on facilities, where schools are only one of many agencies and not necessarily the most important, are still rare. The ability of community education to implement interagency collaboration and high levels of community participation is essential if this facet of the Flint Program is to come to dominate more than the theory of the movement.

Theoretical Dimensions

Underlying the various conceptualizations of community education that have had some prominance during this century, the community school of the Depression, the Flint Model and the community control schools of the 1960's have had quite different theoretical positions concerning the nature of social change and the source of learning. Making explicit some of these more pervasive assumptions about key aspects of reality can clarify the differences among these conceptualizations and enable the reader to evaluate the approaches more precisely.

Social Change

Social change theory is usually seen as a continuum going from emphasis on the status quo to evolutionary change to revolutionary change. All of the community schools described above see change as occurring largely in an evolutionary context. Physical force is not supported by any of the approaches. Neither is any group satisfied with the status quo; all believe that significant groups of people have not had an equitable share of America's resources and deserve more extensive opportunities.

Within these broad limits, however, there are important differences. Social change can be seen as being caused by top-down pressures (e.g., government or other institutional incentive or directive) or bottom-up pressure (nonviolent resistance, strikes, citizen lobbying, etc.). Change can also be seen as occurring largely through economic growth fostered by existing institutions or as a result of structural change occurring within major institutions.

The community school and, to a large extent, the community education movements have emphasized top-down change strategies and have relied on the growth of existing institutions to produce change. Change agents in the early days of the Flint Program were school administrators such as Frank Manley (Decker, 1972) and, perhaps most importantly, the Mott and Kellogg Foundations. The strategy used by the Mott Foundation in the 1960's established the Mott Inter-University Clinical Preparation Program and a series of regional resource centers with ties to a national center in Flint. The theory implicit in such an approach is that change will occur through leadership training of key personnel such as future community school directors and university professors of education and administration.

The same top-down approach is also key to understanding the federal incentive funding established in the Community Schools Acts of 1974 and 1978. A priority under the act is establishing and reinforcing the potential of state community education departments. The theory is that change will be more likely to occur through the ripple effect emanating from strong state leaders. The Mott Foundation has also been instrumental in strengthening state departments of community education and has strengthened the federal role by financing an additional position within the federal Community Education office. However, in the 1980's federal support of community education became part of block grants and thus is subject more to state than federal control.

All of these change efforts envision the school as being important to reform. Change comes through expansion of the school's programs (wider use of facilities by greater numbers of people), not through major structural changes in the schools themselves.

Recently, however, community educators who see themselves as somewhat different from community schools directors have moved to a more intermediate position on these two dimensions. Community educators, by emphasizing process issues, imply that change needs to come from the bottom as well as the top. Greater citizen participation and collaboration with other institutions are bottom-up philosophies. Similarly, community education sees the school as only one of the institutions involved in delivering community education. Though theoreticians do not envision major institutional change, the notion of a collaborative of local agencies being the vehicle of change implies at least different roles for existing institutions. As was noted above, however, community education is still more of an idea than an established educational approach. Major funding agencies (local schools, the Mott Foundation, and the federal government) continue to support a more usual top-down change process.

In contrast, community control schools advocated some degree of institutional change as well as a major role for consumers of education. Parents, citizens, community groups, and/or students were the initiators of these schools. The lack of continued support from the top by established institutions (public schools, foundations, teacher unions, or government) is theorized to be one of the reasons for their decline (Ornstein, 1974). The very fact that change began with citizen groups implied institutional change.

Traditional urban schools are not structured to permit parent decision making on significant issues such as curriculum, staffing, and funding.

Learning Theory

Two of the pervasive themes of community schools, the importance of the concept of community and of participation, have important implications for the learning theory used. As noted above, many of the Progressivist ideas on learning derive from the importance those theorists give to the community. Education occurs in many institutions besides schools, and immediate community concerns should be a focus of the curriculum (Dewey, 1900, 1916). The learning theory proposed by the Progressivists and congruent with these ideas sees learning occurring through interacting with the significant people, organizations, and problems of their communities (Dewey, 1902). Though the phrase "learning by doing" is an oversimplification, it has an element of the essential active nature of the process.

In similar fashion, participation connotes an active process. Participants have been empowered to create an active role for themselves in the institutions that affect their lives. Modern critics of formal schools, notably Freire (1970, 1973) and Illich (1971), have made the explicit connection between participation as a political concept and participatory learning as its necessary corollary.

The concepts of community and of participation have been interpreted very differently by the different types of community schools, and, therefore, it is understandable that the learning theory and methodologies based on the theory also differ. The Flint Program saw a need for the school to serve more groups within the community and to make better use of community resources to enrich the curriculum. The community was used more as an addition or enrichment rather than a substitution for other school concerns; consequently, it is not unusual for a very typical, formal K-12 curriculum to co-exist with more nonformal afternoon and evening programs for adults in these schools. In contrast, in some of the early community schools founded during the Depression, immediate community concerns like obtaining food and shelter were the curriculum; the methodologies used in those schools were quite different from those used in formal schools.

Similarly, the different implementation of participation has an impact on learning theory. In the Flint Model, citizens are encouraged to be involved in school programs through such devices as volunteering and serving on advisory councils; they do not control the schools through direct decision making mechanisms. In contrast, the community control movement did involve citizens in many more direct and crucial decisions. The greater levels of participation have often been accompanied by more frequent use of active learning processes.

One characteristic that seems common to most community schools has had a somewhat negative effect on the development of coherent learning theory. Most community schools have been initiated in response to political, social, and economic concerns; the two periods of rapid growth in the 1930's and 1960's support the importance of those concerns as does the emphasis on community and participation. Less important and less frequently explored by theoreticians and practitioners in any of the movements has been the work of the developmental psychologists on both children and adults. There is enormous potential for integrating the societal concerns of the community schools with the psychological perspectives of the developmentalists, but that integration is only at the very beginning stages. Until such an integration is available, the learning theory of community schools will continue to be fragmentary and, too often, contradictory.

Delivery Variables

The delivery of an educational program is not a singular but a highly complex phenomenon. Elements include choice of learners, background of staff, nature of the curriculum, teaching-learning approaches, various resources (materials, facilities, funding) and organizational patterns. Variation of any of these elements can substantially change the total impact of the program. This section will describe the community schools that developed from the Flint Program, referring to other community school approaches only in order to place that program in perspective. Though some theorists advocate a much wider delivery system using many community agencies, the reality at present is a delivery system based on the local school.

Learners

Community schools ideally attract learners of all ages. From the earliest days of the Flint Program, cradle-to-grave or lifelong learning has been a major element (Totten and Manley, 1969). In practice, however, the fact that different groups of learners are selected by different criteria has a strong effect on the kinds of programs offered. Learners for K-12 school programs are the same as learners in other formal school programs. Attendance is mandatory; children from a given geographic area must attend that school unless their parents pay tuition for a private education. Thus, a school will contain learners of widely different ability and motivational levels, and if it is an integrated neighborhood, of different cultures as well. Typically these children will be grouped by age into grade levels, though some community schools have ungraded programs particularly for young children.

On the other hand, programs for preschool and adult populations are not mandatory and attract a different population. A far smaller proportion of the eligible population enrolls in these programs, and they are for the most part more motivated than their counterparts who do not enroll. It is estimated that even adult basic education classes aimed directly at the least educated segment of society, attract only the most able and motivated of that group (Hunter and Harman, 1979).

There is often more cultural homogeneity in after school programs than there is in the K-12 programs. In Boston's community schools, for instance, busing for integration has meant that much of the day school population comes from a different part of town while evening programs serve the immediate neighborhood. That factor, along with the natural tendency of friends to enroll together, generally means that after school programs, while less selective on age criteria, often represent more restrictive self-selection on the basis of culture and motivation.

Staff

Similarly, the staff serving these two distinct groups are different. Staff for the K-12 program are professional, certified, and at the high school level, highly skilled in their subject areas. They see their job as being full time and career-oriented, and in most areas of the country, their pay and fringe benefits place them securely in the middle class. Staff for after school programs, on the other hand, consider their work as part time; it is more of an avocation or means of supplementing their jobs. They are paid by the course or hour, are frequently not certified, and often have little more formal schooling than their clients. There are virtually no opportunities for advancement since generally the only full-time position, the community school director, is filled by someone holding a teaching credential and frequently graduate training in community education administration (Totten and Manley, 1969).

A great deal of research has been conducted on the role of the community school director. Perhaps the most widespread conclusion is that the presence of a trained, full-time director is a factor in program success (Kelley, 1975; Tremper, 1974). A recent statewide evaluation of all state funded community education programs in Texas showed a significant positive correlation between the amount of training of the coordinator and the number of participants and variety of activities in the program (Stenning, Cooper-Stenning and Berridge, 1979). There is less agreement on the competencies needed (Cwik, King, and Van Voorhees, 1975) though authors frequently advocate a participatory leadership style (Burden and Whitt, 1973). No research to date has been conducted on the social class, race, and sex of community school directors. However, a look at various books and journals which provide pictures (*The Community School and Its Administration*, 1962-72; *The Community Education Journal,* 1971-present; Hickey and Van Voorhees, 1969) leads one to surmise that white males dominate this field of educational administration, as they do others in the United States.

The Curriculum

The curricula of the day community school and the after school program are also different. The day program in practice resembles the range of programs available in regular schools, with a greater emphasis on enrichment or Progressivist programs. Irwin and Russell illustrate the thrust of this program in the title of their book, *The Community Is The Classroom* (1971). However, the programs described do not take this concept literally, but rather include a wide variety of community-based enrichment activities (field trips, work-study, community projects) and innovations (flexible scheduling, multi-aged grouping, etc.). In general, community schools must follow the same state requirements as do other schools, and the majority of them offer a core of very similar, age-graded, carefully sequenced, largely cognitive studies emphasizing acquisition of basic skills.

The curriculum of the afternoon and evening program is quite different. While basic skill acquisition is offered through adult literacy, GED, and English as a second language programs, the bulk of the curriculum contains more avocational courses: enrichment and recreation for adults and children, career skills, club meetings, and community improvement projects (Seay and Associates, 1974). Most of these latter courses meet psychological and physical needs of learners more than cognitive needs and tend to be offered to any interested person with few prerequisites.

As the idea of community education as a process becomes established, one might envision an even greater difference between the two programs. For the most part, after school programs today are school-based and resemble innovative adult education programs. As community members become more involved in community-centered educational processes, one would imagine programs occurring at other agencies and community sites, as well as at the school. Olsen and Clark (1977) describe such a curriculum as "life-centering," including such concerns as "securing food and shelter, adjusting to other people, sharing in citizenship, controlling the environment" (p. 107). The curriculum, in other words, will include many more items of specific local and personal concern, projects which if implemented would substantially improve the community environment.

Teaching-Learning Approaches

The flexible, less cognitive and more immediate curriculum of the after school program obviously demands different teaching-learning methodologies than does the skill-based program of the K-12 program. Time units are more flexible (the length of a basketball game or an entire evening or day) rather than the 45-60 minute periods of regular schools. Adults take a more active role as learners in both recreational courses and particularly as instigators of community projects. Teachers tend to facilitate learning, advising and demonstrating rather than managing the class. Grades are rare; at most a student prepares for a credential offered by some other agency such as the GED Exam or a real estate certificate. Even the largely cognitive courses like adult basic education tend to be offered in more flexible forms; individualized learning and flexible scheduling are almost universal in these programs rather than the exception as is the case in K-12 programs.

Resources

Most community education programs use the same facilities and often the same materials for day and after school programs. That double or triple use is a major element in the economic efficiency widely discussed in the movement. During the 1960's and early 70's when many new schools were being built, an effort was made to build multipurpose buildings. It was economical to include gymnasiums, well-equipped media centers, art and music studios, and swimming pools, because such facilities served the community as well as the school. Various social service agencies had offices in the school, thus drawing the adult population into the school and more effectively serving children (Passantino, 1975).

The resources for these new schools, then, tend to be located in quite costly, permanent buildings with high maintenance costs. Materials often use a high level of technology and are commercially produced. Both are purchased through a combination of local, state, and federal financing.

Of course, not all community schools are located in new buildings. Other programs are in older city buildings and have to use nearby facilities for after school programs. Worcester, Massachusetts's Woodland Community School offers an example of using the YMCA pool and gym for some programs and other social agencies for others. Ironically, the much discussed but seldom implemented interagency cooperation is practiced out of necessity by personnel in these older facilities.

Administration

Management of community schools is similar to that in other American schools. Ultimate authority rests with the state which usually exercises that authority over graduation requirements, certification of staff, and accreditation of programs. The remaining authority is delegated to local school boards which, in turn, delegate most day-to-day management to a superintendent and his or her staff. Typically, a principal is in charge of the day school program and a community school director of vice-principal status heads the program after school hours. Community schools must conform to the same fiscal accountability as other school programs and require similar services of personnel knowledgeable about budgetary matters.

Funding, however, is only partially dependent on the local and state resources which finance public schools. Day school programs are funded through these sources and occasionally, in an established district, the position of the community school director as well. The remaining funds come from a variety of sources. In some cities, like Boston, the community school budget comes from municipal funds. In other districts, numerous programs such as recreation programs and services for the elderly are financed from the city's budget. Also, social services which are housed in community schools fund their own programs. Other schools finance programs largely through user fees.

Two other sources have been particularly important as sources of incentive funding for beginning new programs, expanding existing ones, and financing innovative approaches to community education. The Mott Foundation has been the most important of these; the strength of the program in Mott's home town of Flint and the State of Michigan is testimony to the constant support of the Foundation. Since the early 1960's, the Foundation has expanded its funding nationwide, funding university training programs and resource centers in several federal regions, financing the beginning of a professional association and journal, as well as funding numerous local programs.

From 1974-1982 the federal government made available a limited amount of seed money for the concept. It was important in strengthening a state's capacity to offer technical assistance to local programs and for support of innovative ideas in the field. Beginning in 1982, however, funding was returned to the states as part of block grants.

Fiscal support for community schools, though from more varied sources than regular schools, still comes largely from governmental sources. It is not surprising then that the accountability movement in community education has been as important as in other educational programs. Major research programs have been undertaken to develop competencies for community school directors (Miller, Paddock, and McCleary, 1979) and to develop and test appropriate evaluation programs (Burback and Decker, 1977).

Because community schools resemble other schools in their management, funding, and evaluation procedures, it is perhaps not surprising that two of the major objectives of community education, increasing citizen participation and collaboration with other agencies, have had only limited success. The governmental structure of the community school restricts community participation to those avenues already open — voting in school bond elections, serving on school boards, volunteering, and offering advice. Community schools have maximized the potential of the latter two devices through the use of community advisory councils and active community volunteer programs. However, these avenues have not proved totally satisfactory and increasing the participation is still identified as the major training need of directors (C.S. Mott Foundation, 1979).

Interagency collaboration has largely been fostered via training the community school director in "enabling" leadership styles (Ringers, 1977). However, most community schools see themselves as umbrella agencies and not surprisingly have engendered fears of "turf encroachment." Neither training nor past experience has prepared directors to serve as participants as one of many agencies in a collaborative project, nor is there firm legal precedent for this role (Wood, 1974).

Community schools, like other schools, function as bureaucracies with vertical patterns of authority, division of labor, and strict standards of accountability. The emphasis is how to "use not abuse" bureaucracies (Ringers, 1977). This management pattern is successful to the extent that it is successful in other schools. However, it tends to be less effective in such areas as increasing participation and collaboration where more horizontal and more participatory patterns of management are needed.

Conclusion

The purpose of the community education movement has been to maximize the contact between the school and its community both by facilitating use of the school by all members of the community and by increasing the school's use of community resources. However, at various times during the movement's history, different types of community schools have emphasized different goals and have employed different means. The early schools during the Depression were a major force in a number of community development projects and often supported opposition to existing social institutions. Similarly, the development of particular minority communities was an aim of the community control schools, and direct citizen control of major decisions posed a serious threat to existing educational administrative practices.

In contrast, the community school, which developed from the Flint Model and is by far the most dominant form of community education in the United States today, has as its primary goal lifelong education of individuals in the community. Means include greater participation of citizens in the schools but no major change in the usual administrative control of decisions. Interagency collaboration is a stated goal, but a goal which is frequently undermined by bureaucratic management methods which make real horizontal connections difficult.

The movement provides a clear example of what a community-based learning approach can become when it is embedded in the dominant characteristics of the American culture, individualism, and when it is delivered by the preponderant public institution, the bureaucracy. It is no accident that challenges to these dominant modes have been short lived. However, their brief existence also has provided interesting examples of alternative forms of community education which might be possible were one to question some of these underlying assumptions governing American society.

Suggested Resources
Community Education

Bibliography

Baillie, S., Dewitt, L., and O'Leary, L. The potential role of the school as a site for integrating social services. Syracuse, New York: Educational Policy Research Center, 1972.

Bernard, T.L. Community education in international perspective. East Longmeadow, MA: International Association of Community Educators, 1979.

Burback, H.J., and Decker, L.E. (Eds.). Planning and assessment in community education. Midland, Michigan: Pendell Publishing Company, 1977.

Burden, L., and Whitt, R.L. The community school principal: New horizons. Midland, Michigan: Pendell Publishing Company, 1973.

Campbell, C.M. Toward perfection in learning. Midland, Michigan: Pendell Publishing Company, 1969.

Clapp, E.R. Community schools in action. New York: The Viking Press, 1939.

Clark, M. Meeting the needs of the adult learner: Using nonformal education for social action. Convergence, 1978, 11, 44-53.

The Community School and Its Administration, October 1962-June 1973.

Crinshaw, W.F. Mott Foundation announces creation of a community education journal. Community Education Journal, March-April, 1974, 4, 32-3:

Cwik, P.J., King, M.J., and Van Voorhees, C. The community advisory council. Monographs of the Office of Community Education Research, 1975, 1, (No. 2).

Cwik, P.J., King, M.J., and Van Voorhees, C. Community education issues and answers. Monographs of the Office of Community Education Research, 1975, 1, (No. 3).

Cwik, P.J., King, M.J., and Van Voorhees, C. Community education and recreation.

Monographs of the Office of Community Education Research, 1975, 2, (No. 1).

Cwik, P.J., King, M.J., and Van Voorhees, C. The community school director. *Monographs of the Office of Community Education Research,* 1975, 1, (No. 1).

Deaver, P.F. *The futures—Direction, process, and the five year plan for community education.* Washington, D.C.: National Community Education Association, 1980.

Decker, L.E. *Foundations of community education.* Midland, Michigan: Pendell Publishing Company, 1972.

Dewey, J. *The child and the curriculum; The school and society.* Chicago: The University of Chicago Press, 1956. (Originally published 1902 and 1900).

Dewey, J. *Democracy and education.* New York: Macmillan Company, 1916.

Educational Facilities Laboratories, Inc. *Community/school sharing the space and the action.* New York: Educational Facilities Laboratories, Inc., 1973.

Everett, S. (Ed.). *The community school.* New York: D. Appleton Century Company, 1938.

Fantini, M., Loughran, E., and Reed, H. Toward a definition of community education. *Community Education Journal,* 1980, 7, 11-14, 33.

Freire, P. *Pedagogy of the oppressed.* New York: The Seaburg Press, 1970.

Freire, P. *Education for critical consciousness.* New York: The Seaburg Press, 1973.

Grant, C.A. *Community participation in education.* Boston: Allyn and Bacon, Inc., 1979.

Hart, J.K. *Discovery of intelligence.* New York: The Century Company, 1924.

Hickey, H.W., and Van Voorhees, C. *The role of the school in community education.* Midland, Michigan: Pendell Publishing Company, 1969.

Hunter, C. St. J., and Harmon, D. *Adult illiteracy in the United States.* New York: McGraw-Hill Book Company, 1979.

Illich, I. *Deschooling America.* New York: Harper and Row Publishers, 1971.

Irwin, M., and Russell, W. *The community is the classroom.* Midland, Michigan: Pendell Publishing Company, 1971.

Kelly, R. The determination and description of a set of variables in the administration structure of public school districts necessary for development of the community education concept (Doctoral dissertation). *Dissertation Abstracts International,* 1975, 36, 2538A.

LeTarte, C.E., and Minzey, J.D. *Community education: From program to process.* Midland, Michigan: Pendell Publishing Company, 1972.

Manser, G., and Cass, R.H. *Volunteerism at the crossroads.* New York: Family Service Association of America, 1976.

Miller, B.P., Paddock, S.C., and McCleary, L.E. *Competency-based community education administration.* Tempe, Arizona: Southwest Center for Community Education Development, Arizona State University, 1979.

C.S. Mott Foundation. *Tabulation of group renewal inservice questionnaire.* Flint, Michigan: C.S. Mott Foundation, September 1979.

Oliver, D.W. *Education and community.* Berkeley, CA: McCutchen Publishing Company, 1976.

Olsen, E.G. *School and community.* New York: Prentice-Hall, Inc., 1945.

Olsen, E.G., and Clark, P.A. *Life-centering education.* Midland, Michigan: Pendell Publishing Company, 1977.

Ornstein, A.C. *Metropolitan schools: Decentralization vs. community control.* Metuchen, NJ: The Scarecrow Press, Inc., 1974.

Passantino, R.J. Community/school facilities: The school house of the future. *Phi Delta Kappan,* January 1975, 56, 306-9.

Peshkin, A. *Growing up American: Schooling and the survival of community.* Chicago, Illinois: The University of Chicago Press, 1978.

Ringers, J. Jr. *Community schools and interagency programs: A guide.* Midland, Michigan: Pendell Publishing Company, 1976.

Ringers, J. Jr. *Creating interagency projects: School and community agencies.* Charlottesville, VA: Community Collaborators, 1977.

Scribner, H. Personal communication, January 10, 1980.

Seay, M.F. *Community education: A developing concept.* Midland, Michigan: Pendell Publishing Company, 1974.

Seay, M.F., and Meece, L.E. *The Sloan experiment in Kentucky.* Lexington, KY: University of Kentucky, 1944.

Stenning, W.F., Cooper-Stenning, P., and Berridge, R. *Relationship of education and community education training to effectiveness of community education programs in Texas.* Paper presented at the NCEA Convention, Boston, November 1979.

Totten, W.F., and Manley, F.J. *The community school basic concepts: Education and organization.* Galien, Michigan: Allied Education Council, 1969.

Tremper, P.W. A comparison of charactertistics of school districts considered to have more successful community education programs with those considered to have less successful programs (Doctoral dissertation, Western Michigan University, 1974). *Dissertation Abstracts International,* 1974, *35,* No. 6415A.

Wood, E.F. An identification and analysis of the legal environment for community education. *Journal of Law and Education,* January 1974, *3,* 1-31.

Journals

Community Education Journal

NASSP Bulletin, November 1975, *59.*

Phi Delta Kappan, November 1972, *54.*

Resource Centers

Community Education Resource Center
School of Education
University of Massachusetts
Amherst, MA 01003

C.S. Mott Foundation
510 Mott Foundation Building
Flint, Michigan 48507

National Center for Community Education
1017 Avon Street
Flint, Michigan 48503

National Community Education Association
1201 16th Street, N.W.
Suite 305
Washington, D.C. 20036

National Community Education Clearinghouse
1201 16th Street, N.W.
Suite 305
Washington, D.C. 20036

13
ADULT BASIC AND CONTINUING EDUCATION

Horace B. Reed

Adult Basic Education

On a rainy, cold evening in New York City, several people are straggling into a public school building to attend classes in basic literacy and computation. They are a diverse ethnic group, but have major commonalities: most are economically poor, unemployed, and many are on welfare. Each takes a classroom seat and waits for the adult education teacher to arrive. Once class starts, additional learners arrive, with minimal interruptions. One senses a feeling of a social gathering, unlike the atmosphere of most elementary and secondary classrooms. Yet, the actual learning sequence is quite structured. This particular class is using elementary school reading texts, and there is rather limited attention to varied differences of competencies the adults bring to this setting.

This is not meant to be a characterization of all Adult Basic Education (ABE) programs in North America or the world. Yet, it does capture some of the common elements. Especially important is the emphasis on learning printed communication and computational skills. Where English (or its equivalent in other nations) for speakers of other languages (ESL) is provided, oral learning is an additional skill. Also common is the frequent tie-in with public schooling. Given the relationship between lower economic status and illiteracy (not necessarily causal in nature), one expects to also find a higher percentage of the disadvantaged in ABE.

Adult Noncredit Programs

The parking lot at the local junior high school in a small New England town is overflowing with cars on a Saturday morning. Inside is a large crowd of adults and older youths lining up to register for a potpourri of workshops, seminars, and classes. The offerings range from Chinese Cooking, to Auto Mechanics, to Family Planning, to Literature on Civil Disobedience. There is considerable noise, for many of the people are chatting together, relevant and not relevant to the signing-up procedures. It is obvious that there are common bonds among many of the people here; snatches of conversation indicate that several have had previous experiences with this Adult and Continuing Education Program. The types of cars outside, and the appearances of the people inside, provide clues to the middle-class, advantaged qualities of these learners. There is a very relaxed atmosphere, quite unlike the hectic scene of registration day at the local university. The fact that the learning will take place during what these adults call their leisure time, and that these are noncredit experiences, helps explain this casual scene.

A friendly tone characterizes a telephone call from a farmer in a Midwestern state to his County Agent. The purpose of the farmer's call is to request information on a forthcoming evening meeting at the Grange Hall. While the announcement of the meeting indicated the topic was "Conservation: Friend or Foe of Farmers," the caller was not at all clear whether this was worth his time to attend. The friendly conversation between the extension worker and the farmer manifested the informal nature of the many years of their work-oriented relationship. While most such contacts are focused on solving problems concerning the nuts and bolts of farming and farm life, there are also more personal bonds built-up through mutual respect and sharing. As an adult educator, the County Agent knows the importance of merging interpersonal needs with the vocational needs of farmers and their families.

Adult Credit Programs

A middle-aged, well-dressed woman has an appointment with a university professor of education. She explains that the youngest of her three children has started school, thus freeing her from some of her homebound duties. Several years ago, she graduated from college as an English major, but married soon after and has been employed since then in the household. Now she wants to obtain a certificate to teach in a secondary school. But because of her continued employment at home, she cannot enroll in the university's full-time teacher preparation program. The professor advises her to talk with the staff at the university's Continuing Education Division. There she will find a program specially constructed for part-time, adult students seeking credit level offerings.

Community college and university based Continuing Education Programs are widespread throughout the fifty states. Parallel with continuing education programs connected with public schools, there is a rich variety of noncredit offerings. But there are also many opportunities on a credit basis.

Some of these latter offerings can be tied into an undergraduate or graduate degree program. In some instances, courses are specially designed for those who have lifestyles that make it very difficult for them to use the traditional patterns of higher education.

Definitions and Distinctions

A programmatic description of adult education is intended in this essay. Included are Adult Basic Education (ABE) and Continuing Education in schools and universities that offer credit and noncredit programs in the United States.

There is a lively dialogue in the theoretical literature and at universities' adult education centers that sees the field as similar to lifelong learning. This view encompasses all planned adult learning including nearly every agency and institution in society: industry, military, churches, government services, labor, etc. (Knowles, 1970).

The distinction between the programmatic and the theoretical view is important for analysis purposes. The attempt by theorists to make adult education mean all things to all people and to all groups has the purpose of trying to establish underlying characteristics that cut across all organized adult learning. What gets lost are important differences in socioeconomic implications, in specific purposes, and in processes among the multitude of adult learning settings. These differences go unexamined in the global, theorists' presentations (Boyd and Apps, 1980).

In addition, the global description does not reflect the general public's and practitioner's understanding about adult education. For example, the Coalition of Adult Education Organizations (CAEO) had, by 1976, some nineteen member organizations. With few exceptions (churches, libraries) these groups represented the more programmatic use of the term. Other organizations serving very large numbers of adult learners such as business, military, or government services are not part of the coalition and have not seen themselves as a part of the traditional adult education movement.

The number of adults served by ABE and Continuing Education efforts is only a fraction of the total number of adults who are engaged in organized learning experiences. The purpose of this essay is to focus on efforts that are currently perceived by the general public as characteristic of the movement. Many of the other efforts such as human services, community education, self-help programs, and museums are treated in separate essays of this book.

The Historical Context

The history of Continuing Education has its U.S. origins in the ninteenth century with the development of lyceums, libraries, and the Chautaugua movement. The lyceums offered discussion forums, lectures and a wide range of literature to the public. The public library system provided a ready source of reading material for the continued education of adults. In addition, many libraries offered other services similar to those of the lyceums: debates, discussions, exhibits, and lectures. The Chautaugua movement had its start through religious auspices. It soon broadened its base from a major religious workers' training emphasis to nationally known speakers on popular topics as well as more specialized areas in the humanities, arts and sciences.

Closely related to university Continuing Education is the Cooperative Extension Service, one of the best known adult education programs in the United States. Starting with the Smith-Lever Act of 1914, this provision for the continued education of rural men and women made a profound impact on the nation's agricultural and family life. In recent years, the extension process has been expanded somewhat to include suburban and urban concerns.

Adult Basic Education is of recent origin, receiving federal funds in the mid-1960's. Aimed at the approximately 59 million out-of-school Americans who had not completed high school, ABE has been administered at the state and local level. It came into existence as part of the War on Poverty, with a strong emphasis on reducing functional illiteracy in the nation. This program is one of the most focused, highly organized adult education efforts in the United States.

Theoretical Issues

The many decades of study and practice of education for adults has given rise to a number of significant issues having major implications for programmatic and implementation concerns. These issues are categorized here under five headings: the cultural environment, philosophical groundings, social change, learning theory, and the world scene.

The Cultural Environment

The continued interest in and growth of adult education is a reflection of several forces in the culture: industrialization, minority pressures, and increased leisure.

Inherent in our modern industrial society are demands for specialized worker skills. It may not be feasible to pick up on-the-job, the skills and information needed for employment in the modern workplace. Thus, there has developed a vast array of educational programs aimed at training and retraining adults to fit the requirements of business, industry, and service agencies. Much of this training activity lies outside the parameters of this essay (such as training in the service and business/industrial sector). Yet, there are connections between these demands in the culture and selected objectives of ABE and Continuing Education.

Minority pressures for adult education opportunities come from two sources. One is the demand for literacy by those for whom English is a second language. The other source comes from those in the culture who are not in a personal or social position to meet their educational needs through formal schooling. These latter groups include many of the disadvantaged minorities: Blacks, Hispanics, Native Americans, poor whites. The impact of the Civil Rights Movement in recent years has heightened the consciousness of minority groups. One consequence is their organized efforts to find alternative educational paths. Much of the federal legislation since the 1960's is in response to these pressures on the social system; the Adult Education Act of 1966 was one specific federal response.

Over the past several decades, there has been a significant increase in the leisure time available to many adults. The decrease in the work week hours and the increase in standards of living combine to create an ambiance that encourages adult participation in continuing education programs. This increase is reflected in both noncredit and credit experiences in school and university-based extension activities.

Philosophical Groundings

The value assumptions of adult education in the United States include a belief in the importance of education for purposes of upward social mobility; the right of all to equal opportunities for growth and advancement; the connections between education and democracy; faith in the industrial/scientific model for constructing and implementing adult education programs; an interest in incorporating group dynamics approaches in the delivery of programs; and faith in the potentials for continued growth of adults (Boone, Shearon, and White, 1980).

The origins of these assumptions are complex with contributions coming from many sources. Three persons, each representing one or more of these beliefs, are frequently referred to by historians of adult education: John Dewey, Ralph Tyler, and Kurt Lewin. The interactions concept of Dewey and his philosophy relating education to the daily life in a democracy were instrumental in providing a foundation for the adult education movement. His impact on adult education may have been greater than on formal public schooling. The impact of Tyler has been his emphasis on the usefulness of a detailed, logical sequence of steps to be followed in designing and implementing educational programs for adults. Also, in recent years, the importance of group interactions to promote the growth of humane interpersonal relations has been recognized by adult educators. The work of Kurt Lewin has provided a theoretical base through the group dynamics movement. Ideas from change theory, the human potential movement, and systems theory are also attracting significant attention (Long and Hiemstra, 1980).

One of the foremost champions of a belief in the potential of adults to change and grow is Malcolm Knowles (1970). While partly basing this value assumption on psychological evidence, there is also a major premise about the nature of human nature. Implicit is a faith in the inherent dignity of all persons at all ages. Related to this concept is a generous view of what is important to learn, a view that includes not only material-based objectives but those of a psychic, intellectual, and spiritual nature.

All this mix of varied influences results in considerable dialogue among adult educators, for these value assumptions are not fully in harmony with one another. Some of the values may be in direct contradiction. As a consequence, some programs have a highly eclectic theoretical base while others are more coherent.

Of special interest for the future is the recent impact of Paulo Freire's work (1973). The origins of his thinking lie in Third World situations, but there is growing interest in his concepts among industralized nations. Most relevant is his emphasis on the importance of the education of the adult population towards understanding the forces of one's society, how these forces impact on personal and community life, and ways of redirecting those forces to lend dignity and enfranchisement to the masses of people.

Social Change

Much of the emphasis in adult education is on individual growth. While some of this emphasis may be seen as potentially relevant to modifications of economic and political forces in the society, there is not much that is explicitly stated about such implications. An upfront emphasis on the relation of adult education programs to community development is difficult to find.

The attack on illiteracy in Adult Basic Education and on quality of rural life in the Cooperative Extension approaches come the closest to any explicit concern with social change issues. The development of functional literacy by individuals from the lower social strata of the nation is designed partly to meet the employment needs in an industrial, corporate society. Literacy also is seen by the federal legislative acts and by some ABE program staff as the empowerment of the disenfranchised. It is assumed that this empowerment would be expressed by the aggregate influence of literate individuals demanding changes in social structures so as to realize their economic and social rights (Cook, 1977).

Whether social change is likely to evolve by providing individuals with literacy competencies is debatable. An excellent examination of this issue is made by Hunter and Harman (1979). They forcefully present the position that making education available is only part of the picture. Along with adult education efforts, there must be planned changes made in the overall social and cultural systems of society. Without substantial modifications in economic, political, health, and environmental elements of social structures, literacy gains will do relatively little to make a positive impact on the quality of community life for those in the lower strata of society.

The social change aspect of the Cooperative Extension movement is a double-edged sword. Seen one way, the standard of living and political environment of the agricultural population in the nation has been remarkably improved. Seen another way, within that population there has been a marked trend toward large, agribusiness farms along with a major reduction in the number of farms and the persistence of a significant number of rural poor. Thus, the effects of the social change of this adult education program are mixed so far as reducing the disparity between rural haves and have-nots.

Despite these examples, most continuing education programs, both those that are for credit and noncredit, focus largely on individual development. There is little that is designed explicitly to encourage learner attention to addressing social ills of communities or the nation.

Learning Theory

One statement can be expected in speeches at adult education conferences: "Adult learning is different from youth learning." Behind this statement is psychological research on development. This field has generally focused on childhood and adolescent age periods. But there is now more attention being paid by psychological theorists and researchers on older age spans. Even the nomenclature reflects this trend, with the term *androgogy* being used to emphasize the distinctions of adult education from *pedagogy*. The latter is being used in connection with child and early adolescent education.

The field of adult human development makes two major premises: that you can teach old dogs new tricks, and that the informal and nonformal learning gained through adults' daily life experiences creates distinctive needs, attitudes, problems, lifestyles, expectations, etc. These psychological differences between youth and adults highlight implications for androgogy. Foremost are the amount and variety of firsthand experiences, habits, and convictions; a need for independence; a concern for time and financial issues; physical idiosyncrasies; crucial problems to solve; many preoccupations; established ways of relating to others; firm beliefs; ingrained responses to education; and, resources to share (Davis and McCallon, 1974).

The concept of adult development is an effort to construct logical order over that period of human existence for purposes of description and prediction. One such construction builds on Jean Piaget's system of stages with the idea of predictable sequences of internalized cognitive structures. Another position posits that at various periods of one's age span, there are common issues and tasks that characterize most adults. A third synergistic position explored by Eric Erikson (1978) sees development as a series of stages that represent age relevant crises with the sequence being less rigid than Piaget's. The implications of varied development theories for adult education program design and implementation provide one of the major sources for research and controversy in the field.

The World Scene

While this essay deals only with the narrow definition of adult education in the United States, mention should be made of the general situation in the world. There is some interest in providing learning opportunities for adults in almost all nations. Many international organizations and national ministries of education provide resources and programs for adult education. In general, the emphasis of these efforts is to develop alternative ways for adults to have access to selected elements of the formal school curriculum. Especially of interest is a concern to reduce illiteracy. Where functional literacy is practiced, there may be an effort to tie literacy instruction to the daily life needs of the learners. It is in such instances that one finds national programs in adult education being influenced by the nonformal education movement (Srinivasan, 1977).

Summary

These theory issues are similar in many ways with those of formal schooling. The crucial difference lies in the emphasis in youth education. on a highly standardized package of academic content that is largely compulsory, as contrasted to the emphasis on the diversity of adults' learning needs. The voluntary nature of adult education greatly affects the content and processes that characterize programs. It is to be expected that noticeable differences, as well as similarities will be found worldwide between youth and adult education as regards abstract issues of cultural environment, groundings in ideas, social change, and learning theory.

Pervasive Themes

A review of the panels and workshops offered at adult education conferences suggests themes that engage the professionals. Topic headings include demographic trends, recruitment and retention, literacy approaches, academic and functional education, competency-based education, and funding. These themes attract attention because they are loaded with controversy and because of new findings which spark current interest.

Demographics

In the United States, there is a major shift in the demographic profile of the population, with the percentage of youth decreasing and the percentage of adults increasing. This trend appears to be one that will continue for a number of years. Adult educators refer to this fact as a significant reason for increasing the public and private support that is needed to meet the increased numbers of adults who want learning opportunities.

The numbers of minorities in the nation, along with their growing consciousness of their rights and of the ways they are disenfranchised, is another demographic fact that is a persistent theme in adult education circles. The growing interest in women's rights is an additional, important factor that affects the direction and content of adult education programs.

Adult Education for Whom?

The rhetoric of adult educators in the literature has as one major theme the obligation to address the educational needs of all adults. Some programs such as ABE are especially aimed at those who have the most elementary needs, such as literacy and computational skills. In practice, most adult education programs are not utilized by those who are most in need. Many millions of adults, characterized largely as impoverished minorities, consistently are missing from these programs. There have been repeated attempts to construct program designs that will attract and hold this population of adults. The results have been quite discouraging. It seems likely that the depressed physical and psychic conditions of their daily existence make it almost impossible for these adults to respond positively to even the simpler cognitive aspects of adult education offerings. Until the nation constructs basic reforms in the sociopolitical-economic structures that are the source of the inhuman conditions for these millions of people in the United States, there is little hope that adult education programs can be of much use to them.

This is not to say that adult education is an elite movement. It is not. There are millions of poor minorities who respond to the opportunities available, and large numbers of lower middle-class and middle-class people make up much of the population served by adult education programs.

Yet, the overall picture as to whom is served indicates that large numbers of those most in need are not being reached. A study by the Comptroller General of the United States (1975) in a Report to the Congress is an evaluation of the nation's first nine years of the Adult Basic Education programs. The findings are that in any given year of federal funding, only a very small percentage of the 57 million people in the adult target group participated. Those with less than eight years of schooling (15 million adults) had a four percent level of participation. Of those who did participate, very few achieved an eighth grade equivalency standard.

In a somewhat contradictory report to the federal government, the NACECE (1979) recommends that federal support be provided for adult learners (older than the post-secondary youth group) through continued higher education. The study points out that there is little financial help for the working adult learner who has limited financial security. Their findings are that most federal programs are designed for postadolescent youths, leaving the older adults with little assistance. The majority of older adult participants in higher education programs are employed, have families, and are largely representative of the affluent middle class. With 40 percent of all formal adult learning occurring in higher education institutions, there are millions of taxpaying people who receive no financial help with their desire and need for continuing education. And for the disadvantaged, there is little likelihood of breaking the cycle of inadequate education leading to unemployment.

Conventional or Radical Approaches to Literacy

About 23 million United States adults are so functionally illiterate that they cannot cope with daily life. They are unable to take control of the work and family life decisions that they face and must depend on others for basic survival. The conventional approaches of such programs as Adult Basic Education and the Right to Read have consistently been unable to recruit and retain this large segment of the illiterate population. Efforts to modify these conventional approaches have largely been unsuccessful.

An alternative approach has been proposed by Jonathan Kozol (1980) which may be seen as radical in nature. Drawing on ideas from China, Israel, and Cuba, Kozol suggests adaptations to fit the unique situation of the United States. The specific suggestion is to construct content that appeals to the motivational system of these adults. Such content would use words that are active, that have emotional meaning to the poor, largely urban, disenfranchised minorities; examples are *pain, longing, prison, protest, power, police*. A second specific suggestion is to recruit a large number of volunteers who would work in teams on a one-to-one basis with the target population.

A major controversy about Kozol's proposal concerns why this approach has not been widely used in the United States. One reason may be a fear among those who are in control of social forces that these adults might learn to demand their rights for jobs, a decent place to live, and access to power-sharing. Current efforts to implement Kozol's proposal are being made with little indication of acceptance by funding sources.

Academic and Functional Education

The influence of higher education on the adult education movement is evident in the concern that university faculty have for the offerings of the continuing education units of their institutions. The staff of these units are under pressure to justify the quality and nature of their programs, as they balance traditional academic standards with meeting the functional needs of the outer community. The credit/noncredit issue is a subset problem, having its origins in the attempt to respond constructively to conflicting pressures of "town and gown." The concern for academic standards is also evidenced in pressures from state regulations and accrediting agencies. A number of higher education institutions in North America are exploring nontraditional ways to meet the needs of adults such as University Without Walls, correspondence study, external degree, distance education, prior learning.

The functional needs of adults very often require more modifications in the purposes and delivery systems than formal education is willing or able to meet. A very useful, although as yet uncharacteristic, effort to address this issue is in the Appalachian area of the United States. The possibilities for applying Third World nonformal adult education experiences to several United States higher education institutions is described in Griffin et al. (1977). Another noteworthy effort that has resolved some of the tensions between standards and functionalism is the Agricultural Cooperative Extension movement. Their educational work with adults has made a major national impact. The fact that they emphasize noncredit, nonformal approaches greatly reduces the pressure from the academic community.

Competency-Based Education

In the last 10 years, some adult educators have explored the potentials of the competency-based education (CBE) movement. At issue here is the concern that adult education is not sufficiently addressing the needs of the learners in ways that are effective and meaningful. Competency-based education is perceived by some as one way to meet this criticism. CBE is characterized by being very specific about the learning objectives, how they are to be achieved, and how they are to be assessed. Further, CBE requires that program designers find out what competencies are really needed by the learners, thus helping to insure that the learning objectives are functionally relevant.

There is controversy concerning CBE among adult educators. The dialogue is largely over the possible misuse of this approach by being too specific as to the learning objectives. That possibility can lead to seeing learning as only a series of separate, discrete bits of stimuli. For those who see many important learnings as a gestalt experience with interaction of complex stimuli being involved, the CBE movement is judged to be inane if not outright destructive. The greatest interest in CBE appears to come from the adult basic education segment. Those closer to the continuing education segment, with its ties to higher education, tend to be the most disenchanted.

Funding Uncertainties

From the mid-1960's to 1980, the funding for ABE and English as a Second Language was largely assured by mandated funding, originating from the federal government and administered and monitored at the state and local levels. With the change in several philosophical-political-economic assumptions at the national level in the early 1980's, a dramatic shift in funding evolved. Directors of ABE and ESL programs could no longer feel as secure about adequate government support for their offerings.

Thus, a pervasive issue was precipitated concerning program survival. Involved was whether the directors and other staff could or would learn the survival skills to keep programs going. This was especially relevant to ABE programs where the tactic of charging fees was dysfunctional given that most of the target population was very poor.

It is ironic that tenure should be a significant factor in this issue. Many of the staff members of these programs have tenure through past and present public school employment. For these individuals this is a safety net in case they are unable to continue working with adult programs due to their inability to locate funding. For staff to maintain these programs, they must invent fresh approaches to find funding support. There will be a tension between continuing to provide needed services to the disenfranchised illiterates, and the staff's own needs for secure employment.

Summary

The practitioners of adult education are deeply involved in the complex, often frustrating work of designing useful, fundable programs that will attract a broad range of adult interests. This involvement is carried out with several pervasive themes that influence short- and long-range decisions.

Given the controversies and unknowns surrounding demographics, enrollments, formal versus nonformal approaches, competency-based education, and funding, it is to be expected that there will be some degree of variability in the actual delivery of programs.

Delivery Variables

One of the attractions of working with adult learners is the challenge to find meaningful, effective ways of implementing the overall design of a program. Explorations of the delivery variables provide a profile or picture of the details of such program elements as who the participants and staff are; why, what, and how content is presented; and what organizational patterns are used.

Target Populations

The adult education movement has served nearly every classification of adult clients one can think of: rich and poor, men and women, majorities and minorities, younger and older, educated and illiterate, professionals and unskilled. While the more advantaged have received a disproportionate amount of service, there are programs for nearly every segment of adult learners. There are programs aimed at the aging, women, professionals, managers, illiterate, handicapped, socio-economic disenfranchised, prisoners, military, labor.

The potential number of adult learners who are classified as functionally illiterate in the United States is roughly estimated at 59 million. Yet, less than five percent of this potential target population is being served. And there is much evidence that those who are served represent adults whose life outlook is most similar to middle-class patterns and who accept the ways of formal schooling.

Objectives

There is considerable variation in the objectives of adult education, even when one uses a narrow definition. Adult Basic Education generally has a fairly specific set of objectives with the emphasis on reading, writing, speaking, and numeracy. Where programs are designed around English taught to those for whom it is a second language, the emphasis is even more on literacy. Some ABE programs may aim at additional competencies having to do with life functions in the home, at work, and in the community.

Continuing and Cooperative Extension Education have a much broader array of objectives. These include vocational and career goals for lay learners as well as professionals. There is considerable emphasis on leisure and recreational objectives. Less frequent, but still available, are objectives that concern the sociopolitical-economic issues of the region, nation, and world. Programs that are tied into credit and degree-granting tracks would naturally involve the formal objectives.

Content

The content of adult education programs tends to be on skills and information. Less of the offerings are highly theoretical and abstract. Thus, the messages are more likely to be relevant to the adult learners' interests and concerns. Since adults are voluntary learners, compared with younger compulsory learners, there is considerably more motivation for the adult educators to select and offer content that lay adults will find appealing and useful.

Some adult education objectives do require content that may not be immediately interesting. A good example is in ABE where the early stages of overcoming illiteracy may require mastering content that is not in itself very appealing. The meaning comes later, when literacy skills are no longer the content, but are the tools to learn other content.

Those programs offered by public schools, community colleges, and universities for credit and degrees have much more academically oriented content. The curriculum may have somewhat more latitude than is usual for youth-oriented programs, but the academic traditions set rather firm limits.

Staffing

Much of the teaching in adult education programs is conducted by school teachers or faculty working in a second job. This is frequently the case for ABE programs and is especially the case for credit and degree programs connected to higher education institutions. The continuing education noncredit offerings are frequently led by instructors who have special knowledge, experience, and talents.

There is considerable interest among ABE personnel and other adult educators in developing staff training programs to prepare and upgrade the professional competencies of teachers of adults. This interest comes in part from the recognition that adult learning is distinctive from youth learning, with the implication that adult education staff need academic exposure to the principles and strategies of adult developmental philosophy, psychology, and sociology.

One unresolved issue is whether adult educators should have a special certificate to teach and, if so, what the competencies and criteria should be. This staffing issue gets at another concern which is whether adults are best served by those especially trained or by those who may be less academically informed but more oriented to being facilitators of learning rather than teachers of learning.

There are training programs for adult educators at the graduate level in a number of universities throughout the nation. These prepare personnel to work at national, state, and local levels as administrators, managers, and leaders of adult education divisions and programs. While these graduate programs see adult education much more inclusively than what is commonly labeled as such, those who graduate probably end up working in the more restricted terrain.

Methods and Materials

There is a wealth of material available on the procedures for the delivery of adult education. Some sources use an abstract approach, providing broad guidelines for decision making about methods and materials. Given the variety of clients, purposes, and settings, there is a need for this general approach to help categorize the endless specific activities of programs. The detailed, concrete descriptions of methods and materials may not be applicable in given situations.

Klevins (1976) provides information on several aids to learning: educational technology, adult learning centers, individualized instruction, mass media. A brief overview of teaching methods that include explanation, demonstrations, questioning, drill, and tutoring is discussed by Verduin et al. (1977). An explicit description for the construction of literacy materials developed from the vast experience of UNESCO is offered by Neijs (1965). Broadcasting as a powerful application to adult education is thoroughly developed by Waniewicz (1972), again based on UNESCO experience. One source that focuses on correspondence education describes in detail the writing of materials and techniques for two-way correspondency and the place of radio and television. A rich sampling of methods used in three countries chronicles innovative approaches: problem-centered from Thailand, projective from Turkey, and self-actualizing from the Philippines (Srinivasan, 1977). These have applications for some adult programs in the United States.

Much of the material used in Adult Basic Education and in English as a Second Language is prepackaged by several large publishing houses. While this material is formal in content, it is presented in very imaginative and attractive ways.

Organization

The organization and administration of adult education generally uses the hierarchical model of formal school systems, and the latter are modeled on the corporate structures of our industrial society. One characteristic of this model is top-down decision making by adult education administrators and staff with little decision powers in the hands of the adult learners. Another characteristic is a concern for outcomes. In the case of adult education, this means a concern for accountability, which may lead to efforts at quantitative measures of learnings. A third characteristic is the emphasis on specialization of personnel with the consequent concern for the professionalism and pressures for certification of the adult educators.

The evolution of adult education professional organizations is another key to the development and characteristics of the organizational aspects of the movement. As the number and variety of adult clients increases, as additional and sometimes conflicting goals are established, and as new agencies and institutions become actively involved, some discord is to be expected among the professional groups.

Facilities and Funding

The cow bird lays its eggs in the nests of other unsuspecting birds; adult educators place their programs in the facilities of other institutions and agencies (with the latter's consent though). This flexibility of the movement is one of its great strengths, for it encourages networking and utilizes the principle of shared resources. Further, this placement of adult education programs in varied settings greatly expands its potentials for meeting the needs of diverse populations and the purposes of diverse organizations.

Funding for adult education comes from varied sources: client fees, organization subsidy, public and private grants, public tax support. Three potential new funding sources include voucher plans, entitlement programs, and government loans. The budgets for ABE, Cooperative Extension, and Continuing Education come from the federal government, channeled through state governments, with additional contributions made by the state. With major budget cuts by the federal government during the 1980's, and with many state finances in serious trouble, the future of funding for these programs is uncertain.

Evaluation and Research

Evaluation and research have many similarities, evaluation being more concerned with what happens with program decision making; research is more interested in why something happens, with knowledge building that is not just specific to a program. But both use many common data gathering and investigative techniques. Adult education has much in common with formal schooling regarding these two fields. The main difference stems from the voluntary nature of adult learning and the greater range of purposes, content, programs, and clients. A succinct, clear overview of the evaluation field for adult education is presented by Grotelueschen (1976, 1980). In addition to a discussion of conceptual issues and models for guiding evaluation plans, the author provides examples of information gathering techniques.

A refreshing position on the relative merits of evaluation for adult education is offered by Knowles (1970). Taking to task those who insist on behavioral science rigor, the author states that practitioners are made guilty by the near impossibility of meeting these standards. They therefore tend to shy away from any planned evaluation. The fascination with the natural science model in evaluation has blocked educators' explorations of other useful models, ones that are more appropriate for the complex programs of formal and nonformal education. Knowles' work also offers both conceptual and implementation information on evaluation designs for adult education programs.

The thorough and imaginative set of essays on adult education research by Long and Hiemstra (1980) provide the reader with an encouraging picture of the variety of defensible ways of carrying out explanatory and knowledge building studies. As with the evaluation field, the exclusive emphasis on experimental research has overshadowed the usefulness of other germane research approaches: historical, survey, and field.

In the international arena, the volume by Edstrom et al. (1970) describes three fields of research: basic, applied, and action. The latter is very similar to evaluation. An unusual and promising view of adult education research is presented by Hall and Kidd (1978), focusing on Third World countries. They describe traditional social science research as including the following weaknesses: ignoring the complexity of educational situations, oppressive research methods that alienate the program participants, establishing barriers which prevent client involvement in decision making regarding action, and a general tendency to operate from a value position that is oriented around the researchers' goals rather than the social justice goals of the adult education movement. These rich sources of information from the international scene can be useful to the program directors in the United States.

Summary

The profile of delivery variables for each of the adult education programs (ABE, credit and noncredit Continuing Education) differs to some extent. They all tend to be influenced by the traditions of formal education, with important differences due to the noncompulsory element, and to the practical nature of adults' learning needs.

Conclusion

Adult education is treated here in a programmatic sense with the focus on Adult Basic Education (ABE) and on credit and noncredit Continuing Education. A broader concept that tends to equate adult education with lifelong learning does not lend itself to an analysis of important distinctions among relevant theories and practices.

Continuing Education in the United States has its roots in the 1800's with the development of lyceums, libraries, and the Chautauqua movement. ABE is largely a federally funded program that started in the 1960's. Current programs are engaged in several theoretical issues and pervasive themes, along with implementing concerns. Theory issues revolve around the impact of industrialization, minority rights, the use of leisure time, the value controversies of the how and what of adult learning, and the social significance of the programs. On the whole, the emphasis of most practitioners is a concern for adult individual development and not for community development.

Pervasive themes that engage the adult education professional include funding problems, meeting the diverse needs of target populations, attracting and retaining participants, and finding workable models such as competency-based education.

The actual delivery of programs is where these theory and theme issues are played out. It is in the design and daily implementation of specific programs that staff are faced with the questions of how to attract minorities, promote basic competency objectives of literacy and more abstract aims, make content relevant to adult needs, train personnel, develop creative methods and materials, and deal with administrative problems of organizations, facilities, and funding. While practices are more varied than one finds in schooling for youth, the overall policies and procedures are more formal than nonformal.

Suggested Resources
Adult Basic and Continuing Education

Bibliography

Alinsky, S.D. *Rules for radicals.* New York: Random House, 1971.

Apps, J.W. *Problems in continuing education.* New York: McGraw-Hill Book Company, 1979.

Bennett, C., Kidd, J.R., and Kulich, J. *Comparative studies in adult education: An anthology.* Syracuse, NY: Syracuse University Publications in Continuing Education, 1975.

Boone, E.J., Shearon, R.W., and White, E.E. *Serving personal and community needs through adult education.* San Francisco, CA: Jossey-Bass Publishers, 1980.

Boyd, R.D., and Apps, J.W. *Redefining the discipline of adult education.* San Francisco, CA: Jossey-Bass Publishers, 1980.

Commission on Non-Traditional Study. *Diversity by design.* San Francisco, CA: Jossey-Bass Publishers, 1973.

Comptroller General of the United States. *The adult basic education program: Progress in reducing illiteracy and improvements needed.* Washington, DC: Department of Health, Education and Welfare, June, 1975.

Cook, W. *Adult literacy education.* Newark, Delaware: International Reading Association, 1977.

Cross, K.P. Our changing students and their impact on colleges: Prospects for a true learning society. *Phi Delta Kappan,* 1978, *II,* No. 3-4, 627-630.

Darkenwald, G.G., and Larson, G.A. (Eds.). *Reaching hard-to-reach adults.* San Francisco, CA: Jossey-Bass Publishers, 1980.

Davis, L., and McCallon, E. *Planning, conducting and evaluating workshops.* Austin, Texas: Learning Concepts, 1974.

Dravis, B. *The free university: A model for lifelong learning.* Chicago, IL: Association Press, 1980.

Edstrom, L., Erdos, R., and Prosser, R. (Eds.). *Mass education.* New York: Africana Publishing Corporation, 1970.

Erikson, E. *Adulthood.* New York: W.W. Norton, 1978.

Freire, P. *Education for critical consciousness.* New York: The Seaburg Press, 1973.

Gilligan, C. In a different voice: Women's conception of self and of morality. *Harvard Educational Review,* 1977, *47,* No. 4, 481-517.

Grabowski, S.M. *Preparing educators of adults.* San Francisco, CA: Jossey-Bass Publishers, 1981.

Griffin, W., et al. (Eds.). *The role of education in the lifelong learning process of the Third World and Appalachia.* Washington, D.C.: American Association of Teacher Education, 1977.

Grotelueschen, A.D. Program evaluation. In A. Knox et al., *Developing, administering, and evaluating adult education.* San Francisco, CA: Jossey-Bass Publishers, 1980.

Grotelueschen, A.D., Gooler, D.D., and Knox, A.B. *Evaluation in adult basic education: How and why.* Danville, IL: Interstate Printers and Publishers, Inc., 1976.

Hall, B.L., and Kidd, J.R. *Adult learning: A design for action.* Oxford, England: Pergamon Press, 1978.

Harrington, F.H. *The future of adult education: New responsibilities of colleges and universities.* San Francisco, CA: Jossey-Bass Publishers, 1977.

Houle, C.O. *The design of education.* San Francisco, CA: Jossey-Bass Publishers, 1972.

Hunter, S.T., and Harman, D. *Adult illiteracy in the United States: A report to the Ford Foundation.* New York: McGraw-Hill Book Company, 1979.

Klevins, C. (Ed.). *Materials and methods in continuing education.* Los Angeles, CA: Klevins Publications, 1976.

Knowles, M.S. *The modern practice of adult education: Androgogy versus pedagogy.* Chicago, IL: Follett Publishing Company, 1970.

Knox, A.B. *Adult development.* San Francisco, CA: Jossey-Bass Publishers, 1977.

Knox, A.B. (Ed.). *Teaching adults effectively.* San Francisco, CA: Jossey-Bass Publishers, 1980.

Kozol, J. *Prisoners of silence: Breaking the bonds of adult illiteracy in the United States.* New York: Continuum, 1980.

Long, H.B., and Hiemstra, R. *Changing approaches to studying adult education.* San Francisco, CA: Jossey-Bass Publishers, 1980.

National Advisory Council on Education. *A target population in adult education.* Washington, D.C.: Government Printing Office, 1974.

National Advisory Council on Extension and Continuing Education. *A special report to the President and to the Congress of the United States.* Washington, D.C.: U.S. Government Printing Office, 1979.

Neijs, K. *Literacy primers: Construction, evaluation and use.* Paris, France: UNESCO, 1965.

Peters, J.M. *Building an effective adult education enterprise.* San Francisco, CA: Jossey-Bass Publishers, 1980.

Srinivasan, L. *Perspectives on nonformal adult learning.* New York: World Education, 1977.

Verdun, J.R., Miller, H.G., and Greer, C.E. *Adults teaching adults: Principles and strategies.* Austin, Texas: Learning Concepts, 1977.

Waniewicz, I. *Broadcasting for adult education.* Paris, France: UNESCO, 1972.

Journals

Adult Education
Adult Literacy and Basic Education
Continuing Education

Resource Centers

Adult Education Association of the U.S.A.
810 18th Street, N.W.
Washington, D.C. 20006

Council of National Organizations for Adult Education
1740 Broadway
17th Floor
New York, NY 10019

National Association for Public Continuing and Adult Education

1201 16th Street, N.W.
Suite 429
Washington, D.C. 20036

OTHER PUBLICATIONS AVAILABLE FROM CITP/CERC

Power: A Repossession Manual
Approaches to community organizing for social change, steps to organize for power; exercises and role plays to develop these skills.
Greg Speeter

Planning, for a Change
Guide to planning and program development for citizen groups.
Duane Dale and Nancy Mitiguy

The Rich Get Richer and the Poor Write Proposals
Information, training activities and suggestions for nonprofit organizations and citizen groups about fund raising and grantsmanship.
Nancy Mitiguy

Working Together: A Manual for Helping Groups to Work More Effectively
Provides the tools for group development and teamwork for citizen boards and grass roots organization.
Bob Biagi

We Interrupt This Program . . .
A manual for citizens and citizen groups for using the media for social change.
Robbie Gordon

Playing Their Game Our Way: How to Hold the Political Process Accountable to Citizen Needs
Strategies and techniques for lobbying, organizing referenda, tracking elected officials, and helping citizens develop clout.
Greg Speeter

How to Make Citizen Involvement Work: Strategies for Developing Clout
An action guide for more effective citizen participation in government.
Duane Dale

Beyond Experts: A Guide for Citizen Group Training
The role of the training coordinator/facilitator within a group plus activities for program development, facilitation, evaluation.
David Magnani and Newell McMurtry

Breaking the Boredom: An Annotated Bibliography on Boards and Councils
Lists detailed descriptions of books, pamphlets, papers, journal articles, and manuals on all issues necessary for board and council effectiveness.
David Magnani and Newell McMurtry

Differences: A Bridge or A Wall
A training manual designed to help individuals, groups and organizations examine and understand racial, cultural, and other. differences, and develop strategies to overcome related problems.
Dan Willis

Networking
A trainer's manual including six-step process to enhance group networking and collaboration plus sections on theories and case studies in networking, a bibliography and information about conference planning.
Joan Brandon and Associates, Eds.

Lifelong Learning Manual
A guide to training for effective education, useful for trainers working as educational staff development and organizational consultants in human service agencies, self-help groups, religious institutions, etc.
Michael Frith and Horace Reed, Eds.

Lifelong Learning in the Community
An annotated, cross-referenced bibliography designed to accompany **Beyond Schools.**
Horace B. Reed and Associates, Eds.

Write for information on individual or bulk rates:

Publications, CITP/CERC
Room 225
Furcolo Hall
University of Massachusetts
Amherst, MA 01003

THE CITIZEN INVOLVEMENT TRAINING PROGRAM (C.I.T.P.)

The Citizen Involvement Training Program of the University of Massachusetts School of Education helps citizens and citizen groups, nonprofits and government to become more effective through a variety of services: consultation, technical assistance, training workshops, and 10 nationally-recognized manuals.

THE COMMUNITY EDUCATION RESOURCE CENTER (C.E.R.C.)

The Community Education Resource Center of the University of Massachusetts School of Education is a collaborative group of students and faculty that acts as a resource, research and consulting center to community projects aimed at improving the quality of life through education.